NEIMAN MARCUS COOKS

RECIPES FOR BELOVED CLASSICS AND UPDATED FAVORITES

KEVIN GARVIN

with JOHN HARRISSON

PHOTOGRAPHS BY JODY HORTON

RIZZOLI
NEW YORK

New York Paris London Milan

First published in the United States of America in 2014

by Rizzoli International Publications, Inc.

300 Park Avenue South

New York, NY 10010

www.rizzoliusa.com

© 2014 NMG Media, Inc.

Photographs © 2014 Jody Horton

Design by Blair Richardson, Little Mule Studio

2014 2015 2016 2017 / 10 9 8 7 6 5 4 3 2 1

Distributed in the U.S. trade by Random House, New York

Printed in China

ISBN-13: 978-0-8478-4337-4

Library of Congress Control Number: 2014939020

DEDICATION

To Jody, my wife,
the best cook in our house.

To Patrick, my son,
*an up-and-coming good cook
in his own right.*

To Anita Hirsch,
a maestro of a cook in the kitchen.

And to all the Neiman Marcus
cooks in our restaurants,
*thank you for doing what you do best:
feeding our customers
great food with a smile.*

CONTENTS

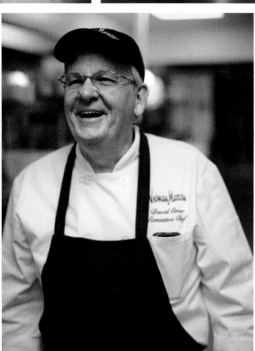

PEOPLE ARE WHAT MAKES THE RESTAURANT BUSINESS COME ALIVE EACH DAY. WE HAVE A SPECIAL GROUP OF COOKS HERE AT NEIMAN MARCUS THAT I WANT TO TELL YOU ABOUT.

Turning on the lights in the kitchen is how all cooks begin their day. The coffee pot is usually the first piece of equipment turned on, followed by the ovens. Once the smell of coffee fills the air the day can officially start. In the Neiman Marcus kitchens the bakers get busy turning on the mixers, beginning with loads of milk and eggs for the popovers and with pounds of butter whipped for the strawberry butter that will soon be smeared all over the warm, piping-hot popovers. The big kettles slowly fill with steam and soon are bubbling slowly with today's chicken broth, while little cheese biscuits are carefully cut from a baker's table filled with the dough. Today's prep sheets will include chicken salad, and like every day, this classic recipe gets the royal treatment with perfectly cooked all-natural chicken white meat. Diced carefully into small cubes by the same person who has made this salad off and on for the past 30 years, it's mixed with chilled extra-heavy mayonnaise, diced celery, splashes of apple cider vinegar, and salt and white pepper to taste. The kitchen staff doesn't speak to one another much in the morning — they're usually sipping a coffee or have found a small muffin to nibble on while they plan their day.

Soon the food deliveries start arriving with fruits, vegetables, locally sourced dairy products, and fresh seafood flown in daily from the docks in Boston. The deliveries add bustle to the kitchen while the cooks and bakers pull together their menu items for the day. Chopping, washing, and mixing adds to the noise level that will soon become what cooks and chefs believe is the "controlled chaos" of daily kitchen life. But for now, the morning is still relatively quiet.

People who work in kitchens want to work in kitchens — unlike most of the servers in restaurants who want to move on to better jobs or the profession they aspire to once they're done with college. Kitchen staff at Neiman Marcus genuinely like what they do. It's the type of job that, if you don't mind working hard, you can excel in and feel secure.

Kitchen staff come to work at Neiman Marcus and stay many years — more than 20 years is the norm. This is one of the primary reasons that we've been able to stay successful for the last 60 years in the restaurant business — it's through the hard work of people like Mary, Lupita, Juan, David, Jose, and Casey in our world. These are the people who cook for the lady eating lunch with her personal shopper, or the French designer in the store for his fall season trunk show, or the two gals meeting up for a quick bite before picking up their kids from school. The kitchen crew at Neiman Marcus are not designer savvy, they don't wear Prada, and typically don't shop in their store. They enter Neimans early in the morning through the back entrance, get dressed in their chef uniforms, and turn out some of the best lunches in the cities where they work. Through this book I hope to shed a small spotlight on this unassuming kitchen group by sharing with our readers the secrets of what has made their food so darn good each and every day for the past 60 years. I hope you enjoy the work of this group as much as I have, as a part of this group, for the past 20 years.

BY POPULAR REQUEST, this book updates and embellishes the classic Neiman Marcus recipes and includes many new recipes that are favorites with our customers across the country. More than a decade has elapsed since the *Neiman Marcus Cookbook* was published, celebrating fifty years of great food by showcasing many of the special recipes that have contributed to the remarkable success of our restaurants.

That book was a best seller and the sequel, *Neiman Marcus Taste*, published several years ago on the occasion of the store's one-hundredth anniversary, paid special tribute to Helen Corbitt, the feisty grande dame of Texas cooking and the initial director of restaurants at Neiman Marcus. Now that we are down to the last few copies of these books — they are well hidden under the desk in my office — and the requests for recipes for some of our classic dishes continue daily, I am reminded that our approach to some of these classics, and to food in general, has changed in the years since we published those books. We introduced our new healthful Go Figure Cuisine and now provide nutritional information for each of our recipes. In notes that accompany most of the recipes, I try to add nuances and guidance to the home cook and tips on methods and ingredients. There's not a single recipe that I don't have a strong opinion about, and I know from our previous books that people love background, and options, when following or adapting a recipe.

Many of our customers will say, "Don't mess with the classic recipes," and I won't. In some cases, you'll get the exact recipe as it's been made for 60 years. But in this new age of information and heightened interest in food, we also offer some worthy variations and twists on longtime favorites. In my job and on my cookbook tours, I have gotten to meet many of you and heard about how you came to know and love the Neiman Marcus restaurants. Many of you explained your own personal motivation for trying to cook more healthfully for your family, and I was frequently asked about best practices for making some of our recipes fit those criteria.

As a chef, I have always been challenged to create healthy menu items and make them available in our dining rooms. But fifteen years ago, these items never sold well and before

![Go Figure icon] GO FIGURE

*Watch for this icon
throughout the book,
denoting our lean and
healthy recipes.*

long, they usually found their way off the menus. It seemed
as though people talked about eating healthy, and liked the
idea, but were rarely willing to go out to a restaurant and
"walk the talk." And so it was that I launched Go Figure
Cuisine at the Neiman Marcus restaurants, and wouldn't
you know, some people got upset. One comment I'll never
forget: A customer sent me a note letting me know that she
came to our restaurant to indulge. She wanted her mayo
thick and her bacon crisp on that chicken salad sandwich.
We also received push-back on items like our classic Orange
Soufflé, which may be 990 calories when served with the
chicken salad and the fresh fruit with poppyseed dressing,
but boy, does it have a following! We realized that the time
was not right, and we put the concept on ice.

Fast forward to 2010 and the passage of the Affordable Health
Care Act, which highlighted health care as a social issue and the
importance of nutrition and eating more prudently. The ongoing
recent campaigns to counter obesity have also had a similar
effect. One of the provisions of the new health care legislation
is that restaurant groups with more than 20 restaurants under
the same name are required to include calorie counts on their
menus. As soon as the bill was passed, we hired a dietitian, and
today we have calorie counts on all of our menus. I also seized
the opportunity to reintroduce our Go Figure Cuisine, which
features menu items with less than 560 calories, and today these
dishes are the best-selling items at Neiman Marcus restaurants.
My motto is "All things in moderation," and the good news is
that you can still indulge at Neiman Marcus on a Monday
and come back later in the week to eat healthfully. Choice is
a wonderful thing!

ABOUT NEIMAN MARCUS RESTAURANTS: Many of you reading this book may not know some of the colorful history of Neiman Marcus and its restaurant business, and it's worth summarizing because it sets some of our recipes — and especially the classics — in context. Neiman Marcus entered the food business in the late 1940s because Herbert Marcus Sr., one of the company's founders, was frustrated by the poor quality of the dining establishments in downtown Dallas, where the flagship store is located. His son, Mr. Stanley (Stanley Marcus was known and addressed as "Mr. Stanley" by everyone in the company), hired a cook to prepare lunches for his father, in a small room on the top floor of the store. Herbert invited vendors and guests to share lunch with him, and it became a popular venue. After Herbert's death in 1950, Mr. Stanley, by then president and chief executive officer of Neiman Marcus, worked to remodel and expand the store. He made the decision to open a full-service restaurant to help keep customers in the store when they made a shopping excursion. Besides, a full and contented shopper is better for business than a hungry one. And so in 1953, the Zodiac Room opened, named by Mr. Stanley.

After a somewhat disappointing start, Mr. Stanley recruited Helen Corbitt in 1955 as the first Neiman Marcus food service director to run the restaurant, and in short order, she made the Zodiac a destination for great food and service. She changed the face of retail dining in America, and the crowds packed the Zodiac to capacity. The great James Beard described Helen as "the queen of the ladies' lunch" in one of his cookbooks. Mr. Stanley wrote, "Under her direction our restaurant gained international attention, for this 'Balenciaga of Food,' as I once introduced her, had the ability to produce new taste sensations and to satisfy the eye as well as the palate by her dramatic food presentation." Mr. Stanley's other pet name for Helen was "my wild Irish genius" — as he put it, "in recognition of her uncontrollability, her genuine Irish temperament, and her sheer genius in the field of food." You can read more about Helen Corbitt on page 9.

Starting in the 1950s and through the 1980s, Mr. Stanley hosted fashion fortnights at the Dallas store; two weeks of special events celebrating the fashion of a particular country combined with a related culinary theme. Sometimes, chefs and kitchen staff were flown in to cook at the events. The fashion fortnights played a major theme in Neiman Marcus restaurants and, to this day, people fondly remember their favorite fortnights and especially how beautifully the store was "dressed up." The

restaurant did a wonderful job transforming itself and creating a unique dining experience to match the country being showcased. Fortnights became the talk of Dallas and beyond. Following Helen Corbitt was my predecessor, Bob Jones, who was the food service director through the 1970s and up to 1994, when I came on board. During the 1970s, Bob oversaw the expansion of Neiman Marcus restaurants beyond the borders of Texas, with further expansion in the 1980s. Today, Neiman Marcus has seven different branded concepts and 43 individual restaurants across the country.

I treasure the many interactions I had with Mr. Stanley after I joined Neiman Marcus in 1994. He was a greatly respected businessman who possessed impeccable taste and a promotional genius. He offered many words of advice and encouraged me to be creative, yet mindful of old recipe favorites especially if they could be given a modern twist that our customers would enjoy. Mr. Stanley was always appreciative of his restaurant staff and consistently focused on the customer. Although he passed away before my first Neiman Marcus cookbook was published, he left notes for the foreword I had invited him to write.

Here is his list:

CUSTOMERS DO NOT LIKE TO:
1. *Wait more than two minutes to be recognized, four minutes to be seated.*

CUSTOMERS LIKE:
1. *Prompt service of food.*
2. *Prompt service of breads, jams, and butter; and the service of a waiter one minute after being seated.*
3. *Prompt response by the manager if any food has not been eaten.*
4. *The offering of a small dish newly added to the menu without a charge.*
5. *To be known by name and have their habits and taste preferences recognized.*
6. *Prompt response to their eye and head signals, especially when it comes to presenting the check.*

Above all, Mr. Stanley always had a vision of excellence for the Neiman Marcus restaurants, and it is a legacy that I am honored to continue. I am proud to present a selection of recipes that reflect these traditions, often updated and improved to satisfy modern tastes and more sophisticated nutritional awareness, just as Mr. Stanley would have liked.

It's been quite a journey. I'm often asked about my culinary journey and food philosophy. It's my firm belief that good cooks aren't simply trained to be good cooks — they're born into a family where cooking is the center of the family life. A good cook is someone who understands how to build on flavors to create a meal that satisfies everyone around the table, and this comes from a childhood spent in and around the family kitchen. My earliest memories as a child are in my mother Irene's kitchen. It was her space, and we got drawn in by the incredible aromas she created when she cooked. Early in the morning, there was coffee simmering in the percolator, maybe some scrapple and eggs with toast, and on Sundays after church, the full-on breakfast with Polish kielbasa (smoked and natural), scrambled eggs, and Irene's great coffee cake. In my mother's kitchen it always seemed that breakfast led right into lunch, which led into after-school snacks, which led into dinner! I remember coming home after school and being struck by the scents of dinner getting underway. Irene started every dinner with a sautéed onion or pepper, or maybe a few cloves of garlic; this was usually the base for a slow-cooked pot roast, chicken, or seafood stew. Dinner was a family affair that started when Dad arrived home from work. This type of family mealtime in Irene's kitchen continued through my entire childhood and served as the basis of my decision to become a chef.

Another of the truths I hold about good cooks is their willingness to put many hours into their job. There's no such thing as holidays off; Saturday nights are always spent in the restaurant; and relationships usually take a backseat to the job. I only began getting paid to cook at age fourteen, when I got my first job at

Piccolo's Pizza in northeast Philadelphia. Tony Foster and Danny Nejberger were young start-up guys who rolled the dice with every penny they ever had to get Piccolo's up and running. I watched those guys work around the clock for the first year in order to grow their business. After year one, two Oldsmobile Toronados were parked out front at Piccolo's, and it was then that I knew they had made it. Piccolo's taught me the importance of hard work in becoming a good cook.

Good cooks will seek out great chef mentors in order to hone their skills in the kitchen. This means packing up your knife kit and traveling. In Europe, it's called a "stage" in the kitchen — in this country, it's called getting experience. I was fortunate to attend the Culinary Institute of America and graduated in 1978. I didn't realize what a perfect time this was to enter into the culinary field as a young American chef. At the time, European chefs were commanding the best stoves in the United States, and I was able to ride the wave through the late 1970s and early 1980s with the advent of Nouvelle Cuisine, which later launched Regional American Cuisine. It was through this time that I got to work for great European chefs like Uwe Henze at the Waiohai Resort on Kauai in Hawaii, followed by a stint under Daniel Boesiger at the AMFAC Hotel in Minneapolis, and finally with Jean Banchet at the Adolphus hotel in Dallas. Each European mentor not only inspired my culinary skills but also made me the type of chef I remain today, committed to creating and serving only the best quality of food and service for every guest.

Good cooks make their job seem fun. They can't imagine themselves ever doing anything else except spending time in and around the kitchen. At one of the many cooking class dinners I've worked in my career, I had a guest ask me, "When are you going to get a real job?" My response went something like, "This is as real as I ever want to be." And that says it all.

BACK WHEN I MADE THE TRANSITION FROM SOUS CHEF TO CHEF, MY BIGGEST FEAR WAS THAT I WOULD NOT BE ABLE TO WRITE A MENU ON MY OWN. As a sous chef you always have the presence of the chef around to bounce ideas off and to approve the menus that you write. So when I moved to the Netherland Plaza Hotel in Cincinnati for my first chef job in 1986, I was a bit intimidated by the idea of going out on my own. The Netherland Plaza had a fine dining restaurant called Orchids, and it was magnificent in décor, food, and service. It was here, in the Orchids kitchen at dinner service, that I met Anita, the lead cook. The lead cook is someone whose next step up the ladder is sous chef, but in the interim, this position takes charge when the chef or sous chef is absent. I soon realized that in spite of her height (five-foot nothing), Anita was born to love food. Our Cincinnati experience was a great time.

I was happy to find Anita and to jointly write seasonal menus, and Orchids had some of the finest press in the city and won many accolades and awards. If, by chance, you've ever eaten at Cincinnati restaurants such as the Maisonette, Pigall's, or the Gourmet Room at the Hilton, you are likely to recall some of the finest meals ever enjoyed in the entire United States. At one time, Cincinnati had the same number of three-star Mobil Guide restaurants as New York City. It was — and remains — a serious food town.

About a year after I started working at Orchids, I was offered the job as executive chef to open a new hotel in the city that was also opening a fine-dining American restaurant: the Palace Restaurant, located at the Palace Hotel. Here, as we opened the new restaurant and hotel, I promoted Anita to the position of executive sous chef. It was a great experience to open a new restaurant and for it to be so successful. Quickly, the Palace was being called the best restaurant in the city, and we were packed every night. The menu writing was incredible, with both of us collaborating on specials each day and night — exciting times. The mutual respect we had for each other helped build our restaurants as well as boost the people around us — and the Palace Restaurant business itself. After eighteen months of heading up the Palace kitchen, I was lured away to become the executive chef at the Adolphus hotel in Dallas. I'm still thankful to Anita for helping make my transition to executive chef so successful — it was because of her focus and willingness to work hard that I was able to move into the bigger role. Although we parted ways, I knew we would work together again someday.

I remember the day I knew I had to get back in touch with Anita and ask her to work with me again. Sharon Hage, a terrific person as well as a talented cook, was the first chef I hired when I came to Neiman Marcus in 1994, but she had decided to leave for another restaurant. Burt Tansky, our former CEO and a consummate food lover, charged me with finding a replacement of the same high caliber. I called Anita right away. She had accepted a chef job on Martha's Vineyard and at the time was not ready to move on, but a couple of weeks later, Anita was at Neiman Marcus, running the Downtown Dallas Zodiac kitchen. I knew that the Zodiac kitchen wouldn't miss a beat with Anita in charge, and in fact it got better and better as Anita settled into a clear understanding of the history of Neiman Marcus food service.

About 10 years ago, I got the chance to promote Anita to the position of corporate executive chef. Our restaurant business took off and we have never looked back.

HELEN CORBITT *The Balenciaga of the Kitchen*

BACK IN 1955, STANLEY MARCUS — "MR. STANLEY" — PERSUADED HELEN CORBITT TO RUN OUR FLAGSHIP STORE'S ZODIAC ROOM RESTAURANT IN DALLAS. Mr. Stanley recognized Helen as a unique talent and a creative cook with a colorful personality. She was hailed as the best cook in Texas, and spent the next fifteen years establishing Neiman Marcus as an innovative and transformative force on the American culinary scene. Mr. Stanley described the red-headed Corbitt admiringly as "my wild Irish genius" and "the Balenciaga of the kitchen," a reference to a top fashion designer of the time whom he greatly esteemed.

Helen was born in upstate New York to a prosperous Irish-American family and learned baking and dessert making from her mother. After graduating with a bachelor's degree in home economics from Skidmore College, Helen worked as a therapeutic dietitian in Newark, New Jersey, and in New York City. Seeking to broaden her horizons, she took a position as food service manager at the Houston Country Club and then at Joske's department store. While there, she served the Duke of Windsor, the former King Edward VIII of England, and named a menu staple after him — the Duke of Windsor sandwich — that we still proudly serve and that remains a best seller. She established her own catering business and moved to work at the Driskill hotel in Austin, where she began a longtime friendship with Lyndon B. Johnson, who later tried (unsuccessfully) to have Helen manage the White House kitchen.

Stanley Marcus told me it took several years of ardent pursuit before Helen Corbitt agreed to work for him in Dallas. He would send her flowers every now and then to remind her of his intent, and eventually his hard work paid off. One day, Helen called Mr. Stanley and asked him when she could start. The following Monday, Helen Corbitt began her remarkable reign at the Zodiac, and the crowds began to line up for a seat.

Helen was dedicated, fiery, and always creative. She wrote five best-selling cookbooks, won many awards and accolades, and was particularly proud to be named among the ten most influential women in Texas. When Mr. Stanley introduced fashion "fortnights" that highlighted a particular country or region, Helen would adapt the menu and work with guest chefs to host special events and dinners. Dallas citizens and out-of-town visitors could enjoy a noonday feast along with a display of the latest fashions worn by sleek, slim Neiman Marcus models . . . Before long, affluent Texans began driving miles into town to wait in long lines for a Corbitt meal. Not only Texans, but every visiting celebrity who came through Dallas vied for a seat in the Zodiac Room.

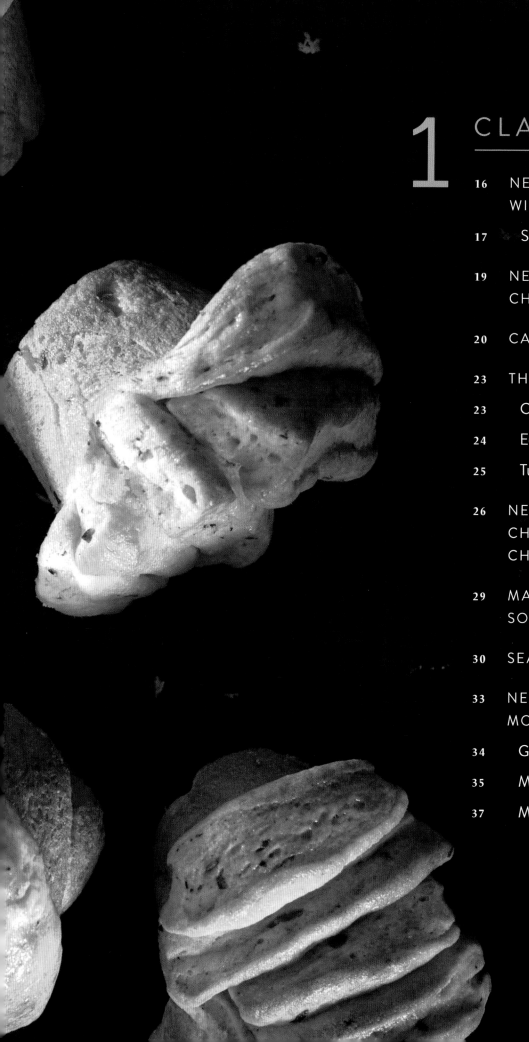

1 CLASSICS

The CLASSICS

Since I started working at Neiman Marcus in 1994, the company has doubled its food service operation by opening almost 20 restaurants in new and existing stores all over the country — now we have 43 in all. This vigorous growth is a real tribute to our customers, and we are very much aware that excellence in customer service is the priority for the Neiman Marcus brand. Clearly, our restaurants and the dining experience play an integral part in the perception of our brand.

Our classic dishes — the perennial customer favorites — play a key role in the success of our restaurant business.

Whenever we open a new restaurant our prospective customers ask, "Will you have popovers and strawberry butter?" Or "What about that little cup with the chicken broth, will you be serving that?" Likewise, "We can't wait for that yummy chicken salad — will you be serving that here, too?" It's amazing to witness how our classic dishes precede us in every new Neiman Marcus market. Over the years, we've temporarily closed a restaurant for upgrades and remodeling, and predictably, in the weeks before we reopen, we will need to reassure callers asking for the relaunch date as they need their popover or their monkey bread fix!

A couple of years ago we were approached by our Neiman Marcus online team to put our famous chocolate chip cookie into the Holiday catalogue. There was a catch: Our team wanted to market the cookies as baked fresh every day and then shipped overnight to customers anywhere in the world. That first holiday season we shipped more than 10,000 cookies, some as far away as Afghanistan to our troops. We're proud to continue to offer our customers these Neiman Marcus classics and we dedicate this chapter to our customers: We deeply appreciate all of your business over the last 60 years.

More than any other single menu item, it is the Neiman Marcus popover that made our restaurants famous.

The Popover

More than any other single menu item, it is the popover that made our restaurants famous. My best advice to home cooks is to practice the recipe a few times before you make them for others — there are so many things to get right and understand about the popover. For example, be sure your popover pans are well seasoned — use them at least three or four times before planning to serve popovers to your guests. (When we open a new restaurant, we make popovers every day for a week before we officially open to perfect them, and then give them away; it's not until a few days in, making countless popover batches, that we get the results we feel deserve the right to be called the Neiman Marcus popover.)

MAKING THE PERFECT POPOVER

The nonstick popover pans we use have twelve 3-ounce compartments, and typically, we spray them with nonstick spray to ensure a nonstick surface. Then, we place the pan on a cookie sheet before transferring to a preheated oven. I'm sometimes asked about the type of oven popovers prefer; our restaurants run the gamut: gas, electric, conventional, and convection. When I first started at Neiman Marcus in the early 1990s, all our kitchens had large, electric, non-convection, triple-deck ovens. They produced fantastic popovers but took up valuable kitchen space and proved very expensive to fix and replace. Today, we like twin-deck convection gas ovens, which have the advantage of halving the baking time to 30 minutes. In today's world, getting fresh popovers to our customers in a timely manner is key.

THE INGREDIENTS

Another key factor in the final outcome is the preparation and quality of the ingredients. For perfect batter, take the time to warm the milk to 120 degrees F. before mixing with fresh eggs that have been left out to warm to room temperature. When combining the eggs and milk in an electric mixer, be sure to beat for up to 10 minutes (on second speed) or until the liquid gets foamy and pale yellow in color. Use a good-quality brand of flour, such as Gold Medal all-purpose bleached white flour, as well as premium baking powder and kosher salt, and allow the batter to rest for about an hour at room temperature before baking.

BAKING THE POPOVERS

Plan on baking the popovers as close to dinnertime as possible, and allow two per guest. The cooking aroma is an added bonus. Once you're ready to bake, preheat the popover pans on a cookie sheet. Bear in mind that popovers do not freeze well, and avoid saving leftover batter in the refrigerator — it's best to bake all the popovers, wrap the leftovers in plastic wrap, and keep them until the next day. Rewarm in a preheated 350 degree F. oven — do not microwave.

SERVING TIPS

As for serving, popovers are designed to be pulled apart with your fingers. Eating a popover is similar to eating the top of a muffin, but popovers are crisp on all sides. Smear strawberry butter on the soft inside part so the bite is crispy and creamy at the same time. Keep in mind that the table will get filled with crumbs so having a small crumber handy is always a good idea — although, you know what? I've honestly come to think of crumbs on a table as a good thing; they signify that bread has been broken, which to me is the true sign of the start to a fine meal.

POPOVER POSTSCRIPT

For best results every time, your work isn't over yet! After baking, once the pans have cooled down, wipe them with a soft cloth; try to avoid washing the pans in soapy water if at all possible. In case you do get popover bottoms that stick to the pan, soak the pan in warm water and gently remove the stuck-on popover with a dishcloth or a small knife, being careful not to scratch the pan. You will need to re-season the pan after washing and drying. Spray the pan with nonstick spray and heat it in a 350 degree F. oven for 30 minutes. Let it cool then wipe it with a clean cloth.

Neiman Marcus Popovers with Strawberry Butter

Yields 12 popovers

We serve our classic popovers with strawberry butter and take special care to make sure it's served slightly soft to ensure the perfect smearing capability. To achieve the perfect shape and size for the strawberry butter, I recommend placing the softened butter in shallow ice cube trays and then refrigerating or freezing overnight. When you're ready to serve, you can dip the trays in warm water and turn out the butter portions on a clean surface before serving them alongside the hot, fresh popovers.

FOR THE POPOVERS

3½   cups milk

4   cups all-purpose flour

1½   teaspoons kosher salt

1   teaspoon baking powder

6   large eggs, at room temperature

FOR THE STRAWBERRY BUTTER

1½   cups butter, at room temperature

1   cup good-quality strawberry preserves

SUGGESTED WINE PAIRING

Bollinger Special Cuvée Champagne

CHEF'S NOTE

It is important to begin with a top-notch butter and high-quality strawberry preserves. We prefer preserves with seeds — this way the end result both looks fresh and tastes exquisite.

To prepare the popovers, place the milk in a bowl and microwave on high for 2 minutes, or until warm to the touch. Sift the flour, salt, and baking powder together into a large mixing bowl. Crack the eggs into the work bowl of an electric mixer fitted with a whisk and beat on medium speed for about 3 minutes, until foamy and pale in color.

Turn down the mixer to low and add the warm milk. Gradually add the flour mixture and beat on medium speed for about 2 minutes. Pour the batter through a wire-mesh strainer into a container. Cover and leave at room temperature for 1 hour.

Meanwhile, prepare the strawberry butter. Place the butter in the work bowl of an electric mixer fitted with the paddle attachment and beat on high speed for 4 or 5 minutes, until light and fluffy. Add the preserves and beat until well combined. To serve, use a pastry bag or small spatula and form a small mound of the butter in a serving dish. Alternatively, place the softened butter in shallow ice cube trays and freeze so the butter hardens. When you're ready to serve, dip the trays in warm water and turn out the butter.

Preheat the oven to 450 degrees F. Spray a well-seasoned popover pan with nonstick spray. Place the empty popover pan on a cookie sheet and place in the preheated oven for 10 minutes.

Remove the pan from the oven and fill the cups almost to the top with the batter. Transfer to the oven and bake for 15 minutes. Turn the oven temperature down to 375 degrees F., rotate the pan, and bake for an additional 30 to 35 minutes, or until the popovers are a deep golden brown on the outside and airy on the inside. Carefully turn out the popovers onto a rack and serve hot, with the strawberry butter alongside.

NUTRITION FACTS —*1 popover*

230 calories	2G saturated fat	35G total carbohydrate	340MG sodium
5G total fat	100MG cholesterol	4G sugars	10G protein

NUTRITION FACTS —*2 tablespoons strawberry butter*

140 calories	8G saturated fat	9G total carbohydrate	0MG sodium
12G total fat	30MG cholesterol	8G sugars	0G protein

Savory Parmesan Popovers

Yields 12 popovers

It's good to try new things and introduce some diversity to the popover universe. Besides, I'm more of a savory guy than a sweet guy, so this one works for me. When you have a winning recipe like the Neiman Marcus popover, you have to be careful how you change it up so as not to offend anyone. This savory version is often used in our catering business to accompany one of our great salads.

Popover batter *(opposite)*
1½ cups grated Parmesan cheese
¼ cup mixed dried herbs, such as thyme, rosemary, and parsley
4 tablespoons unsalted butter, cut into 12 pieces

SUGGESTED WINE PAIRING

Berlucchi Cuvée 61 Sparkling Wine

Prepare the popover batter, cover, and leave at room temperature for 1 hour.

Preheat the oven to 450 degrees F. Spray a well-seasoned popover pan with nonstick spray. Place the empty popover pan on a cookie sheet and place in the preheated oven for 10 minutes.

Remove the pan from the oven and fill the cups almost to the top with the batter. Sprinkle each popover with 1 tablespoon of the cheese and 1 teaspoon of the herbs. Add a piece of the butter to each cup.

Transfer to the oven and bake for 15 minutes. Turn the oven temperature down to 375 degrees F., rotate the pan, and bake for an additional 30 to 35 minutes, or until the popovers are a deep golden brown on the outside and airy on the inside. Before carefully transferring the popovers to a rack, sprinkle with the remaining cheese.

CHEF'S NOTE

My preference is to use Parmigiano Reggiano cheese from the Reggiano region of northwestern Italy. It's expensive but worth every cent.

NUTRITION FACTS —*1 popover*

280 calories	37G total carbohydrate
8G total fat	4G sugars
4G saturated fat	490MG sodium
110MG cholesterol	14G protein

For those who have never heard the urban myth about the Neiman Marcus chocolate chip cookie, I'll take this opportunity to enlighten you. Before I came aboard here at Neiman Marcus there was a chain letter circulating around the country complaining that a Neiman Marcus lunch customer was charged $250 for the chocolate chip cookie recipe after asking their server to mail it to them. As the story goes, along with the recipe came a bill for $250. You guessed it — it was an elaborate hoax, an urban myth. Needless to say, many folks sent letters to our corporate offices to complain and to let us know they were on a personal mission to send as many people as they knew the free recipe that circulated with each letter. I received one of these in my first week of employment back in the fall of 1994. After asking around, I soon realized we didn't even have an official chocolate chip cookie recipe! Many of the powers-that-be at Neiman Marcus weren't interested in creating one, thinking it would just fuel the urban myth fire. However, I was convinced that we did need a chocolate chip cookie recipe and went about creating one. I was all too aware that the new Internet (as it was then) was giving this old chain letter a new life. Fast forward to today: Neiman Marcus restaurants sell more than 100,000 chocolate chip cookies every year, not only in our stores but also on the Neiman Marcus website, which are shipped all over the world. And we never charge for the recipe, not then, not now, not ever!

Honestly, we've never charged for this recipe. It's just an urban myth!

Neiman Marcus Famous Chocolate Chip Cookies

Yields about 3 dozen cookies

½ cup unsalted butter

1 cup light brown sugar

3 tablespoons granulated sugar

1 large egg

2 teaspoons vanilla extract

1¾ cups all-purpose flour

½ teaspoon baking powder

½ teaspoon baking soda

½ teaspoon kosher salt

1½ cups semisweet chocolate chips

1½ teaspoons ground Sanka coffee

Preheat the oven to 300 degrees F. Spray a cookie sheet with nonstick spray. Place the butter, brown sugar, and granulated sugar in the bowl of an electric mixer fitted with a paddle attachment. Beat on medium speed for about 6 minutes, until the mixture is light and fluffy. Beat in the egg and vanilla for 30 seconds longer, until well combined.

In a mixing bowl, sift together the flour, baking powder, baking soda, and salt. Add the flour mixture to the mixer while beating on low speed. Beat for about 15 seconds, and then stir in the chocolate chips and ground coffee.

Using a 1-ounce scoop, drop the cookie dough onto the prepared cookie sheet in dollops about 3 inches apart. Gently press with the back of a spoon to spread out into 2-inch circles. Bake for about 20 minutes, until browned around the edges. Transfer the cookies to a cooling rack. Cool and grease the sheet before baking more batches.

NUTRITION FACTS —*1 cookie*

120 calories	19G total carbohydrate
6G total fat	12G sugars
3.5G saturated fat	85MG sodium
10MG cholesterol	1G protein

Caramel Soufflé

Yields 10 servings

This classic recipe was first introduced by the legendary Helen Corbitt in the mid-1950s as a spring fashion show dessert. Helen, one of the first chefs in the United States to identify modern American cooking, wanted a dessert that was light and airy, not filling, and not a cake-type dessert. Her creation, the caramel soufflé, was a huge hit that secured its place on Neiman Marcus menus for the next 50-plus years.

FOR THE CARAMEL SAUCE

1   cup heavy cream

⅓   cup sugar

¼   cup unsalted butter, chopped

FOR THE VANILLA CUSTARD SAUCE (OPTIONAL)

2½   cups milk

2   teaspoons vanilla extract

5   large egg yolks

⅓   cup sugar

FOR THE SOUFFLÉ

12   large egg whites

½   teaspoon cream of tartar

2   cups sugar

¼   cup warm water

SUGGESTED WINE PAIRING

Nino Franco Primo Franco Prosecco Superiore

To prepare the caramel sauce, place the cream in a small heavy-bottomed saucepan and gradually bring to a simmer over low heat. Keep warm while cooking the sugar: Combine the sugar with 3 tablespoons of water in a separate heavy-bottomed saucepan and bring to a boil over high heat. Turn down the heat to medium and simmer for 10 minutes or until the sugar just turns a light golden brown; do not stir or disturb the sugar while it's cooking. Once the sugar turns golden brown, remove the pan from the heat. Slowly and carefully ladle the hot cream into the caramelized sugar. Add the butter one piece at a time and stir until it is all incorporated. Let the sauce cool to room temperature.

To prepare the optional vanilla custard sauce, place the milk and vanilla in a heavy-bottomed saucepan and bring to a simmer over low heat. Combine the egg yolks and sugar in a mixing bowl and vigorously whip with a wire whisk until the sugar has dissolved. Add about ⅓ cup of the hot milk mixture to the sugar-egg mixture and whisk vigorously to temper. Pour the tempered mixture into the saucepan containing the hot milk mixture and continue cooking over low heat, stirring continuously with a large serving spoon, until the sauce coats the back of the spoon. Remove from the heat, strain into a bowl, and let cool.

To prepare the soufflé, place the egg whites in the bowl of an electric mixer fitted with the whisk attachment. Add the cream of tartar and beat on high speed for about 45 seconds, until soft peaks form. Add 1 cup of the sugar, turn down the mixer speed to medium, and beat until stiff peaks form, about 2 minutes. Turn off the mixer. Place the remaining 1 cup sugar with the ¼ cup warm water in a small heavy-bottomed saucepan and cook over medium-high heat for 4 to 5 minutes or until the sugar is a deep golden brown. Turn on the mixer again to low speed and slowly and carefully add the caramelized sugar to the egg whites. When all of the caramelized sugar has been added, turn up the mixer to medium-high speed and whip for 3 minutes longer.

Preheat the oven to 300 degrees F. Using a rubber spatula, evenly coat the bottom of a Bundt cake pan with ¾ cup of the cooled caramel sauce. Fill the Bundt pan with the soufflé mixture and level off with the spatula. With your spatula, press the air pockets out of the soufflé mixture. Place the Bundt pan inside a large baking pan and fill with about 2 inches of warm tap water. Transfer to the oven and bake for 1 hour, until the top

of the soufflé is nicely browned and has risen 2 to 3 inches over the top of the pan. Remove the pan from the water bath and place on a wire rack to cool.

To serve, run a paring knife around the inside rim of the Bundt pan to release the soufflé. Invert the pan over a platter and gently shake to remove. If it sticks, use a rubber spatula to assist in removing the soufflé from the pan. Spoon a small amount of the caramel from the Bundt pan on each dessert plate. Cut the soufflé into 10 slices and serve a slice on top of the sauce. Drizzle the remaining caramel from the Bundt pan and the custard sauce, if using, over each serving of the soufflé.

CHEF'S NOTES

When making the caramel sauce, be sure not to overcook the sugar or the sauce will taste burnt and bitter.

We've included the vanilla custard recipe to be used as an alternative garnish if so desired. Many of our restaurants use either one, or both, when serving the soufflé.

NUTRITION FACTS —*1 serving*

480 calories	58G total carbohydrate
22G total fat	57G sugars
11G saturated fat	110MG sodium
325MG cholesterol	11G protein

The Neiman Marcus Trio:
Chicken Salad / *Egg Salad* / *Tuna-Pecan Salad*

Yields 5 cups (10 servings)

Making chicken salad is easy but time consuming, and while it's rewarding to make at home, I'm sure the salad will continue to be enjoyed in our restaurants for many years to come. Using all-white meat is sometimes questioned by aficionados as the dark meat has more flavor than white. If you would like to use dark meat by all means do so. Here at Neiman Marcus, customers come into the restaurants just for a simple scoop of the chicken salad that we serve on a bed of lettuce with some ripe tomato slices.

2	pounds boneless, skinless chicken breasts, cleaned of sinew and fat
½	cup diced celery
1	tablespoon cider vinegar
½	cup mayonnaise
3	tablespoons heavy cream
1½	teaspoons kosher salt
⅛	teaspoon freshly ground white pepper

Rinse the chicken breasts under cold running water and place in a small saucepan filled with enough water to cover the chicken by 2 inches. Bring to a boil, turn down to a simmer, and poach the breasts for 20 minutes. Pour off the cooking liquid when finished and, holding with tongs, rinse the breasts under cold running water until cool to the touch. Place the breasts on a serving plate, cover tightly with plastic wrap, and refrigerate for 2 hours.

Remove the plastic wrap and dice the chicken into ½-inch cubes. Transfer to a mixing bowl and add the celery, vinegar, mayonnaise, cream, salt, and pepper. Mix together and then cover with plastic wrap. Chill for about 2 hours before serving.

SUGGESTED WINE PAIRING

Sanford Santa Rita Hills Chardonnay

CHEF'S NOTES

If you plan to keep the cooking liquid from the poached chicken breasts for soup or stock, then be sure the liquid never boils excessively, or it will become cloudy. Rinsing the raw chicken meat under cold running water before boiling will also help keep the liquid clear.

Slicing the celery lengthwise before dicing is the key to uniformly diced celery.

Be sure you taste and season the salad before refrigerating. And most likely, you'll need to re-season the salad just before serving as flavors marry and get softer in a salad like this. Be sure the flavors are right on — salt and pepper are your friends in the kitchen. Remember, seasoning is usually the biggest "miss" when people cook at home.

NUTRITION FACTS *— ½ cup*

210 calories	3G saturated fat	1G total carbohydrate	510MG sodium
14G total fat	65MG cholesterol	0G sugars	19G protein

The Neiman Marcus Trio:
Chicken Salad / **Egg Salad** / *Tuna-Pecan Salad*

Yields 4 cups (8 servings)

This is one of those dishes that's comfort home cooking all the way. I remember putting an egg salad sandwich on a menu many years ago and instantly it became one of our best sellers. It's too bad that not many people take the trouble to cook and peel eggs and then make the salad and serve it. Allow time to make this recipe but know that you're not alone if the egg shells don't peel away easily. We've all been there when the shells are attached to chunks of the egg white, and there's no fun in that. Take comfort in the knowledge that this invariably happens to me when I'm making deviled eggs for a hundred people!

8	large eggs
2	tablespoons mayonnaise
1	teaspoon brown mustard
¼	cup minced celery
	Kosher salt and freshly ground white pepper

SUGGESTED WINE PAIRING

Sanford Santa Rita Hills Chardonnay

Place the eggs in a small saucepan and cover with cold water. Place the pan over medium heat and bring to a boil. Turn off the heat and let the eggs cool for about 1 hour or until you can remove the eggs and peel the shells with your fingers.

Dice the peeled eggs and place in a small mixing bowl. Add the mayonnaise, mustard, and celery and mix together. Season to taste with salt and white pepper. Cover the mixing bowl with plastic wrap and let chill in the refrigerator for at least 1 hour before serving.

NUTRITION FACTS —*½ cup*

110 calories	2G saturated fat	2G total carbohydrate	340MG sodium
8G total fat	200MG cholesterol	1G sugars	7G protein

The Neiman Marcus Trio:
Chicken Salad / *Egg Salad* / *Tuna-Pecan Salad*

Yields 4 cups (8 servings)

There's a choice when it comes to tuna between white and dark meat, just like chicken. About three years ago, we made the switch at our restaurant to dark tuna meat, and although we got some "push back" at a couple of our restaurants and needed to switch back to white albacore by popular demand, my preferred type is tongol tuna, a darker canned tuna. Taxonomists (really smart people!) will tell you that tongol is also called longfin or Northern bluetail tuna, and is native to the Pacific and Indian oceans. Because tongol is more moist and naturally oilier, it has more flavor and you need less mayonnaise in the salad. This in turn reduces the calorie count, which makes it a healthier dish. There is no particular brand I'd recommend, but don't even think about using fresh tuna for tuna salad. I tried that many years ago when living in Hawaii and the texture of cold poached tuna mixed with mayo didn't go over well at all with our guests. However, when it comes to mayonnaise brands, I do have some stronger opinions. Hellman's extra heavy is my first choice, followed by Duke's (mostly found in the Southern part of the United States).

¾ cup pecan pieces

18 ounces chunk white albacore tuna *(packed in water)*, thoroughly drained

1¼ cups mayonnaise

½ cup sliced canned water chestnuts

½ cup minced celery

⅛ teaspoon kosher salt

⅛ teaspoon freshly ground white pepper

SUGGESTED WINE PAIRING

Sanford Santa Rita Hills Chardonnay

Preheat the oven to 350 degrees F. Place the pecan pieces on a cookie sheet and toast in the oven for about 10 minutes or until fragrant and golden brown. Stir the nuts once or twice to avoid burning the edges. Remove from the oven and let cool.

Place the tuna in a mixing bowl and break it up using a fork. Add the toasted pecans, mayonnaise, water chestnuts, celery, salt, and white pepper and mix well. Cover the mixing bowl with plastic wrap and let chill in the refrigerator for at least 1 hour before serving.

Because tongol tuna is more moist and naturally oilier, it has more flavor and you need less mayonnaise in the salad. This in turn reduces the calorie count, which makes it a healthier dish.

NUTRITION FACTS —*½ cup*

370 calories	4G saturated fat	3G total carbohydrate	250MG sodium
33G total fat	40MG cholesterol	1G sugars	15G protein

Neiman Marcus Chicken Broth with Cheddar Biscuits

Yields 10 cups broth and 24 biscuits (8 servings)

Back in the mid-1950s, Stanley Marcus — "Mr. Stanley," as he was affectionately known by staff — challenged Helen Corbitt (see page 9) to come up with a complimentary starter dish to serve when people were first seated at the Zodiac Room, our Dallas flagship store restaurant. It was a brilliant move: Mr. Stanley wanted to get a small dish in front of each guest right away. Back in those days, Zodiac didn't take reservations and seating was first come, first served. Long lines were the norm and having the chicken broth served immediately when guests were seated took the edge right off the long wait and settled the guests into the meal quite nicely.

FOR THE CHICKEN BROTH

5   pounds mixed chicken parts
2   cups coarsely chopped celery
1   cup peeled and chopped carrots
2   cups peeled onion wedges
3   cloves peeled garlic
5   whole black peppercorns
1   dried bay leaf
3   sprigs fresh thyme
1   bunch fresh Italian parsley
2   chicken bouillon cubes

FOR THE CHEDDAR BISCUITS

2½   cups all-purpose flour
1   teaspoon salt
1½   tablespoons baking powder
1   cup vegetable shortening
1   cup grated sharp cheddar cheese
1   cup buttermilk

Kosher salt and freshly ground white pepper

To prepare the broth, rinse the chicken pieces under cold running water and place in a heavy-bottomed stock pot. Add the celery, carrots, onion, garlic, peppercorns, bay leaves, thyme, parsley, and bouillon cubes. Add about 1 gallon cold water or enough to cover the ingredients by about 2 inches. Bring to a boil over medium-high heat and turn the heat down to medium-low. Partially cover the pot with a lid, but do not let the stock cook above a simmer to ensure a clean, clear stock. Simmer for 3 to 4 hours, skimming the surface of the broth occasionally to remove any fat and impurities.

Prepare the biscuits while the broth is cooking. In a mixing bowl, combine the flour, salt, and baking powder. Using a dough cutter, cut in the shortening until the mixture is pea-size. Add the cheese and incorporate. Slowly add the buttermilk and mix together. Turn out the dough onto a lightly floured work surface and gently knead for several minutes until it is no longer sticky to the touch. Return the dough to a clean bowl, cover with plastic wrap, and refrigerate for 1 hour.

Preheat the oven to 350 degrees F. Turn out the dough onto a lightly floured work surface and roll out with a rolling pin to a thickness of 1 inch. Using a 1½-inch round cookie cutter (or a crescent-shaped one) cut out the dough and place the biscuits on an ungreased cookie sheet. There should be approximately 24 biscuits. Transfer to the oven and bake for 20 minutes or until golden brown. Transfer the biscuits to a rack to cool.

Pass the broth through a fine-mesh strainer into a clean saucepan and skim again. Taste and adjust the seasoning before serving. Serve hot in your favorite small demitasse cups accompanied by a few cheese biscuits.

NUTRITION FACTS —*10 ounces broth, strained*

| 15 calories | 0G saturated fat | 1G total carbohydrate | 50MG sodium |
| 1G total fat | 0MG cholesterol | 0G sugars | 1G protein |

NUTRITION FACTS —*1 biscuit*

| 170 calories | 4G saturated fat | 11G total carbohydrate | 240MG sodium |
| 12G total fat | 10MG cholesterol | 1G sugars | 4G protein |

Mandarin Orange Soufflés

Yields 6 servings

For more than 60 years this dish has been the number-one selling dish in all Neiman Marcus restaurants across the country. When I first came aboard and tasted the Orange Soufflé for the first time, I wondered, "What is this about?" At that moment I realized one important thing about my job — it's not about my taste but about the taste of our customers. It will be my job for as along as I'm in charge of Neiman Marcus food service to be sure we deliver in all of our restaurants exactly what it is that our customers expect. And let me tell you something: The expectations are great.

1¼ cups fresh orange juice

1 tablespoon *(1 envelope)* unflavored gelatin

1 cup sugar

2 large egg yolks

1½ tablespoons fresh lemon juice

1 cup heavy cream

½ cup canned mandarin orange sections, drained *(4-ounce can)*

SUGGESTED WINE PAIRING

Seven Daughters Moscato

Pour ¼ cup of the orange juice into a small bowl, sprinkle with the gelatin, and stir to dissolve. Set aside to let the gelatin soften. Prepare an ice bath in a large bowl. Pour the remaining orange juice into a small heavy-bottomed saucepan and stir in the sugar and egg yolks. Cook over medium heat, stirring continuously until the mixture begins to steam and is slightly thickened; do not allow the mixture to boil. Add the softened gelatin mixture (which will have a rubbery texture) and the lemon juice. Stir until incorporated and then transfer to a clean mixing bowl; set the bowl in the ice bath to cool. While the custard is cooling, stir it occasionally.

Using a wire whisk or an electric whisk, whip the heavy cream in a mixing bowl until soft peaks form. With a spatula, gently fold some of the whipped cream into the cooled custard mixture to loosen it. Then add the rest of the cream mixture and fold in until fully incorporated.

> **CHEF'S NOTE**
>
> I like to serve the soufflés simply by themselves on pretty plates but feel free to dress them up by serving on crisp lettuce leaves with fanned strawberries for garnish.

Place 3 or 4 mandarin orange sections in the bottom of six individual 5-ounce fluted plastic molds and fill the molds with the orange soufflé mixture. Place the molds on a cookie sheet and cover with plastic wrap. Transfer to the refrigerator and chill for at least 4 hours, or preferably overnight, until firm.

NUTRITION FACTS —*1 soufflé*

340 calories	10G saturated fat	44G total carbohydrate	45MG sodium
17G total fat	115MG cholesterol	41G sugars	5G protein

Seasonal Fresh Fruit

Yields 3 cups (6 servings)

Many years ago, our restaurants embarked on a concerted effort to purchase local produce and fruits whenever they became available, and today, we go through massive amounts of fresh fruit daily. In addition to desserts, fresh fruits garnish many sandwiches and salads, our best-selling items at the Neiman Marcus restaurants. It's typical, when I'm making restaurant visits around the country, that I take the time to review with my chefs how the fruits we use are most easily cut and presented in the most attractive ways. I've always had a passion for *garde manger* — the cold food preparation area in the kitchen — and still to this day I love making food look beautiful and presenting it in a way that makes people smile.

¾	cup ¾-inch diced honeydew melon
¾	cup ¾-inch diced cantaloupe melon
¾	cup ¾-inch diced golden pineapple
12	strawberries
12	blackberries
12	raspberries
6	fresh mint sprigs

Place the melons and pineapple in a mixing bowl and toss together. Wash the berries under cold running water and drain. In your favorite serving dishes, arrange the melon and pineapple and sprinkle the berries over the fruit. Garnish with mint leaves.

NUTRITION FACTS —½ *cup*

50 calories	0G saturated fat	13G total carbohydrate	10MG sodium
0G total fat	0MG cholesterol	10G sugars	1G protein

Seasonal Fr
Poppyseed D

Neiman Marcus Monkey Bread

Yields 12 buns

One of my favorite food aromas is warm yeast fermenting, usually the first smell that permeates our bakery in the morning as the Monkey Bread and sweet rolls are getting ready to go in the oven. It brings up childhood memories and resonates with me on a deep level. Yeast springs to life when matched with a warm liquid, and I am still fascinated by the process through which this simple micro-organism blossoms into something wonderful. One important thing to remember when working with yeast dough is to allow the dough to double in size, not just once but twice: first, right after mixing the dough, and then again just before baking. This lets the yeast form perfect air pockets in the dough, giving a desirable look as well as flavor. Monkey Bread is very adaptable as the next few recipes illustrate —they are variations on the Monkey Bread theme. We serve this bread in many of our restaurants but in some cases you have to ask for it; it's not widely known that it is usually available every day. Maybe now that the secret is out, our customers will be asking for it every time they dine with us.

2	(¼-ounce) packets active dry yeast
1	cup warm milk
¼	cup sugar
1	teaspoon kosher salt
1	cup butter, melted
3¼	cups all-purpose flour, sifted

To prepare the bread, place the yeast, milk, and a pinch of the sugar in the bowl of an electric mixer fitted with the paddle attachment. Let stand for 5 minutes, until the yeast has dissolved. Add the remaining sugar, the salt, and ½ cup of the melted butter. Stir in the flour to make a soft dough and mix for about 5 minutes.

Transfer the dough to a lightly greased bowl, cover with plastic wrap, and let rise in a warm place until doubled in volume, about 1 hour.

Butter a muffin tin and set aside. Punch down the dough and turn out onto a lightly floured work surface. Using a rolling pin, roll out to a thickness of ½ inch. With a sharp knife cut the dough into 2-inch squares. Gather up four or five squares of the dough and press them together with your fingers; repeat to form 12 buns. Place the remaining melted butter in a shallow bowl and dip the tops of the buns into the butter. Reserve the leftover butter. Place the buns into the buttered muffin tins, buttered side down. Let rise again in a warm place for 30 to 40 minutes or until doubled in volume.

Preheat the oven to 400 degrees F. Transfer the buns to the oven and bake for 15 to 20 minutes or until golden brown. Remove from the oven and brush again with the reserved melted butter.

CHEF'S NOTE
Strawberry butter (page 16) is a natural, winning accompaniment for this recipe.

NUTRITION FACTS —*1 monkey bread*

270 calories	11G saturated fat	29G total carbohydrate	210MG sodium
15G total fat	45MG cholesterol	6G sugars	4G protein

Garlic and Herb Monkey Bread

Yields 12 buns

This recipe was an instant hit when we made it during the holiday season one year to stand in for crisp toast points to accompany the Pimento Cheese Dip from our Holiday Buffet. If the aroma of rising dough and baking bread isn't appealing enough, the garlic and fresh herbs will fill your kitchen with an enticing bouquet to stimulate the appetite.

2	(¼-ounce) packets active dry yeast
1	cup warm milk
¼	cup sugar
1	teaspoon kosher salt
1	cup butter, melted
¼	cup roasted garlic *(page 56)*
1	teaspoon freshly ground black pepper
1	teaspoon minced fresh rosemary
1	teaspoon minced fresh Italian parsley
1	teaspoon minced fresh chives
3¼	cups all-purpose flour, sifted

SUGGESTED WINE PAIRING

Lapostolle Cuvée Alexandre Chardonnay

Place the yeast, milk, and a pinch of the sugar in the bowl of an electric mixer fitted with the paddle attachment. Let stand for 5 minutes, until the yeast has dissolved. Add the remaining sugar, the salt, and ½ cup of the melted butter. Add the roasted garlic, pepper, and herbs and then stir in the flour. Mix for about 5 minutes to make a soft dough.

Transfer the dough to a lightly greased bowl, cover with plastic wrap, and let rise in a warm place until doubled in volume, about 1 hour.

Butter a muffin tin and set aside. Punch down the dough and turn out onto a lightly floured work surface. Using a rolling pin, roll out to a thickness of ½ inch. With a pizza cutter or sharp knife cut the dough into 2-inch squares. Gather up four or five squares of the dough and press them together with your fingers; repeat to form 12 buns. Place the remaining melted butter in a shallow bowl and dip the tops of the buns into the butter. Reserve the leftover butter. Place the buns into the buttered muffin tins, buttered side down. Let rise again in a warm place for 30 to 40 minutes or until doubled in volume.

Preheat the oven to 400 degrees F. Transfer the buns to the oven and bake for 15 to 20 minutes or until golden brown. Remove from the oven and brush again with the reserved melted butter.

NUTRITION FACTS —*1 garlic and herb monkey bread*

300 calories	**10G** saturated fat	**33G** total carbohydrate	**340MG** sodium
16G total fat	**45MG** cholesterol	**5G** sugars	**5G** protein

When you have a dough as versatile as this, you think of your favorite bread recipes and go from there.

Monkey Bread Pretzel Sticks

Yields 36 pretzel sticks

When you have a dough as versatile as this, you think of your favorite bread recipes and go from there. Growing up in Philadelphia, I have always been a big fan of soft pretzels so this seemed like a natural evolution of the Monkey Bread recipe. Even today when I get back to Philly, the first stop I make is a pretzel stand; they're a common sight on many corners throughout the city. Baking fresh pretzels every day, the stands usually sell out by early afternoon. I think you'll find this version to be a big hit, especially for those who know the real thing back East.

Monkey Bread dough *(page 33)*

2   large eggs, beaten

¼   cup kosher salt

¼   cup caraway seeds

SUGGESTED WINE PAIRING

Protea Chenin Blanc

Prepare the Monkey Bread dough and let rise the first time for 1 hour or until doubled in volume.

Punch down the dough and turn out onto a lightly floured work surface. Using a rolling pin, roll out to a thickness of ¼ inch. Cut the dough into 36 one-inch squares and then form the squares into round balls. Set the balls about 1 inch apart on a clean work surface, cover with a damp towel, and let rise for about 30 minutes.

With your fingertips, press each ball into a roughly triangular shape, about ⅛ inch thick; each side of the triangle should be 3 to 4 inches long. Set a triangle on a lightly floured work surface, brush with beaten egg, and sprinkle evenly with salt and caraway seeds. Roll up the triangle and use your fingers to gently twist and elongate the rolled dough into a compact cylinder about 5 or 6 inches long. Set on a cookie sheet lined with parchment paper. Repeat for the remaining dough squares, setting them 2 inches apart on the cookie sheet. Brush again with the egg wash and sprinkle with the remaining salt and caraway seeds. Cover the dough with a damp towel and let rise in a warm place for about 30 minutes or until the sticks have doubled in volume.

Preheat the oven to 350 degrees F. Remove the towel, transfer the pretzel sticks to the oven, and bake for about 30 minutes or until golden brown.

NUTRITION FACTS *—1 monkey bread pretzel stick*

100	calories	10G	total carbohydrate
6G	total fat	2G	sugars
4G	saturated fat	460MG	sodium
25MG	cholesterol	2G	protein

Monkey Bread Cinnamon Rolls

Yields 12 cinnamon rolls

This sweet roll recipe is another easy — and sinfully delicious — twist on the versatile Monkey Bread recipe. The frosting should be spread generously and rolling the sweet cinnamon filling inside guarantees a delectable end result. I always make extra frosting so my guests can choose to add more if they seem so inclined. This is one recipe you'll not have to worry about leftovers!

Monkey Bread dough *(page 33)*

FOR THE CINNAMON FILLING

½   cup unsalted butter, slightly softened

1¼ cups light brown sugar

2   tablespoons granulated sugar

2½ tablespoons ground cinnamon

FOR THE FROSTING

2   ounces cream cheese

1   cup confectioners' sugar

2   tablespoons milk

Prepare the Monkey Bread dough and let it rise.

While the dough is rising, prepare the cinnamon filling. Place the butter, brown sugar, granulated sugar, and cinnamon in a bowl and stir until smooth. Set aside.

To prepare the frosting, place the cream cheese in the bowl of an electric mixer fitted with the paddle attachment and beat on low speed for 3 to 4 minutes. Add the confectioners' sugar and milk and continue to mix until incorporated. Set aside.

Preheat the oven to 350 degrees F. Lightly butter a 9-inch by 11-inch cake pan and set aside. Turn out the dough onto a lightly floured work surface and roll out to a thickness of ¼ inch; the dough will measure about 18 inches by 14 inches. Spread the cinnamon filling evenly over the dough and then roll up a shorter side of the dough to form a long log. Cut the dough crosswise into 12 slices about 1½ inches wide. Lay each slice in the prepared cake pan with a cut side up; it's fine if the rolls are touching one another (use a second pan if necessary). Let the cinnamon rolls rise in a warm place for 20 minutes.

Transfer to the oven and bake the rolls for 15 minutes or until golden brown. Remove from the oven, drizzle the frosting evenly over all the cinnamon rolls, and serve immediately.

NUTRITION FACTS —*1 cinnamon roll*

520 calories	16G saturated fat	68G total carbohydrate	360MG sodium
26G total fat	70MG cholesterol	40G sugars	5G protein

This is one recipe you'll not
have to worry about leftovers!

2 APPETIZERS AND HORS D'OEUVRES

APPETIZERS AND HORS D'OEUVRES

Appetizers and hors d'oeuvres are a key part of my game plan whenever I entertain at home. I'll set out cold appetizers just before my guests arrive, placing them strategically in the room (or rooms) where I'd like them to congregate. About 10 or 15 minutes in, I'll put the warm appetizers in the oven so they're ready about 30 minutes into the gathering. This is usually perfect timing and sets the stage for the rest of the evening. I suggest you practice making these dishes ahead of time, and develop a repertoire of favorite appetizers you can rely on. This takes a lot of the stress out of the equation and will help you perfect your craft. Have a good feeling about what you're serving, knowing it will look and taste great. I always advise people at my cooking classes not to serve a dish for the first time when you're trying to impress with your cooking abilities. "Keep your cooking repertoire for entertaining in the fairway," as I like to say, serve what you do best and you'll have terrific results.

In the same way, I rely on my "best of repertoire" appetizers and hors d'oeuvres to take on the road or prepare for VIP events. You will find most of these dishes covered in this chapter. My other tips? When hosting and cooking for a great party, over-prepare: Set the table well before the guests arrive with all the serving utensils and glassware, be sure all the beverages are chilled appropriately, and clean the kitchen before anyone arrives. Take a quick shower and change before your party so you can feel more relaxed and enjoy all of the appreciation for your efforts!

At Neiman Marcus, appetizers and hors d'oeuvres play an important role in catering events as well as on our menus. These in-store events represent a big piece of our restaurant business every year. Typically, they're centered on a personal appearance by a designer, and usually showcase new merchandise for the upcoming season. Over the years we've hosted designers such as Giorgio Armani, Tom Ford, Carolina Herrera, and Ralph Lauren, just to name a few. In some cases, the designers ask to approve the menu beforehand; in a few cases they will send recipes and rely on us to deliver them accurately. On more than one occasion, designers have sent chefs from Italy or Paris to really make the evening's meal as authentic as possible. These are the type of events I love the most, the ones where people get really involved and the experience is "over the top" for all involved. The only downside is that sometimes the setup for guest chefs requires us to prepare food at another location — in hallways behind the scenes or even in kitchens we've never been in before. Never a dull moment, as they say!

Truffle Parmesan French Fries

Yields 6 servings

Making French fries at home is simpler than you might think. All you need is a candy thermometer, a large, heavy-bottomed saucepan, and enough olive oil, peanut oil, or grapeseed oil to fill the pan halfway. I was first introduced to fried food at home in the early 1990s, when I got my first FryDaddy electric deep-fryer for my birthday. I believe it held about four cups of oil and was fine for making simple fries at home. These days, home fryers come with all sorts of bells and whistles, so tackling some of the recipes in this chapter that call for deep-frying shouldn't present any problems at all. Whether you decide to go "old school" or invest in an electric fryer is your choice.

FOR THE FRIES

2	quarts peanut oil, for deep-frying
6	large russet potatoes, washed, and peeled
1	teaspoon truffle oil
½	cup freshly grated Parmesan cheese
½	tablespoon kosher salt

Roasted Garlic Aioli
(see variation to Simple Aioli, page 227)

Smoked Tomato Ketchup
(page 229)

Caramelized Onion Dip
(page 228)

SUGGESTED WINE PAIRING

Rutherford Hill Chardonnay

To prepare the fries, pour the peanut oil into a deep-fryer or a large, heavy-bottomed saucepan set over high heat; there should be at least 4 inches between the oil and the top of the pan as the oil will bubble up once you add the fries. Heat the oil to 325 degrees F. Cut the potatoes into long strips, ¼ inch wide and ¼ inch thick. Transfer to a large bowl of water to keep from turning brown. Rinse until the water runs clear. Transfer the potatoes to a colander to drain and pat dry completely with paper towels. Working in batches and using a skimmer or large slotted spoon, lower the fries into the hot oil and cook until they appear limp and just start to take on a light golden color. Remove with the skimmer and transfer to a cookie sheet lined with paper towels. Repeat for the remaining potatoes. Note that at this stage, the fries will only be blanched and not cooked through and crisp. Be sure to check your thermometer to keep the temperature of the oil at 325 degrees F.

> **CHEF'S NOTE**
>
> Be sure to follow the instructions for frying twice at different temperatures to get the crispiest fries.

After all the potatoes have been blanched, raise the temperature of the oil to 375 degrees F. and repeat the cooking process until all the fries and have turned brown and crispy, about 5 minutes. Drain on clean paper towels for 30 seconds, transfer to a bowl, and drizzle with the truffle oil. Sprinkle with the Parmesan cheese and salt. Serve immediately with the aioli, ketchup, and onion dip.

NUTRITION FACTS —*1 serving*

550 calories	6G saturated fat	60G total carbohydrate	420MG sodium
33G total fat	5MG cholesterol	3G sugars	8G protein

House-Made Pizzas

Yields dough for two 8-inch pizzas or 3 thin-crust pizzas

Like many of you, I've been watching how popular outdoor kitchens have become, and like you, I want one too! From the outdoor pizza ovens to the high-powered grills, and of course the 52-inch HD TV — all of this has made at-home, backyard entertaining so much more enjoyable, particularly when you can take it outside and prepare the meal as if you were in your very own kitchen. There's nothing quite like cooking in comfort outside, under the stars. Pizza is one of those dishes that I've moved outside to my grill. The Lynx grill that I own reaches 1,000 degrees F., maybe a bit too hot for the average home cook to bake their pizza in. But no worries if you don't have yours yet — all you really need is a good pizza stone and an oven or grill heat that can reach at least 500 degrees F. Whether you make the pizzas inside or outside, you won't be disappointed with the Neiman Marcus classic pizza recipes that follow.

¼	ounce active dry yeast *(1 package)*
2	tablespoons plus ½ teaspoon sugar
1¼	cups warm water *(100 degrees F.)*
2	cups bread flour
½	cup semolina flour
1	teaspoon kosher salt
2	tablespoons olive oil

Place the yeast, ½ teaspoon of the sugar, and ½ cup of the warm water in the bowl of an electric mixer fitted with the dough hook attachment. Mix briefly to break up the yeast and let rest for 5 minutes. Add the bread flour, semolina flour, the remaining 2 tablespoons sugar, the salt, and 1 tablespoon of the olive oil. Mix on medium speed for about 3 minutes until all the flour is incorporated and the dough does not stick to the sides of the bowl. If the dough is still a little sticky, add about 2 tablespoons more bread flour. Continue to knead the dough in the mixer for 5 or 6 minutes. Place the remaining 1 tablespoon olive oil in a large bowl (it should be big enough to accommodate the dough once it has doubled in volume). Roll the ball of dough in the olive oil. At this point you can refrigerate or freeze the dough ball. If freezing, you will need to allow 3 or 4 hours to thaw out the dough ball when you're ready to make your pizza, giving the dough enough time to proof again to double its size before rolling out to finish the pizza. Cover the bowl with plastic wrap and let the dough rise in a warm place for about 1 hour or until it has doubled in volume.

CHEF'S NOTES

I like to have my guests make their own pizzas at my house. To make things easy, I roll out the dough and set out various toppings on my kitchen island and let my guests "build their own."

Bread flour vs. all-purpose flour? Bread flour contains more protein, helping to make the end result a bit more chewy and dense, the type of pizza crust I prefer. However, all-purpose flour also works fine.

Remove the dough from the bowl and place on a clean work service sprinkled with a little flour so the dough does not stick when rolled out. Punch the dough down and divide into 2 pieces. With the first piece, press down and push out to form a flat circle. With a rolling pin or by hand, continue to push the dough out to form an 8-inch crust; sprinkle more flour on the work surface if the dough begins to stick. Repeat for the second piece of dough. Once the second pizza is rolled out, you're ready for your pizza toppings.

Smoked Salmon Pizza

Yields two 8-inch pizzas or 3 thin-crust pizzas

For this recipe, I prefer a thinly sliced hot-smoked salmon, preferably smoked over alder wood, which lends a delicate, slightly sweet quality and is well suited to pizza. There are some great domestic local goat cheeses available these days, and I encourage you to use one you like.

2	teaspoons olive oil
	Pizza dough *(page 44)*
1½	cups shredded mozzarella *(or mozzarella-provolone mixture)*
6	ounces goat cheese *(preferably a good-quality imported chèvre)*
½	teaspoon freshly ground black pepper
4	ounces thinly sliced smoked salmon
6	sprigs fresh dill *(or ½ cup mixed greens)*
½	teaspoon fresh lemon juice

SUGGESTED WINE PAIRING

Bollinger Special Cuvée Champagne

Preheat the oven to 500 degrees F. or prepare the grill to reach its hottest temperature. Place a pizza stone in the oven or on the grill grate. For the pizzas, drizzle 1 teaspoon of the olive oil over the two rounds of dough. Sprinkle the mozzarella evenly over the dough leaving a 1-inch border around the edge. Evenly spread out the goat cheese, then drizzle the remaining 1 teaspoon olive oil and sprinkle with the pepper. Carefully transfer the dough rounds to a pizza stone or pizza pan. If using the oven, bake for 6 to 8 minutes or until the crust is brown and crispy. If using a grill, close the lid and grill the pizza over medium-high heat for 7 or 8 minutes. Remove the pizzas, top with slices of smoked salmon and the dill sprigs, and drizzle with the lemon juice. Cut each pizza into 8 slices and serve.

NUTRITION FACTS *—1 eight-inch pizza*

1600	calories	**145G**	total carbohydrate
69G	total fat	**14G**	sugars
35G	saturated fat	**2150MG**	sodium
215MG	cholesterol	**94G**	protein

CHEF'S NOTES

Use a low-moisture mozzarella as it works best for melting and melding with the flavors of the goat cheese and salmon.

This recipe also works well as a breakfast pizza along with some softly scrambled eggs. I like to top the pizza with a little bit of caviar.

I'm a thin-crust guy, starting back at Mack and Manco's in Ocean City, NJ.

Deli Pizza

Yields two 8-inch pizzas or 3 thin-crust pizzas

This is an upscale version of the classic pepperoni pizza. Of course, here at Neiman Marcus, we use only the best meats and in this recipe we call for upscale imported types. Soppressata is a rustic dry ham salami and a specialty of southern Italy; it sometimes contains spicy chile. Genoa salami is an American salami in the Genoese style that is made with either pork or beef. If one or the other is unavailable, simply increase the other meat toppings accordingly.

Pizza dough *(page 44)*

1   teaspoon olive oil

3   tablespoons tomato-basil sauce *(preferably San Marzano)*

2   ounces thinly sliced Soppressata

1   ounce thinly sliced Genoa salami

1   ounce thinly sliced prosciutto

1   cup grated mozzarella

1   cup grated provolone cheese

1   tablespoon freshly grated Parmesan cheese

Preheat the oven to 500 degrees F. or prepare the grill to reach its hottest temperature. Sprinkle the two rounds of pizza dough with the olive oil and top with the tomato-basil sauce, leaving a 1-inch border around the edge. Evenly place the soppressata, Genoa salami, and prosciutto over the sauce and sprinkle evenly with the mozzarella and provolone. Carefully transfer the dough rounds to a pizza stone or pizza pan. If using the oven, bake for 6 to 8 minutes or until the crust is brown and crispy. If using a grill, close the lid and grill the pizza over medium-high heat for 7 or 8 minutes. Remove the pizzas and sprinkle with Parmesan before cutting each pizza into 8 slices.

CHEF'S NOTE

If you prefer, use 2 cups of either the mozzarella or the provolone cheese.

SUGGESTED WINE PAIRING

Goretti Sagrantino di Montefalco

NUTRITION FACTS —*1 eight-inch pizza*

| 1420 calories | 27G saturated fat | 148G total carbohydrate | 3180MG sodium |
| 60G total fat | 140MG cholesterol | 15G sugars | 66G protein |

Margherita Pizza

Yields two 8-inch pizzas or 3 thin-crust pizzas

The key to this recipe is a great sauce, and the most important ingredient is the canned tomato-basil sauce. My favorite is the San Marzano brand.

Pizza dough *(page 44)*

¾   cup canned tomato-basil sauce *(such as San Marzano)*

6   ounces fresh mozzarella *(buffalo mozzarella, if available)*, thinly sliced

2   tablespoons freshly grated Parmesan cheese

10   fresh basil leaves, torn, for garnish

SUGGESTED WINE PAIRING

Il Poggione Rosso di Montalcino Sangiovese

Preheat the oven to 500 degrees F. or prepare the grill. Top the two rounds of dough with the tomato-basil sauce, mozzarella, and Parmesan, leaving a 1-inch border around the edge. Carefully transfer the dough rounds to a pizza stone or pizza pan. If using the oven, bake for 6 to 8 minutes or until the crust is brown and crispy. If using a grill, close the lid and grill the pizza over medium-high heat for 7 or 8 minutes. Remove the pizzas and top with the torn basil leaves. Cut each pizza into 8 slices and serve.

CHEF'S NOTE

Feel free to get creative with your cheese when making pizza. I, for one, love a mild blue cheese on my pizza.

NUTRITION FACTS *—1 eight-inch pizza*

1180	calories	153G	total carbohydrate
41G	total fat	19G	sugars
17G	saturated fat	2050MG	sodium
70MG	cholesterol	46G	protein

Shrimp and Vegetable Rice Paper Rolls

Yields 12 rolls (6 servings)

It was hard deciding which spring roll appetizer to include in the book: Crispy or soft? So I opted for the easy way out and kept them both; they've both been best sellers in our San Francisco Rotunda over the years. Both recipes make for great sharing when dining as a group. I particularly like the soft rolls because only the shrimp and noodles are cooked — everything else in the filling is fresh, making it a healthy dish. I've been known to make a hundred of these rolls at a time and bring them to a party as the appetizer; creating an assembly line with a friend speeds the process and usually, not one is leftover, they're that good. Be sure you make enough of the dipping sauce — it'll go fast as well.

3 tablespoons peanut butter

3 tablespoons low-sodium soy sauce

¼ cup sweet chile garlic sauce *(such as Mae Ploy)*

FOR THE RICE PAPER ROLLS

2 tablespoons extra-virgin olive oil

1 pound extra-small *("gumbo")* shrimp, peeled and cleaned *(60 shrimp)*

4 ounces vermicelli rice noodles, cooked *(follow the directions on the package)*

2 teaspoons sweet chile garlic sauce *(such as Mae Ploy)*

1 teaspoon low-sodium soy sauce

12 rice papers

2 cups cored and finely julienned Napa cabbage

1 cup julienned carrots

2 scallions, thinly sliced on an angle *(green part only)*

1 cup fresh cilantro leaves

SUGGESTED WINE PAIRING

Shimizu-No-Mai "Pure" Sake

For the sauce, place the peanut butter, soy sauce, chile garlic sauce, and ¼ cup water in a blender and blend until smooth. Set aside at room temperature until ready to use. If not using right away, you can refrigerate for up to a month.

For the rice paper rolls, heat the olive oil in a heavy-bottomed sauté pan over medium heat. When hot, add the shrimp and sauté for 5 to 7 minutes until fully cooked and pink in color. Remove from the heat and let cool to room temperature.

Place the noodles in a bowl, add the chile garlic sauce and soy sauce, and toss together. Half-fill a large bowl with hot water. Remove a rice paper sheet from the package and cover up the remaining papers with a damp towel so they do not dry out. Place the rice paper in the hot water and let sit for 20 seconds, making sure it is completely submerged. Remove from the water and place on a dry paper towel for a few seconds to drain. Transfer to a clean work surface. Evenly lay 5 shrimp, side by side, on the lower bottom of the wrapper about 2 inches from the bottom edge.

Divide the noodle mixture, cabbage, carrots, scallions, and cilantro into 12 equal portions. Place one portion in the rice wrapper; do not overload the filling or the roll will break apart. Starting at the bottom of the wrapper, begin to roll up the lower edge over the ingredients. Once the filling is enclosed, tuck in the sides of each wrapper. Finish rolling tightly and place the roll on a plate, seam-side down. Cover with another damp towel and repeat for the remaining rice paper wrappers and filling ingredients.

After all the rolls are completed, cut in half and place on a serving platter. If not using immediately, transfer to an airtight container and be careful not to let the rolls touch or they will stick to each other and tear when separated. Serve with the peanut sauce.

NUTRITION FACTS —*2 rolls*

290 calories	1.5G saturated fat	34G total carbohydrate	950MG sodium
10G total fat	95MG cholesterol	10G sugars	16G protein

Crispy Shrimp and Vegetable Spring Rolls

Yields 12 rolls (6 servings)

I'm telling you, these crispy spring rolls are addictive! Unlike the previous rice paper wrapper recipe, the ingredients are precooked. As with that recipe, have all your ingredients for the filling ready to go as you need to stir-fry the mixture quickly, all in about 1 minute. It's a good idea to "volunteer" a friend to help because it will make the preparation go a lot quicker. This is one case where many hands make light work, rather than too many cooks spoiling the broth!

FOR THE DIPPING SAUCE

¼   cup low-sodium soy sauce

¼   cup sweet chile garlic sauce *(such as Mae Ploy)*

FOR THE SPRING ROLLS

1   tablespoon sesame oil

1   teaspoon minced garlic

1   teaspoon peeled and minced fresh ginger

1   pound extra small *("gumbo")* shrimp, peeled and cleaned *(60 to 70 shrimp)*

2   cups julienned carrots

2   cups bean sprouts

2   cups cored and finely julienned Napa cabbage

2   scallions, thinly sliced on an angle *(white and green parts)*

1   teaspoon low-sodium soy sauce

2   teaspoons sweet chile garlic sauce *(such as Mae Ploy)*

½   cup fresh cilantro leaves

12   spring roll wrappers *(found in the frozen food section)*

1   egg, lightly beaten

     Peanut oil, for frying

To prepare the dipping sauce, mix together the soy sauce and sweet chile sauce in a bowl and set aside. The sauce will keep in the refrigerator for up to 1 month.

To prepare the spring rolls, set a large, heavy-bottomed sauté pan or wok over medium-high heat. Add the sesame oil and when hot and almost smoking, add the garlic and ginger. Stir-fry for 10 seconds, making sure not to burn. Add the shrimp and stir continuously for 30 seconds. Add the carrots and stir-fry for 15 seconds longer. Turn off the heat and add the bean sprouts, cabbage, scallions, soy sauce, and sweet chile sauce. Transfer the mixture to a large roasting pan, spread out, and let cool. Once cool, fold in the cilantro leaves and drain excess liquid.

To assemble the spring rolls, remove a wrapper from the package and cover the remaining wrappers with a damp towel so they do not dry out. On a clean work surface, lay the wrapper with one corner facing you and place 1 heaping tablespoonful of the filling on the lower bottom part of the wrapper, about 2 inches from the edge. Do not overload the filling or the roll will break apart. Whisk together the egg and 2 tablespoons water in a bowl. Use a pastry brush to dampen the sides of the wrapper with the egg wash to seal it. Starting at the bottom, tightly roll the lower edge over the ingredients. Once the filling is enclosed, tuck in the sides of each wrapper and continue rolling. Place the roll on a plate, seam side down, and cover with another damp towel. Repeat for the remaining spring roll wrappers.

Pour 4 inches of oil into a large saucepan and heat to 350 degrees F. Using a strainer, carefully lower 4 spring rolls at a time into the oil. Deep-fry the spring rolls for about 4 minutes or until golden brown, checking the temperature of the oil and adjusting the heat as necessary. Remove from the pan with the strainer or a slotted spoon and drain on paper towels. Repeat for the remaining spring rolls. Serve with the dipping sauce or prepared Chinese hot mustard sauce.

NUTRITION FACTS —*2 rolls*

229 calories	1G saturated fat	22G total carbohydrate	890MG sodium
6G total fat	150MG cholesterol	8G sugars	29G protein

Homemade BBQ Potato Chips with Pimento-Cheese Dip

Yields 2½ cups (5 servings) potato chips and 2¼ cups dip

The hardest part about making fresh potato chips is setting them aside and avoiding the temptation of eating them before your dining companions get the chance to enjoy them! We've been known to tape the container closed with a note attached warning of dire consequences in the event passersby have a hard time keeping their hands off! The pimento cheese dip is a recipe that has been worked over for years in our kitchens. There's always someone telling us they have a slightly better version, so we test it out and tweak our recipe now and again.

FOR THE PIMENTO-CHEESE DIP

4	ounces cream cheese, softened
¼	cup sour cream
¼	cup mayonnaise
1	cup grated cheddar cheese
½	teaspoon garlic powder
½	teaspoon onion powder
¼	teaspoon celery salt
1	tablespoon grated onion
½	teaspoon paprika
1	teaspoon kosher salt
	Pinch of cayenne
1	teaspoon Worcestershire sauce
3	tablespoons diced bottled pimentos

FOR THE BBQ SPICE

1	teaspoon paprika
1	teaspoon pure red chile powder
½	teaspoon ancho chile powder
½	teaspoon garlic salt
½	teaspoon onion salt
½	teaspoon freshly ground black pepper
⅛	teaspoon cayenne
1	teaspoon kosher salt

SUGGESTED WINE PAIRING

The Federalist Zinfandel

FOR THE POTATO CHIPS

2	quarts peanut, grapeseed, or canola oil
4	large Idaho or russet potatoes *(about 3 pounds)*, washed, peeled, and dried

To prepare the pimento-cheese dip, place the cream cheese in the bowl of an electric mixer fitted with the paddle attachment and add the sour cream and mayonnaise. Mix on low speed until smooth. Add the cheddar cheese, garlic powder, onion powder, celery salt, grated onion, paprika, cayenne, salt, and Worcestershire sauce and mix for about 1 minute on low speed. Add the pimentos and mix just enough to incorporate.

To prepare the BBQ spice, mix all the ingredients together in a small bowl and set aside.

To prepare the chips, pour the peanut oil into a large, heavy-bottomed saucepan set over high heat; there should be at least 4 inches between the oil and the top of the pan as the oil will bubble up once you add the potato chips. Using a deep frying/candy thermometer, heat the oil to 350 degrees F. Meanwhile, using a mandoline slicer, finely slice the potatoes and transfer to a large bowl of water to keep them from turning brown. Rinse until the water runs clear. Transfer the potatoes to a colander to drain and pat dry completely with paper towels. Working in batches and using a strainer or large slotted spoon, lower the chips into the hot oil and cook until they start to take on a light golden color, 3 to 5 minutes. Remove with the strainer and transfer to a cookie sheet lined with paper towels. Repeat for the remaining potatoes. Be sure to check your thermometer to keep the temperature of the oil at 350 degrees F. Transfer the chips to a mixing bowl and dust with the BBQ spice to coat thoroughly and evenly. Serve with the dip.

NUTRITION FACTS —*½ cup potato chips*

480	calories	55G	total carbohydrate
28G	total fat	2G	sugars
4.5G	saturated fat	630MG	sodium
0MG	cholesterol	5G	protein

NUTRITION FACTS —*½ cup pimento-cheese dip*

300	calories	10G	total carbohydrate
27G	total fat	4G	sugars
12G	saturated fat	470MG	sodium
65MG	cholesterol	4G	protein

Hummus Three Ways with Garlic-Herb Grissini

Yields about 30 breadsticks

Our hummus is another one of the recipes in the book with popular variations that we couldn't decide among — so we included all the variations! I love to serve the dips together to show off their taste and color combinations. The basic chickpea hummus recipe also forms the basis of the red pepper hummus. The edamame recipe uses an alternative base. As good as the recipes are, I'll admit all three hummus recipes are simply vehicles for the *grissini* (Italian for "breadsticks"). They are simply "to die for," and another item you'll need to hide to avoid having them eaten before they even get to the table. As an alternative, offer vegetable sticks.

FOR THE ROASTED GARLIC

12   cloves garlic, peeled

½   cup olive oil

FOR THE BREADSTICKS

¼   ounce active dry yeast *(1 package)*

1   cup warm water *(100 degrees F.)*
    Pinch of sugar

3½ cups bread flour

1   cup semolina flour

1   tablespoon kosher salt

1   tablespoon butter, softened

3   tablespoons chopped mixed fresh herbs *(such as Italian parsley, thyme, and oregano)*

    Kosher salt

SUGGESTED WINE PAIRING

Hanna Sauvignon Blanc

Preheat the oven to 325 degrees F. To prepare the roasted garlic, place the garlic and olive oil in a small, ovenproof skillet and cover with foil. Roast in the oven for 25 minutes or until the garlic is soft. Turn off the oven, remove the skillet, and let the garlic cool. Remove the garlic from the oil and puree in a food processor; set aside. Save the oil to prepare the grissini.

To prepare the breadsticks, in the bowl of an electric mixer fitted with a dough hook, combine the yeast, ½ cup of the warm water, and sugar. Mix on low speed for 5 seconds to combine and then let rest for 5 minutes.

In a mixing bowl, combine 3 cups of the bread flour with ½ cup of the semolina flour and the salt. With the mixer running at low speed, add the flour mixture to the yeast mixture and add the butter, 2 tablespoons of the reserved roasted garlic oil, and the mixed herbs. Add the remaining ½ cup of warm water and 2 tablespoons of the pureed roasted garlic. Increase the mixer speed to medium and continue to mix for 10 minutes; if the dough becomes too sticky, add a little more bread flour. Transfer the dough to a clean work surface and shape with your hands into a ball. Drizzle about ½ tablespoon of the reserved roasted garlic oil into a large, clean mixing bowl and roll the dough in it to cover thoroughly. Cover the bowl with plastic wrap and set in a warm place for 1 hour to allow the dough to rise and double in size.

These grissini are tall and elegant with a crunchy texture that simply invites nibblers. Serve so they stand upright to accentuate their visual appeal.

In a bowl, mix together the remaining ½ cup bread flour and ½ cup semolina flour. Remove the dough from the bowl and place on a clean work surface. Divide the ball into 4 pieces.

Brush a large cookie sheet with olive oil and sprinkle with 1 tablespoon of the flour mixture. Sprinkle ¼ cup of the flour mixture on the work surface and roll out the dough pieces into rectangles 10 inches long, 6 inches wide, and slightly less than ¼ inch thick. In a small bowl, mix 2 tablespoons of the roasted garlic oil with 1 tablespoon water and brush the dough rectangles with the mixture. Lightly sprinkle the dough with kosher salt. Using a paring knife or pizza wheel, cut ¼-inch strips and carefully lift them onto the prepared cookie sheet, leaving the strips ½ inch apart. When you have filled the cookie sheet, let the grissini rise for about 8 minutes longer.

Preheat oven to 350 degrees F. Transfer the grissini to the oven and bake for 10 to 12 minutes until the breadsticks are golden brown and slightly crisp. Repeat for the remaining dough. After the grissini has cooled, transfer to an airtight container and keep at room temperature.

CHEF'S NOTE

If you keep grissini in an airtight container, they will stay fresh for up to 3 days. They're best slightly reheated after the second day.

NUTRITION FACTS —*1 grissini*

70 calories	12G total carbohydrate
1.5G total fat	0G sugars
0G saturated fat	200MG sodium
0MG cholesterol	2G protein

Chickpea Hummus

Yields 2½ cups (5 servings)

2   *(15½-ounce)* cans chickpeas, drained

1   cup tahini paste

3   cloves garlic, smashed

3   tablespoons fresh lemon juice

2   teaspoons ground cumin

¼   cup olive oil, plus more for drizzling

2   teaspoons kosher salt

½   teaspoon za'atar *(see Chef's Note)*

Place the chickpeas, tahini, and garlic in the bowl of a food processor fitted with a metal blade. Process for about 3 minutes, until the mixture is smooth. Add the lemon juice, cumin, olive oil, and salt. Continue to process for 1 minute longer. Adjust the seasoning as necessary.

When serving the hummus, make a small indentation in the middle of the hummus with the back of a teaspoon and drizzle with a little olive oil. Sprinkle with the za'atar. Serve with Grissini (page 56).

NUTRITION FACTS *— ½ cup*

260 calories	**19G** total carbohydrate
18G total fat	**0G** sugars
2.5G saturated fat	**550MG** sodium
0MG cholesterol	**7G** protein

CHEF'S NOTE

Za'atar is a Middle Eastern spice and herb blend. It is available in specialty grocery stores and markets. The tahini paste, made from sesame seeds, can also be purchased at most health-food stores.

Edamame Hummus

Yields 3 cups (6 servings)

16   ounces frozen shelled edamame, defrosted

½   cup tahini paste

2   cloves garlic, smashed

¼   cup olive oil, plus more for drizzling

2   tablespoons fresh lemon juice

1   teaspoon ground cumin

1   tablespoon kosher salt

½   teaspoon za'atar *(see Chef's Note, opposite)*

Bring a large saucepan of water to a boil. Place the edamame in a colander or metal strainer that can fit in the saucepan. Dip the edamame in the water for 45 seconds. Remove the colander, rinse with cold running water, and drain well. Transfer the edamame to the bowl of a food processor fitted with a metal blade and add the tahini, garlic, olive oil, lemon juice, cumin, salt, and ½ cup of water. Process for 2 minutes and then stop the processor to scrape down the sides of the bowl. Process for 2 minutes longer, until completely smooth. Adjust the seasonings as necessary.

When serving the hummus, make a small indentation in the middle of the hummus with the back of a teaspoon and drizzle with a little olive oil. Sprinkle with the za'atar. Serve with Grissini (page 56).

CHEF'S NOTE

Edamame — the Japanese word means "beans on branches" — are soy beans harvested when they are soft, just before they fully mature and harden.

NUTRITION FACTS *— ½ cup*

310 calories	13G total carbohydrate
24G total fat	2G sugars
3G saturated fat	980MG sodium
0MG cholesterol	13G protein

Roasted Red Bell Pepper Hummus

Yields 3 cups (6 servings)

Chickpea Hummus *(see recipe, previous page)*

1   *(12-ounce)* jar roasted red bell peppers, drained

Prepare the Chickpea Hummus. Add the roasted red peppers to the hummus in the food processor and process for about 30 seconds or until thoroughly incorporated and the mixture is very smooth.

When serving the hummus, make a small indentation in the middle of the hummus with the back of a teaspoon and drizzle with a little olive oil. Sprinkle with the za'atar. Serve with Grissini (page 56).

NUTRITION FACTS *— ½ cup*

310 calories	13G total carbohydrate
24G total fat	2G sugars
3G saturated fat	980MG sodium
0MG cholesterol	13G protein

Anita's Chopped Chicken Liver with Pickled Red Onions and Grilled Flatbread

Yields 6 servings

We just had to include this recipe in the book. Anita Hirsch's famous chopped liver is a favorite, especially around the holidays in late December. Have you ever said, "This is one recipe I'll only make certain times of the year"? Well, this is one of those recipes. It's truly decadent and worth every calorie — and no, we will not offer a healthier version! You need to be "all in" on this one.

FOR THE PICKLED RED ONIONS

1   cup apple cider vinegar

¼   cup sugar

1   large red onion, thinly sliced *(julienne)*

FOR THE CHICKEN LIVERS

1   pound chicken livers, rinsed and drained

1   onion, quartered, plus 2 tablespoons diced onion

3   cloves garlic, peeled

3   cups prepared chicken broth

3   hard-boiled eggs

2   teaspoons kosher salt

1   teaspoon freshly ground black pepper

¼   cup mayonnaise

2   tablespoons schmaltz *(optional, see Chef's Notes)*

FOR THE GRILLED FLATBREAD

¼   cup olive oil

2   cloves garlic, finely minced

1   teaspoon kosher salt

3   tablespoons za'atar *(see Chef's Note, page 58)*

3   plain naan breads

3   pita breads *(no pocket)*

To prepare the pickled onions, pour the vinegar and ¼ cup water into a small saucepan and set over medium-high heat. Stir in the sugar and bring to a boil. Place the red onion in a bowl and pour the hot liquid over the onion to completely cover. When cool, transfer to an airtight container and let marinate in the refrigerator for at least 4 hours or overnight.

To prepare the chicken livers, place the chicken livers, quartered onion, garlic, and chicken broth in a small saucepan; the broth should cover the livers. Bring to a boil over high heat, then turn down the heat to a simmer. Continue to simmer for 20 to 25 minutes until the livers are no longer pink. Drain and let cool; reserve the livers, garlic, and quartered onion.

Using a grinder with a small hole attachment (alternatively, a food processor fitted with a metal blade), grind the reserved cooked liver, garlic, and quartered onion into a small mixing bowl. Then grind the 2 tablespoons diced onion, and 2 of the hard-boiled eggs. Add the salt and pepper, and fold in the mayonnaise and schmaltz (if using). Mix well and transfer the mixture to a serving dish. Grate the remaining hard-boiled egg. Garnish the liver mixture with the grated egg and pickled red onion.

To prepare the flatbread, prepare the grill (alternatively, use a toaster oven or broiler). Combine the olive oil, garlic, salt, and za'atar in a bowl. Using a pastry brush, spread the olive oil mixture evenly on both sides of the naan and pita breads. Grill over medium-low heat for 3 to 4 minutes on each side or until golden brown. Cut into small triangles and serve with the chopped chicken liver.

SUGGESTED WINE PAIRING

M. Chapoutier Côtes-du-Rhône Belleruche Rouge

NUTRITION FACTS —*1 serving*

550 calories	5G saturated fat	54G total carbohydrate	2360MG sodium
25G total fat	360MG cholesterol	11G sugars	24G protein

Ahi Tuna Tartare on Wonton Crisps

Yields about 48 crisps (16 servings)

This is one of those recipes that people love because it's conveniently small and just a bite or two. It's important you follow our lead and use the best raw tuna available. When you ask your fishmonger or supermarket seafood honcho to prepare you a couple of pounds of tuna for this recipe, be sure to request that they don't sell you any raw tuna loin that has the blood line in the fillet. This is the darker red area you see sometimes in fresh tuna. What you want is "sushi grade," light red to almost opaque, letting you know it's as fresh as possible.

FOR THE WONTON CHIPS

Peanut, grapeseed, or canola oil, for frying

24 frozen wonton wrappers, cut in half to form triangles

FOR THE AHI TUNA TARTARE

2 pounds center-cut ahi tuna fillet

½ tablespoon peeled and minced fresh ginger

1 teaspoon finely minced garlic

¼ cup soy sauce

1 teaspoon sesame oil

1 teaspoon Sriracha sauce

2 teaspoons teriyaki sauce

1 tablespoon fresh lime juice

¼ cup sweet chile garlic sauce *(such as Mae Ploy)*

3 tablespoons seeded and finely minced jalapeño

2 tablespoons finely minced fresh cilantro

1 tablespoon finely minced shallot

1 tablespoon chopped fresh chives

1 avocado, halved, pitted, peeled, and finely diced, for garnish *(optional)*

Wasabi Mayonnaise *(page 117),* for garnish *(optional)*

To prepare the wonton chips, heat the peanut oil in a deep-fryer or a large, heavy-bottomed saucepan over high heat; there should be at least 4 inches between the oil and the top of the pan as the oil will bubble up once you add the wonton wrappers. Heat the oil to 350 degrees F. and follow the directions on the wrapper package for frying spring rolls. The wrappers should be golden and crisp. Remove and drain on paper towels.

To prepare the ahi tuna tartare, use a very sharp knife to cut the tuna into ¼-inch dice. Transfer to a bowl set inside another bowl containing ice; it is important to keep the tuna very cold. In another small bowl, mix the ginger, garlic, soy sauce, sesame oil, Sriracha, teriyaki sauce, lime juice, and sweet chile sauce. About 30 minutes prior to serving, add the jalapeño, cilantro, shallot, and chives to the tuna and mix thoroughly. Add the soy sauce mixture to the tuna and gently fold together. Place about 1 ounce of the tuna tartare on each wonton crisp and garnish with the avocado and Wasabi Mayonnaise if desired.

> Be sure to ask for "sushi-grade" tuna for this recipe — it should have a light red, almost opaque color.

CHEF'S NOTES

If you prefer, serve good-quality sesame crackers instead of making wonton chips.

The shelf life of this recipe is short, once you mix the ingredients together — you should serve the same day.

NUTRITION FACTS —*3 wonton crisps and tartare*

120 calories	1.5G saturated fat	8G total carbohydrate	830MG sodium
8G total fat	0MG cholesterol	3G sugars	6G protein

SUGGESTED WINE PAIRING

Santa Margherita Prosecco

Gorgonzola Walnut Tartlets

Yields 30 tartlets (15 servings)

If you like blue cheese you'll love these tartlets. I think warm blue cheese is one of the better pleasures of life. Another bonus with this recipe is that it's one of the easiest you'll ever find — and it can be prepared ahead of time. Once you try it, it is sure to become one of your go-to appetizers for any party.

¼   cup walnut pieces

30   small phyllo pastry shells
(see Chef's Note)

1   cup Gorgonzola cheese, crumbled

1¼ cups sour cream

2   teaspoons minced fresh chives

½   teaspoon freshly ground
black pepper

Preheat the oven to 300 degrees F. Place the walnut pieces on a cookie sheet and toast in the oven for 5 minutes or until they start to darken and become fragrant. Remove from the oven and set aside. Place the phyllo shells on a large cookie sheet or in a roasting pan. In a bowl, mix together the Gorgonzola, sour cream, chives, and pepper. Using a small spoon, fill each tart shell with the Gorgonzola mixture and top with the toasted walnuts. If not serving immediately, reserve the tartlets in the refrigerator.

Transfer the tartlets to the oven and bake for 8 minutes until they are warm and the cheese is melted.

SUGGESTED WINE PAIRING

Bollinger Special Cuvée Champagne

NUTRITION FACTS —*2 tartlets*

130	calories	6G	total carbohydrate
10G	total fat	1G	sugars
6G	saturated fat	230MG	sodium
25MG	cholesterol	5G	protein

CHEF'S NOTE

The phyllo pastry shells can be found in the frozen food section of larger supermarkets or specialty markets.

Chicken Quesadillas with Guacamole and Roasted Tomato Salsa

Yields 4 servings

Having lived and worked in Texas for the past 25 years, there are not many types of quesadillas I haven't tasted. As more and more Mexican restaurants pop up around the country, the humble quesadilla has become artisan in nature, and creative cooks are filling tortillas with all sorts of ingredients. Here, we keep it simple and straightforward with our chicken filling and lots of cheese. By all means get creative with your fillings, but when you need a simple Tex-Mex fix, this recipe will not disappoint.

FOR THE ROASTED TOMATO SALSA

8	plum tomatoes, halved lengthwise
½	large onion, diced *(about 1 cup)*
3	cloves garlic, smashed
1	jalapeño, seeded and minced
1	tablespoon olive oil
¼	cup roughly chopped fresh cilantro leaves
1	teaspoon kosher salt
1	teaspoon freshly ground black pepper

FOR THE GUACAMOLE

4	avocados, halved, pitted, and peeled
2	cloves garlic, smashed and roughly chopped
1	serrano chile, roasted, peeled, seeded, and roughly chopped
3	tablespoons roughly chopped fresh cilantro leaves
	Juice of 1 lime
1	teaspoon kosher salt

FOR THE QUESADILLAS

8	small *(6-inch)* flour tortillas
2	cups shredded Monterey Jack cheese
1	jalapeño, seeded and thinly sliced
2	cups diced cooked chicken breast *(or store-bought rotisserie chicken)*
2	tablespoons olive oil

SUGGESTED WINE PAIRING

Markham Chardonnay

Preheat the oven to 400 degrees F. To prepare the salsa, place the tomatoes in a mixing bowl, add the onion, garlic, and jalapeño, and toss with the olive oil. Transfer to a roasting pan and roast in the oven for 25 minutes. Remove from the oven and let cool. Transfer the tomato mixture to a food processor fitted with a steel blade. Add the cilantro, salt, and pepper and pulse until the salsa is smooth but still with a few small chunks in it. Adjust the seasonings and transfer to an airtight container. Keep refrigerated; the salsa will keep for up to 5 days.

To prepare the guacamole, place the avocados, garlic, and serrano in a mixing bowl. Add the cilantro, lime juice, and salt and mash with a fork, leaving it a little chunky. Keep covered in the refrigerator until ready to serve so it does not discolor.

To prepare the quesadillas, lay out 4 of the tortillas on a clean work surface. Sprinkle them with half of the shredded cheese and the sliced jalapeño. Top with the chicken, add the remaining cheese, and top with the remaining tortillas. Set a griddle pan or a large, heavy-bottomed skillet over medium-low heat. Add 1 tablespoon of the oil to the pan, making sure the entire surface is covered by the oil. (If you want to decrease the calories, use nonstick spray instead of the oil.) Add 2 of the quesadillas and cook for about 2 minutes on each side until the tortillas begin to brown and the cheese is melted. Remove the quesadillas from the pan and repeat for the remaining quesadillas. Cut each quesadilla into 4 triangles. Serve with the salsa and guacamole.

CHEF'S NOTE

To roast the serrano chile, use tongs to hold it over a gas flame until the skin becomes charred and blackened. Let cool and remove the charred skin with your fingers; cut in half lengthwise and remove the seeds.

NUTRITION FACTS —*1 quesadilla*

840 calories	17G saturated fat	51G total carbohydrate	1290MG sodium
52G total fat	110MG cholesterol	6G sugars	44G protein

Flash-Fried Calamari with Thai Chile Dipping Sauce

Yields 4 servings

This recipe is another great reason to bust out your home fryer. Calamari have become one of the most popular "shared appetizers" in many of our restaurants. In some, we garnish our entrée salads with the warm calamari. We call it "flash-fried" because the calamari take less than a minute in the hot oil to crisp up and get their addictively crunchy quality.

FOR THE THAI CHILE DIPPING SAUCE

1   cup mayonnaise

3   tablespoons soy sauce

½   cup sweet chile garlic sauce *(such as Mae Ploy)*

FOR THE CALAMARI

1½   pounds calamari *(rings and tentacles)*

1   cup buttermilk

     Vegetable oil, for deep-frying

2   cups all-purpose flour *(or Wondra flour; see Chef's Notes)*

2   teaspoons kosher salt

1   teaspoon freshly ground black pepper

     Pinch of cayenne

1   tablespoon chopped fresh cilantro leaves

1   lemon, cut into 8 wedges

SUGGESTED WINE PAIRING

MAZZONI Vermentino Chardonnay

NUTRITION FACTS —*1 serving*

930 calories	74G total carbohydrate
52G total fat	17G sugars
8G saturated fat	2650MG sodium
425MG cholesterol	36G protein

To prepare the dipping sauce, place the mayonnaise in a mixing bowl, add the soy sauce and chile garlic sauce, and combine thoroughly. Transfer to an airtight container and keep in the refrigerator for up to 1 week.

To prepare the calamari, place the calamari in a glass or ceramic mixing bowl and add the buttermilk; add more if necessary to cover the calamari. Cover the bowl with plastic wrap and let marinate in the refrigerator for at least 2 hours or overnight.

Pour the vegetable oil into a deep-fryer or large, heavy-bottomed saucepan set over high heat; there should be at least 4 inches between the oil and the top of the pan as the oil will bubble up once you add the calamari. Heat the oil to 350 degrees F. Place the flour in a bowl and season with the salt, pepper, and cayenne. Drain the calamari, discarding the buttermilk, and transfer to the seasoned flour, shaking the calamari so they are completely covered. Transfer the calamari to a sieve, and shake off the excess flour. In two batches, carefully transfer the floured calamari to a fry basket (or use a skimmer or large slotted spoon) and lower into the oil. Deep-fry for 45 seconds, carefully lift out of the oil, and drain the calamari on paper towels. Sprinkle the calamari with a little salt and pepper. Repeat for the remaining calamari. Transfer to serving plates, garnish with the chopped cilantro and lemon wedges, and serve the dipping sauce on the side.

CHEF'S NOTES

After removing the calamari from the packaging, check for any cartilage and discard. If the calamari comes frozen, defrost overnight in the packaging and drain of any excess water.

Wondra is a bleached, enriched all-purpose wheat flour that dissolves easily and results in lump-free gravies and sauces. Because it has been precooked and then dried (much like instant rice), it dissolves without seizing up when stirred into hot liquid. Its low protein content and baby powder–like consistency also make it great for other uses. It's one of those little kitchen secrets to keep in your back pocket. It makes an excellent light and crispy crust for fish fries, pan fries, or breading and frying other meats and vegetables.

Pan-Fried Eastern Shore Crab Cakes with Rémoulade

Yields 6 servings

When we shared this recipe a few years back in our original *Neiman Marcus Cookbook* we explained that it was an East Coast recipe since we use Dungeness crabmeat at our West Coast restaurants. This recipe has become so popular with our guests everywhere that reproducing it here is a no-brainer. Growing up on the East Coast I learned to love the sweetness of the hard-shell blue crab that my grandmother Stephanie would cook; she'd clean the crab from the shell for me. I guess you could say I was a bit spoiled on those occasions!

1   cup mayonnaise

1   tablespoon minced fresh Italian parsley

1   tablespoon minced fresh tarragon

1   tablespoon capers, drained and minced

1   tablespoon minced cornichons *(or sour dill pickles)*

1½ teaspoons minced shallot

FOR THE CRAB CAKES

1   pound jumbo lump crabmeat

1   large egg, beaten

¼   cup mayonnaise

1½ teaspoons Dijon mustard

¼   cup plus 1 tablespoon fine plain bread crumbs

¼   cup thinly sliced scallions *(white and green parts)*

2   tablespoons minced fresh Italian parsley

1   tablespoon Old Bay seasoning

1   teaspoon Worcestershire sauce

     Dash of Tabasco sauce

     Vegetable oil, for frying

¼   cup fresh parsley sprigs, for garnish

SUGGESTED WINE PAIRING

Jack Nicklaus Private Reserve White Blend

To prepare the rémoulade, place the mayonnaise in a mixing bowl and add the parsley, tarragon, capers, cornichons, and shallot. Stir gently with a whisk until thoroughly incorporated. Transfer to an airtight container and reserve in the refrigerator.

To prepare the crab cakes, place the crabmeat in a mixing bowl and add the egg, mayonnaise, mustard, bread crumbs, scallions, parsley, Old Bay seasoning, Worcestershire sauce, and Tabasco sauce. Mix together gently, taking care not to break up the crab too much. Form the mixture into 12 patties. Heat about ¼ inch of vegetable oil in a large sauté pan or heavy skillet set over medium-high heat. Carefully add the crab cakes, in two batches if necessary, allowing plenty of room in the pan. Cook for about 2 minutes on each side or until well browned and heated through. Transfer the crab cakes to a plate lined with paper towels and let drain. To serve, place a dollop of the rémoulade on top of each crab cake and garnish with the parsley sprigs.

Rémoulade, which originated in France and flourishes in Louisiana cooking, makes a tasty accompaniment to shrimp, seafood, and fish.

CHEF'S NOTE

Many times, I'll use very small dollops of caviar, if I have it around, to garnish the crab cakes.

NUTRITION FACTS —*2 crab cakes*

| 470 calories | 6G saturated fat | 5G total carbohydrate | 710MG sodium |
| 41G total fat | 105MG cholesterol | 1G sugars | 18G protein |

Deviled Eggs Three Ways

Yields 6 servings (12 halves)

Whenever we make deviled eggs we get to see a lot of happy faces in the crowd. I suppose it's because most people like deviled eggs but relatively few will take the time to cook and peel the eggs and then make the egg mousse for a party — it is a lot of work! Regardless of the effort involved, these recipes always impress for their color and flavor, and you'll be appreciated for taking the trouble.

6   large eggs

3   tablespoons mayonnaise

1   teaspoon dry mustard

½   teaspoon prepared horseradish

⅛   teaspoon celery salt

½   teaspoon cognac *(or brandy; optional)*

4   sprigs fresh Italian parsley

SUGGESTED WINE PAIRING

Cusumano Insolia

Gently place the eggs in a large saucepan and cover with water. Bring to a boil, turn down the heat to a simmer, and cook the eggs for 7 minutes. Turn off the heat and let the eggs stand in the water for 5 minutes longer. Drain and when cool enough to handle, peel them and cut in half crosswise. Remove the yolks, transfer them to a small bowl, and add the mayonnaise, mustard, horseradish, celery salt, and cognac if desired. Mash with the back of a fork until thoroughly combined. Spoon the yolk mixture back into the egg white halves and transfer to a serving platter. Garnish with parsley leaves.

NUTRITION FACTS —*2 halves*

120 calories	**1G** total carbohydrate
10G total fat	**0G** sugars
2.5G saturated fat	**130MG** sodium
190MG cholesterol	**6G** protein

Truffled Deviled Eggs

Yields 6 servings (12 halves)

6   large eggs

3   tablespoons mayonnaise

1   tablespoon truffle oil

½   teaspoon Dijon mustard

    Kosher salt and freshly ground
    black pepper

¼   ounce black caviar *(optional)*

Gently place the eggs in a large saucepan and cover with water. Bring to a boil, turn down the heat to a simmer, and cook the eggs for 7 minutes. Turn off the heat and let the eggs stand in the water for 5 minutes longer. Drain the eggs and let cool. When the eggs are cool enough to handle, peel them and cut in half crosswise. Remove the yolks and transfer them to the bowl of a food processor fitted with a metal blade. Add the mayonnaise, truffle oil, mustard, and salt and pepper to taste and blend until smooth. Spoon the yolk mixture back into the egg white halves and transfer to a serving platter. Garnish with the caviar if desired.

NUTRITION FACTS —*2 halves*

140 calories	2.5G saturated fat	0G total carbohydrate	120MG sodium
12G total fat	190MG cholesterol	0G sugars	6G protein

Smoked Salmon Deviled Eggs

Yields 6 servings (12 halves)

6   large eggs

1   tablespoon cream cheese

2   slices smoked salmon *(about
    2 ounces)*, plus more for garnish
    (optional)

¼   cup minced fresh dill

½   teaspoon Worcestershire sauce

    Kosher salt and freshly ground
    black pepper

Gently place the eggs in a large saucepan and cover with water. Bring to a boil, turn down the heat to a simmer, and cook the eggs for 7 minutes. Turn off the heat and let the eggs stand in the water for 5 minutes longer. Drain the eggs and let cool. When the eggs are cool enough to handle, peel them and cut in half crosswise. Remove the yolks and transfer them to the bowl of a food processor fitted with a metal blade. Add the cream cheese, salmon, dill, Worcestershire sauce, and salt and pepper to taste and blend until smooth. Spoon the yolk mixture back into the egg white halves and transfer to a serving platter. Garnish with more salmon if desired.

NUTRITION FACTS —*2 halves*

100 calories	2.5G saturated fat	1G total carbohydrate	190MG sodium
7G total fat	220MG cholesterol	1G sugars	9G protein

Risotto Cakes with Shrimp Scampi

Yields 8 servings

This is where you get to make risotto, which is straightforward but takes time, like any risotto recipe. Trust me when I tell you that this is a very good recipe from the start — and it's one of the first recipes I taught my son when he became old enough to begin cooking at our house. I set him up with the hot chicken stock and had him stirring vigorously for 20 minutes. He loved it, and we loved the end result. To this day he can make an excellent risotto that makes his Dad proud. Keep in mind this recipe is probably one that can serve as an entrée but when it comes to entertaining at Neiman Marcus, we pull out all the favorites!

FOR THE RISOTTO CAKES

5	cups prepared chicken broth or vegetable broth
1	tablespoon olive oil
1	tablespoon unsalted butter
3	tablespoons minced onion
1½	teaspoons minced garlic
1	cup Arborio rice
½	cup freshly grated Parmesan cheese
3	ounces fresh mozzarella, finely diced
3	large eggs
2	tablespoons chopped fresh Italian parsley
2	teaspoons kosher salt
½	teaspoon freshly ground black pepper
½	cup all-purpose flour
3	tablespoons milk
1	cup plain bread crumbs

FOR THE GARNISH

8	large fresh basil leaves
2	tablespoons olive oil

CHEF'S NOTE

The risotto cakes can be fully cooked and then frozen. Bring to room temperature and then reheat in an oven set to 300 degrees F.

FOR THE SHRIMP SCAMPI

½	tablespoon olive oil
½	teaspoon minced garlic
1	teaspoon minced shallot
8	large shrimp, about 8 ounces, peeled, deveined, and butterflied *(tail on)*
¼	cup white wine
2	tablespoons unsalted butter
3	tablespoons fresh lemon juice
1	tablespoon chopped fresh Italian parsley
½	teaspoon kosher salt
½	teaspoon freshly ground black pepper

SUGGESTED WINE PAIRING

Santa Margherita Pinot Grigio

To prepare the risotto cakes, pour the broth into a large saucepan set over medium heat and bring to a gentle simmer. Meanwhile, set a saucepan over medium-low heat and add the olive oil and butter. When the butter is melted, add the onion and garlic and sauté for 5 or 6 minutes or until translucent. Stir in the Arborio rice with a wooden spoon and sauté for 2 minutes longer. For the next 20 minutes add 1 cup of broth at a time so the rice is covered, and stir continuously. Let each addition of the broth be totally absorbed by the rice before adding the next cup; if the rice absorbs all of the broth before it is cooked, warm some more broth. After about 35 minutes, or when the rice is creamy and tender, turn off the heat and spread the risotto in a large roasting pan so that it can cool evenly. (The risotto can be cooked up to a day in advance and kept in the refrigerator.)

Transfer the risotto to a mixing bowl and add the Parmesan, mozzarella, 1 of the eggs, the parsley, salt, and pepper. Mix to thoroughly incorporate. With your hands, form the mixture into eight small discs about 1 inch thick and 2 inches across. Place the flour in a bowl, crack the remaining 2 eggs in a separate bowl and whisk with the milk. Place the bread crumbs in a third bowl and lightly season with salt and pepper. Keeping one hand dry, take a risotto cake and dip first in the flour; using the same hand, drop into the whisked eggs. With your other hand, lift the risotto cake from the egg mixture and place in the bread crumbs. Shake the bread crumbs so the risotto cakes are immersed and completely covered. Pat the risotto cakes on all sides to secure the bread crumbs so that they stick. Transfer to a clean plate and repeat for the remaining risotto cakes. If not cooking immediately, keep refrigerated and remove from the refrigerator 30 minutes so they come to room temperature.

To prepare the garnish, place the basil leaves in a small sauté pan, cover with the olive oil, and set over high heat. When the leaves are crispy, remove with tongs and drain on paper towels and reserve.

Preheat the oven to 200 degrees F. Transfer ½ tablespoon of the oil used for the basil leaves to a large nonstick skillet set over medium heat. Warm the oil but do not overheat or the bread crumbs will burn. If the risotto cakes lose their shape, keep forming them with your hands and press them back together. Carefully place the risotto cakes into the skillet and sauté for 3 to 4 minutes on each side until golden brown. Transfer to a plate lined with paper towels, let drain, and then place on a large cookie sheet or roasting pan. Transfer to the oven to keep warm while preparing the shrimp scampi.

To prepare the shrimp scampi, using the skillet in which the risotto cakes were cooked, discard any excess oil and bread crumbs. Set the skillet over medium-high heat and add the olive oil. When hot, add the garlic and shallot and sauté for about 30 seconds. Add the shrimp, taking care not to overcrowd them, and sauté for 1 minute on each side. Deglaze the pan with the white wine and cook until the liquid is reduced by half. Turn down the heat to low and add the butter, lemon juice, parsley, salt, and pepper. Swirl the skillet around so the butter evenly coats the shrimp. Remove the skillet from the heat.

Remove the risotto cakes from the oven and arrange a risotto cake in the middle of each plate. Top each cake with 1 shrimp and drizzle the butter sauce over and around the shrimp. Garnish with the reserved crisped basil leaves.

NUTRITION FACTS —*1 serving*

350 calories   8G saturated fat   32G total carb   1940MG sodium
16G total fat   110MG cholesterol   2G sugars   20G protein

Chicken Charmoula Skewers

Yields 4 servings (16 skewers)

This is our adaptation of a method for flavoring chicken with a classic marinade from northern Africa. Feel free when making the marinade to make plenty, as it works great on all types of seafood as well as red meat. We like to serve the skewers with the classic Greek tzatziki, a seasoned yogurt dip.

FOR THE TZATZIKI

1	cup plain Greek yogurt
1	large cucumber, peeled, seeded, and finely diced
1	tablespoon olive oil
½	teaspoon minced garlic
¼	cup minced fresh dill
	Juice from ½ lemon
⅛	teaspoon kosher salt
⅛	teaspoon freshly ground white pepper

FOR THE SKEWERS

2	pounds boneless, skinless chicken breast
1½	cups olive oil
¼	cup fresh lemon juice *(about 2 lemons)*
2	tablespoons minced garlic
2	teaspoons ground cumin
2	tablespoons paprika
¼	teaspoon cayenne
1½	teaspoons kosher salt
1	teaspoon ground allspice
6	tablespoons chopped fresh cilantro leaves
6	tablespoons chopped fresh Italian parsley
16	bamboo skewers, 6 to 8 inches long

SUGGESTED WINE PAIRING

Domaine Chanson Viré-Clessé

To prepare the tzatziki, place all the ingredients in a bowl and mix thoroughly. Cover and set aside in the refrigerator.

To prepare the chicken skewers, cut the chicken into 32 strips, about 1 ounce each, and place in a glass or ceramic mixing bowl. In a separate bowl, mix the olive oil, lemon juice, garlic, cumin, paprika, cayenne, salt, allspice, cilantro, and parsley. Pour the marinade over the chicken, making sure the chicken is covered. Cover tightly with plastic wrap and let marinate in the refrigerator for at least 4 hours or overnight.

Soak the skewers in water so they don't burn when cooking. Prepare the grill. Remove the bamboo skewers from the water and thread 2 chicken strips lengthwise on each skewer. Set the threaded skewers on a clean platter as you work. Place the skewers on the grill and cook over medium heat for 3 or 4 minutes on each side or until completely cooked through. Serve the chicken skewers with the tzatziki.

> **CHEF'S NOTE**
>
> Charmoula (sometimes also written and pronounced as "chermoula") is a marinade used in North African cooking, and typically contains olive oil, herbs, garlic, lemon, and cumin or coriander. It's most commonly used with fish and seafood, but as this recipe shows, it makes a fine marinade for chicken too.

NUTRITION FACTS —*4 skewers and tzatziki*

630	calories	7G	saturated fat	3G	total carbohydrate	750MG	sodium
47G	total fat	145MG	cholesterol	0G	sugars	49G	protein

Crispy Polenta Bites with Eggplant Caponata

Yields 54 squares (10 to 12 servings)

Polenta is a great starch that we also pair with entrées at many of our restaurants. It's versatile — it can be served smooth and creamy, or crispy when allowed to set and then seared or grilled. This is one of those recipes that can be changed up on the fly as need be. Once you have the crispy polenta made you have a vehicle for any type of topping. Here we offer a cooked eggplant "salad" that is a Sicilian tradition. Other toppings you might consider are a simple olive tapenade — classic and tasty — or melted goat cheese.

FOR THE POLENTA BITES

- 1   cup milk
- 2   teaspoons kosher salt
- 1   cup polenta *(coarse cornmeal)*
- 1   cup freshly grated Parmesan cheese
- 2   tablespoons unsalted butter
- ½   teaspoon freshly ground black pepper

FOR THE EGGPLANT CAPONATA

- ¼   cup plus 2 tablespoons olive oil
- 1   small eggplant, peeled and finely diced *(about 1 cup)*
- 1   clove garlic, minced
- 2   tablespoons finely diced red onion
- ½   cup black *(Kalamata)* and green olives, pitted and minced
- 2   tablespoons capers, drained and chopped
- 2   tablespoons minced fresh Italian parsley, plus additional leaves for garnish
- 1   anchovy, minced *(optional)*
- 1   teaspoon lemon zest
- 2   tablespoons red wine vinegar

SUGGESTED WINE PAIRING

MAZZONI Barbera

To prepare the polenta, place the milk, salt, and 3 cups water in a saucepan and bring to a boil over medium heat. Slowly start pouring the polenta into the saucepan while whisking. Turn down the heat to low and continue to whisk the polenta for about 12 minutes until it is no longer grainy. Turn off the heat and stir in the Parmesan, butter, and pepper. Spray a roasting pan measuring 13 inches by 9 inches with nonstick spray, pour the polenta mixture into the pan, and spread it out evenly. Refrigerate for at least 2 hours. You can prepare the polenta up to 1 day in advance, covered with plastic wrap.

To prepare the eggplant caponata, heat ¼ cup olive oil in a sauté pan over medium heat. Add the eggplant and garlic and sauté for 2 minutes. Add the red onion and sauté for 1 minute longer. Transfer to a bowl and add the olives, capers, minced parsley, the anchovy (if using), lemon zest, and vinegar.

Remove the polenta from the refrigerator and carefully flip the pan over, releasing the polenta onto a cutting board. With a sharp knife, cut the polenta into 1½-inch squares; you should have about 54 squares. In a nonstick skillet, heat the remaining 2 tablespoons olive oil over medium-low heat. In batches, sear the polenta squares for 1 to 2 minutes on each side or until golden brown. Transfer to a platter, top each polenta square with a teaspoon of caponata, and garnish with parsley.

NUTRITION FACTS —*4 to 5 squares*

150 calories	**12G** total carbohydrate
10G total fat	**2G** sugars
3.5G saturated fat	**530MG** sodium
15MG cholesterol	**5G** protein

CHEF'S NOTES

The caponata can be made ahead of time and will keep refrigerated for up to 1 week in an airtight container.

The polenta squares can also be prepared and then seared up to one day ahead. Reheat in a 300 degree F. oven for 8 to 10 minutes, until warmed through.

Endive Spears with Fresh Ricotta and Lemon Zest

Yields 24 spears (8 servings)

This is such a simple recipe, and so pretty and delicious. Any dinner party or gathering can use a nice platter of fresh endive spears with a good ricotta cheese and lemon zest. It's elegant, it's simple, it's pretty, and it's always a winner. Ricotta is made from the whey after the curds are strained in the cheese making process, and increasingly, it's being made locally in many parts of the country. Its attractively soft, smooth texture and flavor makes ricotta a favorite ingredient for desserts in Italy, such as cannoli and cheesecake.

12 ounces ricotta *(see Chef's Notes)*

Pinch of kosher salt

Pinch of freshly ground black pepper

24 red or white Belgian endive spears, about 2½ inches long *(3 or 4 heads endive)*

2 lemons

Baby watercress leaves, for garnish

In a mixing bowl, combine the ricotta, salt, and pepper and keep chilled. Gently rinse the endive spears under cold running water and then wipe them dry with a paper towel. Lay the endive spears on a clean platter. Scoop the ricotta with a teaspoon and place in the middle of each endive spear, using another teaspoon to help push off the ricotta onto the spear. Using a Microplane or fine grater, grate zest from the lemons over the ricotta and endive spears; top each with a watercress leaf. Serve chilled. This appetizer can be prepared up to 3 hours in advance and kept loosely covered in the refrigerator.

SUGGESTED WINE PAIRING

Boutari Moschofilero

CHEF'S NOTES

You'll find fresh ricotta in finer cheese sections and it's worth the investment if you really want to make an impression with this recipe.

Belgian endive is a form of chicory and one of the most flavorful. When buying heads of endive, prepare by cutting the core from the spears about ½ inch from the bottom; then carefully pull the leaves apart.

NUTRITION FACTS *—3 spears*

60 calories	3G total carbohydrate
3.5G total fat	0G sugars
2G saturated fat	85MG sodium
15MG cholesterol	5G protein

This is such a simple recipe, and so pretty and delicious.

3 SOUPS

SOUPS

You can always tell if a cook really knows their way around the kitchen if they can put together a great tasting soup.

For me, the test of a great tasting soup is wanting two or three bowls and making a meal out of it. One of the questions I ask all cooks when interviewing them for a position at Neiman Marcus is, "What types of food do you like to cook the most?" If someone tells me they love to make soups, my ears perk up. I then lead the conversation into combining ingredients, marrying flavors, layering seasoning, and examples of when it's best to serve soup as-is, or blended and strained. Good soup cooks have the foresight to understand the finished product; even when they start out with different types of ingredients, they'll know exactly what they want in the finished product. Any applicant that strikes a chord with me in this type of conversation usually winds up with the job! While following a recipe can lead to a very good tasting soup, a real cook can check their refrigerator and put together a great soup by combining vegetables and proteins and the ingredients on hand.

I love making soups, especially during the colder months when I can cook them for long periods of time, like the lentil soup or the flank steak gumbo in this chapter. As crazy as it might sound to some, soups that are made today usually taste better tomorrow when the soup has had a chance to cool down overnight and the flavors have had a chance to marry. I often urge our chefs to make tomorrow's daily soup a day ahead; this way, our customers get to taste the soup exactly the way the recipe was intended to taste. As a chef I realize that soups are best made with the season so you have the freshest ingredients.

At our restaurants, we have some soups that never change or leave the menu, like the Atlanta She-Crab Soup, Kahuku Corn Chowder in Honolulu, and the Tortilla Soup. These soups have become mainstays in the daily diets for many of our customers and I would never think about changing them. Some of the Go Figure soups that I've included here have become regular seasonal soups that switch in and out of the menus, making many customers really happy. Then there are the soups in this chapter that I just want to share with you knowing that you'll probably include them in your own repertoire. One thing you will notice in the following recipes — compared to our last two cookbooks, we now use more finished, pre-prepared broths, cooked beans, and other prepared foods. The bottom line is that over the last ten years or so, the amount of fabulous new food products has exploded onto the market. I've never considered myself a food purist, and now more than ever I'm writing recipes that deliver great taste and appearance by using prepared food products. Anything to help save time and deliver quality is good enough for me and I hope you appreciate the time savers as well! Ⓒ

CHEF'S NOTE

The recipes in this chapter typically call for a large saucepan. This refers to a 6-quart saucepan or larger. By all means use a large sauce pot or a stock pot if you wish.

Mediterranean Lentil Soup

Yields 12 cups (9 or 10 servings) ⧗ GO FIGURE

In this recipe we use yellow lentils because I like their peppery flavor and that fact that they hold their shape and don't get mushy as quickly as brown lentils. Green lentils seem to hold up well in this recipe too, so I'd say that's the best alternative. Lentil recipes typically suggest sorting through the lentils before cooking because occasionally you'll find small stones or debris lurking among them. It's probably best to find a stone that way, before the stone finds your back molar. We've made this soup for the Go Figure category knowing that lentils are low in fat and high in protein. Lentils also take well to assertive flavors like cinnamon, smoked paprika, and ground cumin. Keep in mind that this soup, like all soups made with beans or grains, will thicken overnight; having extra chicken stock on hand is a must when reheating these soups the next day.

2	tablespoons olive oil
2½	cups yellow lentils, rinsed and sorted through
2	teaspoons ground cumin
1½	teaspoons smoked paprika
1	teaspoon ground coriander
1	teaspoon red chile powder
½	teaspoon ground cinnamon
1	cup finely diced onion
½	cup finely diced carrot
½	cup finely diced celery
1	teaspoon minced garlic
7	cups prepared chicken broth
½	cup finely chopped fresh Italian parsley
1	teaspoon fresh thyme leaves
1	teaspoon kosher salt
1	teaspoon freshly ground black pepper
¼	cup sour cream, for garnish *(optional)*
2	tablespoons minced lemon zest, for garnish *(optional)*

Heat the olive oil in a large, heavy-bottomed saucepan set over medium heat. Add the lentils, cumin, paprika, coriander, chile powder, and cinnamon and sauté for about 3 minutes, stirring continuously so the lentils do not burn. Add the onion, carrot, celery, and garlic and sauté for 5 minutes longer. Add the chicken broth and bring the mixture to a rapid boil. Turn down the heat to medium-low, cover the pan, and continue to cook at a high simmer for 35 to 40 minutes, until the lentils are soft. Remove from the heat and add the parsley, thyme leaves, salt, and pepper. Garnish with the sour cream and lemon zest, if desired.

> I like yellow lentils because of their peppery flavor.

NUTRITION FACTS —*10 ounces (1¼ cups)*

250 calories	**0.5G** saturated fat	**37G** total carbohydrate	**340MG** sodium
4G total fat	**0MG** cholesterol	**2G** sugars	**16G** protein

SUGGESTED WINE PAIRING

Seven Daughters Pinot Noir

Ribollita

Yields 10 cups (8 servings) ⧗ GO FIGURE

In Italian, *ribollita* literally means "reboiled," because this rustic soup with peasant origins is based on leftover minestrone that's heated up, with some added ingredients thrown in for good measure. There's nothing reboiled in Neiman Marcus restaurants when it comes to this favorite, but it does contain similar, satisfying flavors. This is one of those soups that makes its way back onto our menus every couple of seasons. It reminds me of those well-worn loafers you keep on the shelf and decide to wear on the days you need comfort and a simple style statement to finish your wardrobe. Don't be shy with the pesto garnish — our customers ask for more, and I swear they're taking it home!

2	tablespoons olive oil
1	cup finely diced onion
½	cup finely diced celery
½	cup finely diced carrot
½	cup finely diced fennel
2	teaspoons minced garlic
1	cup finely diced unpeeled zucchini
3	cups canned plum tomatoes, crushed
5	cups prepared low-sodium vegetable broth
1	(15½-ounce) can cannellini or great northern beans, rinsed
1	(16-ounce) can red kidney beans, rinsed
¼	cup chopped fresh Italian parsley
1	teaspoon kosher salt
1	teaspoon freshly ground black pepper
2	cups roughly chopped baby spinach leaves
8	teaspoons Fresh Basil Pesto *(page 222)*
8	shavings Parmesan cheese

Heat the olive oil in a large, heavy-bottomed saucepan over medium-high heat. Add the onion, celery, carrot, fennel, and garlic and sauté for 6 minutes, stirring frequently. Add the zucchini and sauté 3 minutes longer. Add the tomatoes, vegetable broth, and beans, bring to a simmer, and cook for 30 minutes longer. Stir in the parsley, salt, and pepper. Divide the spinach among eight soup bowls and ladle the soup over the spinach. Drizzle about 1 teaspoon pesto over each portion, and garnish with a Parmesan cheese shaving.

CHEF'S NOTE

For the garnish, use a vegetable peeler to shave the Parmesan into uniform pieces.

All soups love crackers and bread. I suggest serving some nice crusty bread and grated Parmesan cheese alongside the soup.

NUTRITION FACTS —*10 ounces (1¼ cups)*

130 calories	0.5G saturated fat	19G total carbohydrate	440MG sodium
4G total fat	0MG cholesterol	4G sugars	5G protein

SUGGESTED WINE PAIRING

Cusumano Nero d 'Avola

Pasta e Fagiole

Yields 13 cups (8 servings)   ⏳ GO FIGURE

The name says it all: This is a soup made with pasta and beans (*fagiole* in Italian). But here we really take advantage of a great time saver — canned cooked beans. I'm not advocating that you stop using dried beans if you prefer, but when there's a really great substitute, you can save tons of time, and easily add more beans later if you want to increase the amount. The other key component that will make the soup shine is high-quality canned tomatoes. I'm partial to the canned tomatoes from Italy, so in my house you'll see loads of those in the pantry. Make sure you have some crusty Italian bread around when serving this to your guests.

2	tablespoons olive oil
1	cup finely diced onion
2	teaspoons minced garlic
4	sprigs fresh thyme *(leaves only)*
⅛	teaspoon crushed red pepper flakes
3	cups canned plum tomatoes, crushed
5	cups low-sodium vegetable broth
1	*(16-ounce)* can red kidney beans, rinsed
1	*(15-ounce)* can cannellini or great northern beans, rinsed
2	cups cooked mini pasta shells
1	teaspoon kosher salt
1	teaspoon freshly ground black pepper
¼	cup chopped fresh Italian parsley *(optional)*
¼	cup grated Parmesan cheese, for garnish *(optional)*

Heat the olive oil in a large, heavy-bottomed saucepan over medium heat. Add the onion, garlic, thyme leaves, and red pepper flakes. Sauté for 6 minutes, stirring frequently, until the onion is translucent. Add the tomatoes, vegetable broth, and beans and bring to a boil. Reduce the heat to a simmer and cook for 30 minutes, stirring occasionally. Remove from the heat, stir in the cooked pasta, and season with the salt and pepper. Ladle the soup into serving bowls and garnish with the parsley and cheese, if desired.

NUTRITION FACTS —*10 ounces (1¼ cups)*

160 calories	**0.5G** saturated fat	**24G** total carbohydrate	**480MG** sodium
3.5G total fat	**0MG** cholesterol	**4G** sugars	**8G** protein

SUGGESTED WINE PAIRING

Colavita Verdicchio di Matelica

Summer Tomato Soup

Yields 14 cups (11 servings)

For me, tomato soup is a true comfort food, evoking memories of my mother opening up a can of Campbell's tomato soup and making a grilled cheese sandwich to go with it. That's exactly how this soup appears on a lot of our menus around the country — with a grilled cheese sandwich. Although you can make a great soup with fresh tomatoes, they can vary in flavor and water content, so using a good-quality canned product is more reliable. At Neiman Marcus, we source heirloom tomatoes when summer garden tomatoes are not in season. Serve with fresh crusty bread.

3   cups chopped onions

6   cloves garlic, smashed

5   fresh ripe plum tomatoes, halved

2   tablespoons olive oil

2   teaspoons kosher salt

½   teaspoon crushed red pepper flakes

1   *(22-ounce)* can good-quality whole plum tomatoes *(such as San Marzano)*

1   *(22-ounce)* can good-quality crushed plum tomatoes *(such as San Marzano)*

4   cups prepared low-sodium chicken or vegetable broth

6   fresh basil leaves

1   cup grated Parmesan cheese, plus more for serving

1   teaspoon Worcestershire sauce

2   teaspoons sugar *(optional)*

SUGGESTED WINE PAIRING

Colavita Valpolicella Ripasso

Preheat the oven to 300 degrees F. Place the onions, garlic, and fresh ripe plum tomatoes in a large bowl, add 1 tablespoon of the olive oil, and toss together. Transfer to a roasting pan and sprinkle with the salt and red pepper flakes. Roast in the oven for 45 minutes.

Heat the remaining 1 tablespoon oil in a large, heavy-bottomed saucepan over medium heat. Add the roasted vegetables and sauté for 3 to 4 minutes, stirring occasionally. Add the canned tomatoes (whole and crushed) and the broth and bring to a boil. Turn down the heat to low, cover the pan, and simmer for 30 minutes.

Remove the pan from the heat and stir in the basil and Parmesan. Using a handheld immersion blender, carefully blend the soup. Strain into a clean saucepan and stir in the Worcestershire sauce. Bring the soup to a boil, turn down the heat to low, and simmer for 8 to 10 minutes. Adjust the seasonings and add the sugar if needed. Serve the hot soup in soup bowls or tureens and sprinkle with additional Parmesan cheese, if desired.

CHEF'S NOTE

The San Marzano canned plum tomatoes (also known as Roma tomatoes) called for in this recipe are sold in 22-ounce cans. Typically, canned tomatoes brands come in the large, 28-ounce cans, or the smaller 14-ounce cans. If using those, choose a large can of whole plum tomatoes and a small can of crushed.

NUTRITION FACTS —*10 ounces (1¼ cups)*

140 calories	**2G** saturated fat	**14G** total carbohydrate	**1170MG** sodium
6G total fat	**5MG** cholesterol	**8G** sugars	**9G** protein

Tortilla Soup: "The Hybrid"

Yields 15 cups (12 servings)

Neiman Marcus restaurants around the country offer their unique versions of our popular tortilla soup and this is my "hybrid" recipe — it's a cross-breed of my favorites. If I ever want to have a passionate conversation about our restaurants, I'll ask one of our knowledgeable customers who regularly shops and dines with Neiman Marcus at several locations around the country about where they'll find the best tortilla soup. I'll get plenty of great feedback on who makes the best and what's special about it. I love our passionate Neiman Marcus foodies!

2	tablespoons canola oil
1	cup finely diced onion
½	cup finely diced celery
½	cup finely diced carrot
1	poblano chile, seeded and finely diced
1	teaspoon minced garlic
4	small *(5-inch)* white corn tortillas, torn in pieces
1	tablespoon red chile powder
2	teaspoons ground coriander
2	teaspoons ground cumin
1	teaspoon dried Mexican oregano
2	cups canned plum tomatoes, crushed
6	cups prepared low-sodium chicken broth
2	cups grated Monterey Jack cheese
1	teaspoon kosher salt
6	cups diced boneless rotisserie-cooked chicken meat

Heat the olive oil in a large, heavy-bottomed saucepan over medium heat. Add the onion, celery, carrot, poblano, and garlic and sauté for about 6 minutes, stirring frequently. Add the tortilla pieces, chile powder, coriander, cumin, and oregano and continue to sauté for 1 minute longer. Add the tomatoes and chicken broth and bring the soup to a boil. Reduce the heat to low and simmer for 20 minutes longer. Stir in the cheese and salt, and using an immersion blender, carefully puree the soup until smooth. Stir in the cooked chicken, warm through, and remove from the heat. Ladle the soup into serving bowls.

NUTRITION FACTS —*10 ounces (1¼ cups)*

260 calories	**4.5G** saturated fat	**9G** total carbohydrate
12G total fat	**75MG** cholesterol	**3G** sugars
		28G protein

420MG sodium

I love our passionate Neiman Marcus foodies!

CHEF'S NOTE

If you wish, garnish with tortilla chips or strips, and diced avocado.

SUGGESTED WINE PAIRING

Tangley Oaks Chardonnay

Flank Steak Gumbo

Yields 24 cups (12 servings)

This recipe provides a lot of servings — you can always enjoy it tomorrow and if need be, it freezes well. My take on people who make a lot of gumbo is that they have a real affection for the pot they make it in — and they usually stick to the same recipe year after year. Chances are they were given the recipe by a relative (maybe their mother) who asked that the recipe stay in the family. If they were lucky enough to be given the family's old cast-iron soup pot, then you know they're really serious gumbo people. I would strongly suggest to you that if you're ever invited to the same party and they agree to make the gumbo — then by all means let them, and know how fortunate you are! Gumbo is not complicated, and this recipe is really easy; it uses poblano chiles for some subtle heat and plenty of dry spices that will pack a punch when the dish is finished.

FOR THE ROUX

1   cup unsalted butter

1½ cups all-purpose flour

FOR THE GUMBO

2   tablespoons olive oil

2   pounds flank steak, cut into ½-inch cubes

1   teaspoon kosher salt

1   teaspoon freshly ground black pepper

4   cups finely diced onions

2   cups finely diced celery

2   cups finely diced carrots

1   cup seeded and finely diced poblano chile

1   tablespoon minced garlic

2   tablespoons gumbo filé powder

2   tablespoons blackened spice seasoning (*such as Paul Prudhomme*)

2   tablespoons red chile powder

2   teaspoons dried oregano

1   teaspoon dried thyme

12 cups prepared beef broth

3   cups canned crushed plum tomatoes

12 ounces frozen okra, sliced

5   cups cooked white rice (*follow directions on package*)

½   cup minced fresh Italian parsley, for garnish

¼   cup sliced scallions, for garnish

SUGGESTED WINE PAIRING

The Federalist Zinfandel

CHEF'S NOTE

I love using flank steak because it's easy to dice into small pieces, has great natural flavor when cooked slowly over a long period of time, and tends to not fall apart when fully cooked.

To prepare the roux, melt the butter in a heavy-bottomed saucepan over medium-low heat; do not let it brown. Stir in the flour and stir frequently for about 20 minutes until the mixture is the color of peanut butter. Set aside.

To prepare the gumbo, heat the olive oil in a large, heavy-bottomed saucepan over high heat. Season the flank steak with salt and pepper and when the oil is hot and almost smoking, add the meat. Do not stir; sear for about 3 minutes on each side, turning the meat each time with tongs. Remove the meat with a slotted spoon and set aside.

In the same saucepan, add the onions, celery, carrots, poblano, and garlic and sauté over medium heat for about 10 minutes, stirring frequently. Stir in the gumbo filé, blackening spice, chile powder, oregano, and thyme and cook for 1 minute longer. Add the broth, tomatoes, and okra, turn up the heat to high, and bring to a boil. Turn the heat to low.

Add the roux in three stages using a spoon; after each addition, stir to completely dissolve the roux. Add the reserved flank steak and continue to simmer the soup over low heat for 20 minutes. Spoon ½ cup cooked rice into each serving bowl and ladle the gumbo over the rice. Garnish with the parsley and scallions.

NUTRITION FACTS *—10 ounces*

590 calories	110MG cholesterol	1810MG sodium
28G total fat	56G total carbohydrate	30G protein
14G saturated fat	8G sugars	

"Quick" Asian Broth, Pho-Style

Yields 12½ cups (10 servings)

Pho is a Vietnamese soup that probably originated in the northern part of the country in the early twentieth century, influenced by Chinese and French traditions. It is a popular street food there and has translated well to Vietnamese restaurants in the United States, where it is enthusiastically embraced by a wide audience. Pho is a basic style of soup typically containing broth, noodles, and meat that gets dressed up or stays peasant-style depending on who's making it and how much you want to spend on the finished product. In this recipe you get a very quick, simple, but excellent-tasting pho using prepared beef broth. In the end it's completely up to you to finish the soup with grilled shrimp, pulled rotisserie chicken, or your favorite cut of tender meat cooked perfectly on the grill. The suggested vegetable garnishes are readily available at any vegetable market.

FOR THE SOUP

2   teaspoons sesame oil

1½ cups diced onion

2   cloves garlic, minced

1   cup diced carrot

1   cup diced celery

1   (2-inch) piece fresh ginger, unpeeled

1   cinnamon stick

1   star anise

1   bunch fresh cilantro

8   cups prepared low-sodium beef broth

1   tablespoon fish sauce

½   cup soy sauce

¼   cup sweet chile garlic sauce (such as Mae Ploy)

FOR THE GARNISH

1   (13-ounce) package rice noodles

4   cups fresh bean sprouts

2   cups fresh cilantro leaves

1   jalapeño, thinly sliced crosswise (with seeds)

1   pound cooked shrimp or cooked and sliced chicken or beef

2   tablespoons finely sliced scallions (white and green parts)

½   cup fresh basil leaves (preferably Thai basil)

SUGGESTED WINE PAIRING

Sokol Blosser Evolution White Blend

To prepare the soup, heat the sesame oil in a large, heavy-bottomed saucepan over medium heat. Add the onion, garlic, celery, carrot, and ginger and sauté for 6 minutes, stirring continuously. Stir in the cinnamon, star anise, and cilantro and sauté for 1 minute longer. Add the broth, fish sauce, soy sauce, and sweet chile sauce and bring to a boil. Turn down the heat to low and simmer for 15 minutes. Strain the broth through a fine strainer into a clean saucepan and keep warm.

To serve and garnish, divide the soup garnishes (except the basil leaves) evenly among ten serving cups. Ladle the soup over the garnish, add the basil leaves, and serve immediately.

CHEF'S NOTE

The Asian ingredients section of most supermarkets will carry the sweet chile sauce, fish sauce, and rice noodles.

NUTRITION FACTS —*10 ounces (1¼ cups)*

110 calories	21G total carbohydrate
1G total fat	5G sugars
0G saturated fat	780MG sodium
5MG cholesterol	4G protein

Chicken and White Bean Chili

Yields 18 cups (12 servings)

I enjoy a bowl of this chili every week here at the Neiman Marcus Dallas store. You could say that by now, I'm an expert on its flavor and consistency after years of taste-testing. It's interesting how many of our customers also make a routine of enjoying certain dishes as part of their weekly Neiman Marcus diet. I find that whenever I change a restaurant menu I can expect several phone calls or e-mails from guests concerned over my changes. Once this recipe makes its way onto a menu at one of our stores, it usually never comes off — it's that good!

3   tablespoons olive oil

3   cups diced onions

1   teaspoon minced garlic

2   teaspoons ground cumin

1½ teaspoons dried oregano

1   teaspoon red chile powder

1   teaspoon ground coriander

¼   teaspoon cayenne

⅛   teaspoon ground cloves

⅛   teaspoon freshly ground black pepper

3   *(15-ounce)* cans cannellini beans

1   cup diced canned green chiles

5   cups prepared chicken broth

3   cups diced rotisserie-cooked chicken
     meat *(½ rotisserie chicken)*

3   cups grated Monterey Jack cheese

     Tortilla chips, for garnish

     Sour cream, for garnish

     Pico de Gallo Salsa
     (page 130), for garnish

SUGGESTED WINE PAIRING

Lapostolle Cuvée Alexandre Chardonnay

Heat the olive oil a large, heavy-bottomed saucepan over medium heat. Add the onions and garlic and sauté for 6 minutes, stirring frequently, until translucent. Add the cumin, oregano, chile powder, coriander, cayenne, cloves, and pepper. Sauté for 2 minutes, stirring continuously. Add the beans, green chiles (and the liquid in which they are packed), and chicken broth and bring to a boil. Turn down the heat to low and simmer, uncovered, for 30 to 45 minutes, stirring occasionally. Add the chicken meat and heat through for about 5 minutes.

Remove the pan from the heat and add 2 cups of the cheese; stir until it is incorporated. Ladle the soup into bowls and top with the remaining 1 cup cheese. Garnish with the tortilla chips, sour cream, and salsa.

CHEF'S NOTE

Great northern or other similar small white beans can be used instead of the cannellini beans.

NUTRITION FACTS —*10 ounces (1½ cups)*

240 calories	3.5G saturated fat	19G total carbohydrate	440MG sodium
9G total fat	40MG cholesterol	3G sugars	21G protein

Once this recipe makes its way onto a menu at one of our stores, it usually never comes off — it's that good!

Butternut Squash Soup

Yields 19 cups (15 servings)

Nothing means fall season like butternut squash soup being served at our restaurants, and so many of our customers adore this version. The hardest thing for a chef is that when you appreciate and love the customers, you don't want to disappoint them or let them down by changing the menu. We usually take it off the menu once fall ends, but if we could find butternut squash year-round, I'm sure it would remain by popular demand! I love the way the squash gets infused with that nutty flavor from roasting.

FOR THE SPICY PECANS

1	tablespoon kosher salt
2	teaspoons celery salt
1	teaspoon garlic salt
¼	teaspoon cayenne
2	tablespoons vegetable oil
1	pound shelled pecan or walnut halves

FOR THE SOUP

2	butternut squashes
1	tablespoon olive oil
2	tablespoons unsalted butter
2	cups diced onions
2	shallots, diced
1	teaspoon chopped fresh thyme
2	teaspoons kosher salt
⅛	teaspoon freshly ground white pepper
8	cups prepared vegetable broth
2	cups heavy cream
½	cup honey

8 to 10 teaspoons sour cream, for garnish

Hanna Chardonnay

To prepare the spicy pecans, mix together the salt, celery salt, garlic salt, and cayenne in a bowl and set aside. Heat the oil in a heavy-bottomed saucepan over medium heat. When the oil is hot, add the nuts and cook for about 2 minutes or until they begin to brown; it is important to keep shaking the pan while the nuts are cooking to avoid burning them. Drain the nuts on paper towels. Transfer the nuts to a bowl while still warm and sprinkle with the salt mixture. Mix thoroughly until the nuts are evenly coated. Let cool to room temperature.

To prepare the soup, preheat the oven to 400 degrees F. Carefully cut the butternut squashes in half lengthwise and remove any seeds. Rub a cookie sheet generously with the olive oil and place the squash on it, flesh-side down. Transfer to the oven and roast the squash until soft, about 45 minutes. Remove from the oven and let cool slightly. Scoop out the squash flesh and set aside.

In a large, heavy-bottomed saucepan, melt the butter over medium heat and add the onions, shallots, and thyme. Add the salt and pepper and sauté for 6 minutes or until translucent. Add the reserved butternut squash and vegetable broth. Bring the soup to a boil and then turn down the heat to low. Simmer for 30 minutes, stirring occasionally. Turn off the heat. Use an immersion blender to blend the soup in the pan; be careful as the soup will be very hot. Add a little of the cream and honey at a time and continue blending until the soup is completely smooth. Taste the soup and adjust the seasonings. Ladle into serving bowls and garnish with the spiced pecans and sour cream.

CHEF'S NOTE

I recommend using an immersion blender; if you don't own one, you can leave the soup unblended.

NUTRITION FACTS —*10 ounces (1¼ cups)*

250 calories	26G total carbohydrate
15G total fat	13G sugars
9G saturated fat	330MG sodium
50MG cholesterol	4G protein

Turkey Chili

Yields 16 cups (12 servings)

This recipe came about when we decided to create a healthier version of the classic beef chili. Ground turkey became more widely available in the early 1990s, and it grew in popularity both because of its flavor and the fact that it is a leaner meat. When we tried it in a chili, it instantly attracted an enthusiastic following among our customers. Now, when we offer turkey chili on the same menu as a good old meat chili, we'll serve twice as many bowls on any given day.

2	tablespoons olive oil
1	tablespoon minced garlic
1	pound ground turkey meat *(preferably both white and dark meat)*
2	tablespoons pure red chile powder
1	tablespoon ground cumin
1	tablespoon blackening spice *(such as Paul Prudhomme)*
1	tablespoon onion powder
1	teaspoon dried Mexican oregano
¼	teaspoon cayenne
2	cups finely diced onions
½	cup diced poblano chile
½	cup diced red bell pepper
½	cup diced yellow bell pepper
1	*(28-ounce)* can crushed plum tomatoes
2	cups V-8 juice
2	teaspoons Worcestershire sauce
2	teaspoons kosher salt
1	teaspoon freshly ground black pepper
¾	cup grated Monterey Jack cheese, for garnish

Heat the olive oil in a large, heavy-bottomed saucepan over medium heat. Add the garlic and sauté, stirring so it does not burn, for about 2 minutes. Add the ground turkey and continue to sauté, stirring frequently, for 7 to 8 minutes or until cooked through. Add the chile powder, cumin, blackening spice, onion powder, oregano, cayenne, and onions. Turn down the heat to low and sauté gently for 5 minutes. Add the poblano, red and yellow bell peppers, tomatoes, V-8 juice, and Worcestershire sauce. Stir together, cover with a lid, and simmer for 20 minutes, stirring occasionally. Season with the salt and black pepper. Transfer the chili to serving bowls and garnish with 1 tablespoon of the Monterey Jack cheese per serving.

NUTRITION FACTS —*10 ounces (1¼ cups)*

170 calories	**1.5G** saturated fat	**20G** total carbohydrate	**600MG** sodium
7G total fat	**25MG** cholesterol	**11G** sugars	**9G** protein

SUGGESTED WINE PAIRING

Protea Red Blend

Kahuku Corn Chowder

Yields 16 cups (12 servings)

Here's a recipe that I predict will never come off the Mariposa restaurant menu at our Ala Moana store in Honolulu. This soup has been with us since the store opened in 1997. It was our local take on the popular corn chowder that we used to make in Dallas. Our chef at the time mentioned that one of the excellent ingredients available to us on Oahu was the corn grown at Kahuku on the North Shore — the same part of the island known for its epic surf. Kahuku corn makes the most delicious, sweet, creamy soup you've ever tasted. Of course, you can still get great results with corn from your local farmer's market. You can also add more flavor by grilling the corn first.

6	fresh corn cobs, husked and silks removed
2	cups prepared chicken broth
1	teaspoon minced fresh thyme
1	bay leaf
¼	cup virgin olive oil
1	cup finely diced onion
1	cup finely diced celery
3	cups peeled and diced Idaho (*russet*) potatoes
½	cup all-purpose flour
4	cups heavy cream
1	teaspoon kosher salt
½	teaspoon freshly ground black pepper

With a chef's knife, remove the corn kernels from the cobs and reserve the kernels and cobs separately. Place the corn cobs in a large, heavy-bottomed saucepan and add the chicken broth, thyme, and bay leaf. Bring to a boil, then turn down the heat to low and simmer for 15 minutes. Strain the chicken broth into a large, clean saucepan and keep warm; discard the solids.

Heat the olive oil in another large, heavy-bottomed saucepan over medium heat. Add the onion and celery and sauté for 6 or 7 minutes, until translucent. Add the reserved corn kernels and the potatoes and sauté for 3 minutes longer. Add the flour to the vegetables and stir well, until incorporated. Add the warm chicken broth to the vegetables and bring to a boil. Turn down the heat to low, add the cream, and simmer for 30 minutes. Season with salt and pepper and ladle into serving bowls.

NUTRITION FACTS —*10 ounces (1¼ cups)*

700 calories	**29G** saturated fat	**49G** total carbohydrate	**150MG** sodium
54G total fat	**165MG** cholesterol	**6G** sugars	**11G** protein

SUGGESTED WINE PAIRING

Chimney Rock Elevage Blanc White Blend

Roasted Red Bell Pepper and Brie Soup

Yields 10 cups (8 servings)

Just the name of this soup sounds yummy. You'll notice that I've made things easier by suggesting store-bought roasted red peppers, but feel free to char fresh peppers on a wire rack over a stovetop gas flame if you'd like. I love the various roasted peppers on the market today. Be sure to use a good-quality Brie in the soup — you will get an appreciative response from around the table if you do. You might want to consider doubling this recipe and making plenty, because tomorrow you'll be looking for leftovers.

2	tablespoons olive oil
2	cups diced onions
5	cloves garlic, peeled
2	shallots, chopped
24	ounces canned or bottled roasted red bell peppers packed in their juice, chopped
5	sprigs fresh thyme
4	cups prepared vegetable broth
1	teaspoon Worcestershire sauce
1	teaspoon kosher salt
1	teaspoon freshly ground black pepper
10	ounces Brie cheese, cut into 8 pieces

SUGGESTED WINE PAIRING

M. Chapoutier Côtes-du-Rhône
Belleruche Rosé

Heat the oil into a heavy-bottomed saucepan over medium-high heat. Add the onions, garlic, and shallots and sauté for 5 minutes. Add the roasted peppers and their juice, thyme, and broth. Bring to a boil, turn down the heat to low, and simmer for 15 minutes, stirring occasionally. Stir in the Worcestershire sauce, salt, and pepper and remove from the heat. Puree the soup with an immersion blender until completely smooth. Ladle the soup into serving bowls and top each serving with a slice of the brie.

NUTRITION FACTS —*10 ounces (1¼ cups)*

200 calories	6G saturated fat	13G total carbohydrate	890MG sodium
13G total fat	35MG cholesterol	3G sugars	8G protein

I love the various jarred
roasted peppers available
at the market today.

Atlanta She-Crab Soup

Yields 13 cups (10 servings)

When we reopened our Neiman Marcus restaurant in Atlanta after a major remodel a few years ago, we decided to bring back a true Southern staple: She-Crab Soup. The gender of the recipe title refers to the preference for female crabs because of their excellent flavor. Originally, the soup got its red color from the female crab roe; now, we use a touch of smoked paprika to add color as well as an interesting flavor. Only the best sherry finishes the soup whenever this recipe is made in Atlanta. You'll need to keep your bar stocked with your favorite sherry once you and your friends try this recipe.

This truly decadent and indulgent soup is full of good things.

2	tablespoons unsalted butter
½	cup finely diced leek *(white part only)*
½	cup finely diced onion
½	cup finely diced celery
2	tablespoons smoked paprika
¾	cup all-purpose flour
1	cup dry white wine *(such as Sauvignon Blanc)*
6	cups canned crab broth or prepared seafood stock
6	sprigs fresh thyme, tied together with twine or string
2	bay leaves
1	teaspoon Worcestershire sauce
2	cups heavy cream
¾	cup dry sherry
1	pound pasteurized lump crabmeat
	Kosher salt and freshly ground white pepper
	Salmon roe or tobiko, for garnish
	Thinly sliced fresh chives, for garnish

Melt the butter in a large, heavy-bottomed saucepan over medium heat. Add the leek, onion, and celery and sauté for 6 minutes, stirring frequently. Stir in the smoked paprika and cook for 1 minute longer. Add the flour and continue stirring for 3 to 4 minutes more. Deglaze the pan by adding the white wine, whisking to prevent any lumps from forming. Whisk in the crab broth, turn down the heat to low, and add the thyme and bay leaves.

CHEF'S NOTES

Rinse the leeks carefully before dicing to remove any sand between the leaves.

The salmon roe is usually sold in small jars.

Continue to simmer the soup for 15 minutes, stirring occasionally. Add the Worcestershire sauce and cream and cook for 10 minutes longer. Remove the thyme and bay leaves from the soup. Add the sherry and gently fold in the crabmeat. Season with salt and pepper. When the crab is warmed through, ladle the soup into serving bowls. Garnish each serving with salmon roe and chives and serve immediately.

NUTRITION FACTS —*10 ounces (1¼ cups)*

300 calories	**12G** saturated fat	**11G** total carbohydrate	**640MG** sodium
21G total fat	**100MG** cholesterol	**1G** sugars	**14G** protein

SUGGESTED WINE PAIRING

Mischief & Mayhem White Burgundy

Chilled Strawberry Soup with Red Wine

Yields 12 cups (10 servings)

I've been carrying this recipe around since my days when I was the chef at the French Room at the Adolphus hotel here in Dallas. My French colleagues in the kitchen helped me come up with the recipe, which explains the technique of adding red wine to help cook down the strawberries. So many chilled fruit soups come out too sweet for my liking, but this one uses savory herbs and saffron, which give it a both sweet and savory finish, a welcome change.

3	pints fresh strawberries, hulled and washed
1	bottle good-quality red wine *(Zinfandel or Merlot)*
½	cup sugar
½	cup lightly packed fresh mint leaves
4	large sprigs fresh thyme
1	cup fresh orange juice
	Zest and juice of 2 lemons
	Pinch of saffron *(⅛ teaspoon)*

Combine all the ingredients in a large, heavy-bottomed saucepan and bring to a boil. Turn down the heat to a simmer and cook until the strawberries begin to soften, about 20 minutes. Remove the pan from the heat and let cool. Remove the mint leaves and thyme. Using a handheld immersion blender, blend the strawberry mixture until smooth. Pass the mixture through a strainer into a clean saucepan and let cool. Refrigerate for at least 2 or 3 hours or overnight before serving.

CHEF'S NOTE

If the soup is too thick, add more red wine or sparkling wine as needed.

SUGGESTED WINE PAIRING

Terlato Family Vineyards Pinot Noir

NUTRITION FACTS —*10 ounces (1¼ cups)*

230 calories	**0G** saturated fat	**43G** total carbohydrate	**55MG** sodium
1G total fat	**0MG** cholesterol	**13G** sugars	**2G** protein

Saffron and strawberries —
who would have thought?!

4 SANDWICHES

SANDWICHES

Over the years, I have come to realize that building — or perhaps "crafting" would be a better word — the perfect sandwich is an art form in itself. By now, the kitchen staffs in our restaurants are familiar with my philosophy on "the art of the sandwich"; they know I have a passion for the subject. Growing up in the Northeast section of Philadelphia, we ate lots of sandwiches, most notably the hoagie or the steak sandwich, and it never crossed my mind that there might be a right and wrong way to put a sandwich together. But it was those sandwiches, synonymous with Philly, that first taught me the importance of building a sandwich correctly, in order of ingredients. My first job when I was 14 was prep person at Piccolo's pizza and hoagie shop. On weekends I would open the shop and bring in the bread that was left by the front door and start pre-slicing it so the grill and sandwich cooks didn't have to do it when they were busy. We got our bread from Amoroso's Bakery — they're still in operation. This was a time before bakeries were using the term "artisan," and Wonder Bread was the big mass-produced bakery in Philly. That was the product we used for a simple peanut butter and jelly sandwich.

Still to this day I search out a great kaiser or hoagie roll when I get back to visit family in Philly. So it's no wonder that the choice and quality of the bread plays a big role in sandwich making at the Neiman Marcus restaurants. One of the fun parts of my job when we open new restaurants is tasting the bread samples from a local bakery hoping to supply us. Bakers bring more samples than any other vendor and I must admit I'm a bread lover through and through, so you can imagine that makes me happy. I hold all artisan bakers up to high standards, being from the East Coast where bread making is a craft handed down through the generations by the earliest immigrants from Europe.

The next building block of a great sandwich is the *schmear* — a term I like to use to describe the spread — derived from Yiddish by way of "deli slang." Mayo, mustard (typically a brown type), maybe an aioli, whatever you decide; the main thing is that the schmear on the bread gives flavor to the sandwich. It's important that you never use so much that the sandwich gets soggy — no one likes a soggy sandwich!

Finally, and more important than anything else, are the fillings. Here at Neiman Marcus, we take pride in using only premium fresh turkey roasted in-house, the leanest roast beef cooked perfectly to medium-rare, and the finest lobster and seafood flown fresh from Boston daily. Building a sandwich means building flavors, using ripened tomatoes, crisp lettuces, seasoning with appropriate herbs and spices, and of course making sure the other ingredients are prepped daily, keeping them fresh as possible.

A good sandwich always starts with a little schmear of mayo, mustard, or maybe aioli.

Many of our sandwiches are served warm and this is done in a variety of ways. Currently we use high-speed ovens (MerryChefs or TurboChefs). These ovens use a combination of induction heat and microwaves to heat and toast the sandwiches quickly with great results. The kitchen toasters in our restaurants get mixed reviews from our chefs, and there are few things worse than the aroma of burnt bread wafting through a retail store because a piece of toast has gotten stuck to the heating element! The panini press is another great kitchen tool we use to heat and toast sandwiches, and they are ideal for the home kitchen. I like the look of the great groove marks they leave in the bread and the way they make the outside of the sandwich crisp and toasty. For cooking the ultimate burger I personally prefer using a griddle rather than a broiler as a griddle helps to retain moisture and therefore texture. My favorite at-home grill attachment is my *plancha*. This flat-top cast-iron griddle attachment fits over the grill grates; once it gets very hot, it sears meats and fish quickly and evenly.

Jumbo Lump Crab Cake Burger with Creamy Coleslaw

Yields 4 crab cake burgers and 5 cups slaw

I was first introduced to crab cakes at Watson's Restaurant in Ocean City, New Jersey, back in the early 1970s when I worked as a prep cook during my school summer break. In those days you spent hours "picking" the crabmeat from the shells — a job that no one liked, but it had to be done. The ultimate no-no was if the chef ever found shell in my picked crabmeat. Today, you rarely find bits of shell left in crabmeat once it's processed, so lucky you!

FOR THE CREAMY COLESLAW

2	cups mayonnaise
¼	cup apple cider vinegar
2	tablespoons sugar
2	tablespoons chopped fresh dill
2	teaspoons Dijon mustard
1	teaspoon caraway seeds
½	tablespoon prepared horseradish *(optional)*
½	teaspoon celery seeds
½	teaspoon celery salt
½	teaspoon kosher salt
½	teaspoon onion salt
½	teaspoon freshly cracked black pepper
6	cups shredded white cabbage
½	cup grated carrot

FOR THE CRAB CAKE BURGERS

1	pound jumbo lump blue crabmeat
1	large egg, beaten
¼	cup mayonnaise
1	scallion, thinly sliced *(white and green parts, about ¼ cup)*
2	tablespoons minced fresh Italian parsley
1	teaspoon Dijon mustard
1	teaspoon Worcestershire sauce
	Dash of Tabasco sauce, or to taste
1	tablespoon Old Bay seasoning
5	tablespoons fine plain bread crumbs
	Vegetable oil, for sautéing
1	tablespoon softened butter
4	soft brioche rolls or hamburger buns
	Lettuce leaves and tomato slices, for garnish *(optional)*

To prepare the creamy coleslaw, place the mayonnaise and vinegar in a mixing bowl and add the sugar, dill, mustard, caraway seeds, horseradish, celery seeds, celery salt, kosher salt, onion salt, and pepper. Mix together the shredded cabbage and carrot in a large bowl, pour the coleslaw dressing over, and mix well. Adjust the seasonings and keep refrigerated until ready to serve.

To prepare the crab cake burgers, place the crabmeat on a cookie sheet and spread it out evenly. Pick through carefully to remove any shell or cartilage. Return the crabmeat to a bowl. In a separate bowl, combine the egg, mayonnaise, scallion, parsley, mustard, Worcestershire sauce, Tabasco, and Old Bay seasoning and mix gently with a fork. Fold the mixture into the crabmeat. Sprinkle the bread crumbs on the mixture and gently stir to combine with a fork so as not to break up the lumps of crab. Form the crab cake mixture by hand into four patties, around 1 inch high and 4 inches wide. Place on a plate, cover with plastic wrap, and reserve in the refrigerator until ready to cook.

Preheat the oven to 200 degrees F. Pour ¼ inch of vegetable oil into a large skillet set over medium heat. When the oil is hot, gently add the crab cakes and sauté for about 2 minutes on each side. Transfer the crab cakes to a plate lined with paper towels. Keep warm in the oven while assembling the sandwiches. Lightly butter the soft rolls and warm in the oven.

Place a crab cake in each warm buttered roll and serve ½ cup of the coleslaw on top of the crab cakes (with the lettuce and tomato, if you like).

NUTRITION FACTS —*1 burger*

660	calories	54G	total carb.
36G	total fat	8G	sugars
10G	saturated fat	1140MG	sodium
200MG	cholesterol	30G	protein

NUTRITION FACTS —*½ cup slaw*

340	calories	7G	total carb.
35G	total fat	5G	sugars
4.5G	saturated fat	510MG	sodium
15MG	cholesterol	1G	protein

Deli-Style Reuben Sandwich with Balsamic-Braised Sauerkraut

Yields 4 sandwiches

I vividly recall the first time I ever ate a Reuben sandwich. I was attending the Culinary Institute of America in Hyde Park, New York, having lunch for the first time in the school's coffee shop. Back then, the coffee shop class was a requirement for all students. Coming from Philly and having eaten in countless diners, this class seemed like "old hat" but believe it or not I had never experienced a Reuben. You'll find a Reuben sandwich recipe in an earlier Neiman Marcus cookbook, but here we give it a makeover. The first time around we didn't say to cook your own corned beef, but taking the time to prepare it is well worth it. The sandwich delivers fork-tender, falling-apart, perfect corned beef with a perfect "schmear" of sauce, tangy kraut, and the finishing touch of thinly sliced Gruyère. Get busy perfecting this sandwich in your home!

FOR THE CORNED BEEF

1   corned beef brisket *(6 to 8 pounds)*

1   cup prepared pickling spice seasoning

2   onions, roughly chopped

6   cloves garlic, smashed

FOR THE SAUERKRAUT

2   tablespoons finely diced bacon

½   cup finely diced onion

1   cup firmly packed prepared sauerkraut

1   tablespoon balsamic vinegar

FOR THE SANDWICHES

8   slices rye bread

8   thin slices Gruyère or Swiss cheese *(about 4 ounces)*

    Louis Dressing *(page 217)*

4   tablespoons softened butter

To cook the corned beef, place the brisket, pickling spice, onions, and garlic in a large saucepan or stock pot and add enough water to cover the brisket by 4 inches. Cover tightly with a lid and bring to a boil. Turn down the heat to low and simmer for 3 to 4 hours or until the brisket is tender but not stringy when sliced. Remove the corned beef carefully from the pan and transfer to a platter large enough to hold it. Let the corned beef cool thoroughly, then cover tightly and keep in the refrigerator. When ready to make the sandwiches, cut against the grain into ¼-inch slices.

To prepare the sauerkraut, sauté the diced bacon in a sauté pan over medium heat for about 3 minutes, until well browned; remove the bacon and set aside. Add the onion to the pan and sauté for 3 or 4 minutes, until lightly browned. Add the sauerkraut, stir to combine, and heat through. Add the balsamic vinegar and reserved bacon and mix well. Remove the pan from the heat.

To assemble one sandwich, place 2 slices of rye bread on a clean work surface. Place a slice of cheese on each slice and top with about 1 tablespoon Louis dressing. Place about 5 ounces corned beef over the dressing on one slice and top with one-quarter of the sauerkraut. Top with the other slice of bread and butter the outside of each bread slice with about ½ tablespoon butter. Repeat for the remaining sandwiches. Place one or two of the finished sandwiches at a time on an electric griddle or in a large skillet over medium heat. Cook until the bread is golden brown and the cheese has melted.

SUGGESTED WINE PAIRING

Seven Daughters Red Blend

NUTRITION FACTS —*1 sandwich*

820 calories	15G saturated fat	47G total carbohydrate	1370MG sodium
62G total fat	75MG cholesterol	10G sugars	19G protein

Barbeque Shrimp Wrap with Vinegar Slaw, Wasabi Mayonnaise, and Avocado

Yields 4 wraps

Shrimp is the most popular protein of customers at Neiman Marcus restaurants. Our cooks today have it easy since we only buy peeled and deveined shrimp from our supplier, which saves a lot of prep time. For this recipe, I like "butterflying" the shrimp — cutting them in half, almost all the way through, so more of the BBQ sauce can cover the entire surface of the shrimp. I don't have a particular favorite BBQ sauce — I like them all, from vinegary to sweet and from thin to very thick. Use your favorite BBQ sauce with this delicious sandwich.

FOR THE WASABI MAYONNAISE

2	teaspoons wasabi powder
½	cup mayonnaise
½	tablespoon fresh lemon juice
¼	teaspoon kosher salt

FOR THE SHRIMP

20	shrimp *(about 1 pound)*, peeled, deveined, and tail removed
2	tablespoons Barbecue Spice *(page 55)*
2	tablespoons olive oil
¼	cup barbecue sauce *(your favorite)*
4	large *(10-inch)* flour tortillas
2	cups shredded white cabbage
3	tablespoons Cilantro-Lime Vinaigrette *(page 215)*
1	avocado, peeled, pitted, and cut into 16 thin slices

SUGGESTED WINE PAIRING

MAZZONI Pinot Grigio

To prepare the wasabi mayonnaise, mix together the wasabi powder and 4 teaspoons water in a bowl to make a smooth paste. Fold in the mayonnaise, lemon juice, and salt. Mix well and set aside; it will keep in the refrigerator, covered, for up to 1 week.

To prepare the shrimp, place the shrimp in a bowl and sprinkle with the spice mix and olive oil. Toss together to coat the shrimp and marinate in the refrigerator for 1 hour. Heat the grill to medium heat. If using a charcoal grill, use the least hot side of the grill. Arrange the shrimp on the grill, taking care not to overcrowd them. Grill on the first side for about 1½ minutes. Turn the shrimp over and brush with the barbecue sauce. Grill the shrimp for 2 minutes longer or until completely cooked through. Transfer to a plate. Heat 1 flour tortilla at a time on the grill, about 15 seconds on each side.

To prepare the shrimp wraps, mix the cabbage with the vinaigrette to make a slaw. Lay each warmed flour tortilla on a cutting board. Spread the wasabi mayonnaise on each tortilla, covering the entire tortilla. Place one-quarter of the slaw in a strip down the middle of each tortilla. Arrange 5 of the shrimp on each tortilla and then 4 avocado slices. Tightly roll up the tortilla like a burrito and cut in half on an angle. Alternatively, cut each wrap into 6 slices for bite-size servings.

Go easy on the wasabi mayo — it's best to use too little to begin with than too much!

CHEF'S NOTE

Feel free to use flavored tortillas such as spinach or tomato tortillas in this recipe, or whole wheat ones.

NUTRITION FACTS —*1 wrap*

630	calories	52G	total carbohydrate
43G	total fat	11G	sugars
7G	saturated fat	1460MG	sodium
50MG	cholesterol	13G	protein

All-Natural Grilled Hamburger with Secret Sauce

Yields 4 burgers

When I first arrived at Neiman Marcus there were no hamburgers or French fries on the menus. At that time, people still referred to the Zodiac Room restaurant as "the tearoom," and you wouldn't dare find these comfort foods on a tearoom menu! Times sure have changed and hamburgers receive prominent attention on all our menus. We even serve them on a special plate with a special garnish so we can showcase the great all-natural patties, fresh-made buns, and piping-hot French fries. And by the way, I can tell you that ladies who lunch do enjoy a good burger too!

1½ pounds coarsely ground beef chuck *(80% lean)*

2 tablespoons Worcestershire sauce

4 tablespoons softened butter

1 teaspoon minced garlic

2 cups sliced button mushrooms

Kosher salt and freshly ground black pepper

4 slices Swiss cheese *(about 4 ounces)*

4 brioche buns, soft rolls, or hamburger buns

4 tablespoons Caramelized Onion Dip *(page 228)*

4 tablespoons Secret Sauce *(page 225)*, or your favorite steak sauce

4 slices ripe tomato *(optional)*

4 Bibb lettuce leaves *(optional)*

SUGGESTED WINE PAIRING

Markham Merlot

Place the ground beef and Worcestershire sauce in a bowl and gently mix together. Form the mixture into 4 patties about 1 inch thick and 3½ inches across. Let the patties come to room temperature before cooking.

Prepare the grill. Set a sauté pan over low heat and melt 2 tablespoons of the butter. Add the garlic and sauté, while stirring, for 3 minutes until the garlic has softened. Add the mushrooms, turn up the heat to medium-high, and season with salt and pepper. Stir once and then let the mushrooms brown for 3 or 4 minutes without stirring. Stir once and then let the mushrooms cook for 3 or 4 minutes longer. Turn off the heat and keep warm.

Season the burgers with salt and pepper on each side and transfer to the grill. Cook for 3 or 4 minutes over medium-high heat; do not move or feel tempted to even sneak a peek. Turn the burgers over and cook for 3 to 4 minutes longer, without disturbing, for medium-rare, or longer for your preferred doneness; the shorter the cooking time, the juicier and more tender the burgers. During the last minute of grilling on the second side, add a slice of cheese. Remove the burgers from the grill and let them rest for a few minutes.

Evenly spread the remaining butter on each side of the brioche or hamburger buns. Toast on the grill over low heat. Place the burgers on the bottom halves. Top each burger with 1 tablespoon of Caramelized Onion Dip and the sautéed mushrooms. Drizzle with the Secret Sauce. Garnish with the tomato and lettuce, if desired, and close with the top half of each bun.

CHEF'S NOTE

Make sure the ground beef is cold. Work gently when handling the ground beef and do not overwork it for a tender and juicier burger. You can keep the formed patties, covered, in the refrigerator for several hours or overnight.

NUTRITION FACTS —*1 burger*

810 calories	24G saturated fat	51G total carbohydrate
48G total fat	210MG cholesterol	10G sugars

1080MG sodium
43G protein

Croque Madame with Sunny-Side-Up Eggs and Frisée Greens

Yields 4 sandwiches

Originally, this sandwich started out as a cool-weather menu item at many of our restaurants, but it soon became so popular that we have a tough time taking it off the menu when the weather begins warming up. Some would say this is the ultimate ham and cheese sandwich, and although it calls for making a béchamel sauce from scratch, it's well worth the effort. If you ever need a homemade *wow!* type of lunch, save this recipe for those special meals. Frisée salad greens dress up the plate. *Bon appétit!*

FOR THE BÉCHAMEL SAUCE

- 1 tablespoon unsalted butter
- 1 tablespoon all-purpose flour
- 1 cup milk
  Pinch of grated nutmeg
  Kosher salt and freshly ground black pepper
- ½ cup grated Gruyère or baby Swiss cheese

FOR THE SANDWICHES

- 8 slices artisan sourdough bread, crusts removed
- 2 cups shredded Gruyère or baby Swiss cheese
- 8 thin slices ham, about 8 ounces *(preferably Black Forest or smoked country ham)*
- 2 tablespoons unsalted butter
- 4 large eggs
- 4 cups frisée greens
  Kosher salt and freshly ground black pepper
- 2 teaspoons olive oil

SUGGESTED WINE PAIRING

Marius Rouge

To prepare the béchamel sauce, melt the butter in a small saucepan over medium-low heat. When melted, whisk in the flour. Continue whisking for 2 minutes and then slowly add the milk while whisking. Turn down the heat to low; the milk will begin to thicken. Continue to cook for 2 minutes longer. Season with the nutmeg, salt, and pepper. Remove from the heat and whisk in the cheese. When ready to serve, warm the sauce over low heat. If not using immediately, transfer to an airtight container and keep refrigerated for up to 3 days.

To prepare the sandwiches, preheat the oven to 400 degrees F. Set 4 of the bread slices on a clean work surface and evenly sprinkle ¼ cup of the shredded cheese on each slice. Place 2 slices of ham on top of the cheese and then add the remaining shredded cheese. Top with the remaining 4 slices of bread.

Set a large nonstick sauté pan over low heat. Spread ¼ tablespoon of the butter on each side of the sandwiches and transfer to the warm sauté pan. Turn up the heat to medium-low and begin browning the sandwiches, about 2 minutes on each side. Transfer the sandwiches to a cookie sheet. Evenly spread about 2 tablespoons of the béchamel on top of each prepared sandwich. Place in the oven until the tops are bubbling and golden. Keep the béchamel warm.

Set the same sauté pan over low heat and add the remaining 1 tablespoon butter. When melted, carefully crack the eggs into the pan, making sure they don't run into each other (cook in two batches, if necessary). Turn up the heat to medium-low and cook the eggs to medium sunny-side-up, about 3 minutes, or to the desired doneness. Transfer the sandwiches to serving plates, and top each with an egg.

Place the frisée in a bowl, season with salt and pepper, and toss with the olive oil. Divide among the serving plates and serve the remaining béchamel in a bowl at the table.

NUTRITION FACTS —*1 sandwich*

680 calories	17G saturated fat	50G total carbohydrate	1370MG sodium
34G total fat	295MG cholesterol	7G sugars	42G protein

Fresh Maine Lobster Club Sandwich with Crispy Bacon

Yields 4 sandwiches

The Neiman Marcus Lobster Club Sandwich originated with our San Francisco Rotunda restaurant, and it's still their single most popular menu item, even when peak New England lobster season in the late summer months is over. We've added this sandwich to other restaurant menus around the country, and guess what? Part of the secret of our success is the consistent source we use — Steve Connolly Seafood in Boston — and best of all, their policy is to use sustainable fisheries so stocks can remain viable into the future. Now, all of our restaurants buy freshly picked lobster meat, fully cleaned, cooked, and ready to serve. As a result of the easier preparation, the lobster club took off and our customers couldn't get enough of it! We could also keep our costs down this way so menu price was never an issue. It's good when everyone wins.

8	slices good-quality, thick-cut smoked bacon
1	pound freshly cooked and cleaned lobster meat *(frozen lobster claw, knuckle, and tail meat can be substituted),* coarsely chopped
¼	cup mayonnaise
2	tablespoons fresh lemon juice
1	teaspoon minced chives
1	teaspoon Old Bay seasoning
	Pinch of freshly ground black pepper
12	slices brioche bread
8	Bibb, green leaf, or butter lettuce leaves
8	large slices ripe tomato
1	ripe avocado, pitted, peeled, and cut into 16 slices

SUGGESTED WINE PAIRING

Rutherford Hill Chardonnay

Preheat the oven to 350 degrees F. Place the bacon in a roasting pan without overlapping the slices. Transfer to the oven and cook the bacon for 20 to 25 minutes until crisp. Drain the bacon fat and keep the bacon warm.

CHEF'S NOTE
Cooking bacon in the oven is a very easy and less messy way to prepare it.

Place the lobster in a mixing bowl and add the mayonnaise, lemon juice, chives, Old Bay seasoning, and pepper. Mix together and keep refrigerated until you are ready to assemble the sandwiches.

Toast the brioche slices and set 4 slices on a clean work surface. Add 4 of the lettuce leaves and top with the tomato slices and half of the lobster mixture. Cover with another slice of the toasted brioche and top with the rest of the lettuce and lobster salad, and then 2 bacon slices and the avocado slices. Close the sandwiches with the last 4 slices of the toasted brioche. Secure the sandwiches with toothpicks and cut in half or quarters.

This is probably the most widely requested sandwich on Neiman Marcus menus.

NUTRITION FACTS —*1 sandwich*

750	calories	64G	total carbohydrate
33G	total fat	8G	sugars
9G	saturated fat	1760MG	sodium
240MG	cholesterol	46G	protein

Mahi-Mahi Fish Tacos with Cilantro-Lime Vinaigrette and Crisp Cabbage Slaw

Yields 4 servings   ⧗ GO FIGURE

Who would have thought that the trendy food-truck fish taco would find its way onto Neiman Marcus restaurant menus? Well, they have, and in a big way. On a whim, we tried this recipe in our Dallas NorthPark Mermaid Bar restaurant and it quickly became one of the top sellers. Putting into practice the principle that whatever's good for one Neiman Marcus restaurant must be good for others, the tacos soon found their way onto the menus of many of our biggest and fanciest restaurants. From "white tablecloth" to "grab-and-go" concepts, this dish sells.

FOR THE FISH

4	mahi-mahi fillets, about 1 inch thick and 5 ounces each
1	tablespoon Cajun blackening spice
3	tablespoons olive oil
1	lime, cut into 8 wedges

FOR THE CHIPOTLE MAYONNAISE

1	cup light mayonnaise
	Juice of 1 lime
2	tablespoons pureed canned chipotle chile and adobo sauce

FOR THE CABBAGE SLAW

2	cups shredded white cabbage
3	tablespoons Cilantro-Lime Vinaigrette *(page 215)*
2	tablespoons roughly chopped fresh cilantro leaves

FOR THE TACOS

8	small *(5-inch)* white corn tortillas
1	avocado, pitted, peeled, and cut into 16 slices
1	jalapeño, thinly sliced

SUGGESTED WINE PAIRING

Terlato Family Vineyards Pinot Grigio

To marinate the fish, place the mahi-mahi fillets in a large dish and sprinkle with the blackening spice and olive oil. Squeeze the lime juice from the wedges over the fish, and toss with the squeezed lime wedges. Transfer to the refrigerator and let sit for 1 hour.

Meanwhile, prepare the chipotle mayonnaise. Place the mayonnaise in a small mixing bowl, add the lime juice and chipotle puree, and mix thoroughly. Cover and keep refrigerated.

To prepare the slaw, place the cabbage in a mixing bowl and add the vinaigrette and cilantro. Toss together and mix thoroughly. Cover and keep refrigerated.

Prepare the grill and spray the grill rack with nonstick spray so the fish does not stick. Place the fillets on the grill and cook over medium-high heat on the first side for 3 to 4 minutes. Turn the fish over and grill for 3 to 4 minutes longer. Remove the fish and reserve. Heat the tortillas on the grill for about 15 seconds on each side to heat through; a little browning is fine and they should still be pliable.

To assemble the tacos, place two tortillas, side by side, on each serving plate. With a fork, gently flake each mahi-mahi fillet into four smaller pieces and place two pieces on each tortilla. Top the fish with the cabbage slaw and then two slices of avocado. Drizzle with the chipotle mayonnaise and garnish with jalapeño slices. To serve, fold the tacos over or serve open-face.

CHEF'S NOTES

The blackening spice is the key to this recipe.

If mahi-mahi is unavailable, use another firm-fleshed fish such as snapper, Gulf redfish, or even fresh tuna.

NUTRITION FACTS —*1 serving*

550	calories	37G	total carbohydrate
32G	total fat	6G	sugars
4.5G	saturated fat	810MG	sodium
105MG	cholesterol	31G	protein

Vegetable Panini with Grilled Peppers and Zucchini with Basil Pesto

Yields 4 servings   ⧗ GO FIGURE

It's always a challenge when you put a vegetarian sandwich on a menu — it's a hard sell. But when you make a sandwich as good as this one and the calorie count gets our Go Figure nod, you sell plenty. It's one of my favorite sandwiches because when you're finished you feel satisfied but not overly full. That's a good thing when you're going back to work for the afternoon. Feel free to load it up with as many fresh veggies as you want — I can't promise the Go Figure numbers, but I will promise a great tasting sandwich. I like to serve the sandwich with a small side salad side and some seasonal sliced fruit.

1	large red bell pepper, stemmed and seeded, cut into ¼-inch rings
1	zucchini, cut into ¼-inch slices on an angle
2	tablespoons olive oil
⅛	teaspoon kosher salt
⅛	teaspoon freshly ground black pepper
4	slices provolone cheese, about 1 ounce each
4	ciabatta rolls, about 3 inches square, cut in half, or 4 slices ciabatta loaf, 3 inches square
4	large slices ripe tomato
1	cup baby arugula
4	bottled artichoke hearts, quartered
4	tablespoons Fresh Basil Pesto (*page 222*)

Preheat the oven to 350 degrees F. Prepare the grill and spray the grill rack with nonstick spray so the ingredients do not stick. Place the peppers, zucchini, olive oil, salt, and pepper in a mixing bowl and toss together to coat. Place the peppers and zucchini on the grill and cook over medium-high heat for about 2 minutes on each side. Transfer the vegetables to a cookie sheet, arranging them in 4 servings, and top with a slice of cheese. Place in the oven for about 3 minutes or until the cheese has melted. Toast the ciabatta bread on the grill for 1 or 2 minutes until toasty brown.

To serve, place a tomato slice on each bottom slice of ciabatta and add the arugula, artichoke quarters, and the zucchini, peppers, and cheese. Spread the pesto on the top halves of the ciabatta and close the sandwiches.

NUTRITION FACTS —*1 sandwich*

520 calories	7G saturated fat	62G total carbohydrate	810MG sodium
23G total fat	25MG cholesterol	5G sugars	19G protein

SUGGESTED WINE PAIRING

Ernie Els "Big Easy" White Blend

CHEF'S NOTE

You can use the grill for this recipe, or a griddle pan or panini sandwich maker. Whichever method you choose, take care not to overcook the vegetables; they should still have a little crispness to them.

Tuscan Grilled Chicken Melt with Fresh Mozzarella and Arugula

Yields 4 servings   ⌛ GO FIGURE

We take creative liberty here with the recipe title of "Tuscan Grilled," but just the idea of grilling in Tuscany over open fire says flavor and good taste. The way we deliver this sense of Tuscany in our kitchens is by marinating our chicken breasts as soon as they are delivered. Adding flavor is a term we speak about often; usually we add lots of chopped fresh herbs and extra-virgin olive oil. Now all you need is a really good glass of chilled white wine and lunch is complete, Tuscan style.

2   boneless, skinless chicken breasts, about 6 ounces each

2   tablespoons chopped mixed fresh herbs *(such as basil, parsley, and oregano)*

1   small lemon, thinly sliced

1   clove garlic, minced

1   tablespoon olive oil

Kosher salt and freshly ground black pepper

1   red bell pepper, stemmed, seeded, and cut into ¼-inch rings

4   ciabatta rolls, about 3 inches square, cut in half, or 4 slices ciabatta loaf, 3 inches square

4   ounces fresh mozzarella, cut into 4 slices

4   large slices ripe tomato

2   cups baby arugula

2   tablespoons Fresh Basil Pesto *(page 222)*

SUGGESTED WINE PAIRING

Cusumano Insolia

Place the chicken breasts on a plate. In a bowl, combine the herbs, lemon slices, garlic, olive oil, and salt and black pepper and then rub the mixture into the chicken. Cover and refrigerate for at least 2 hours or overnight.

Preheat the oven to 350 degrees F. and prepare the grill. Spray the grill rack with nonstick spray so the ingredients do not stick. Grill the pepper rings for about 2 minutes on each side over medium-high heat. Scrape the herbs, lemon, and garlic from the chicken breasts and discard. Spray the grill again and grill the chicken breasts over medium-high heat for 3 to 4 minutes on each side or until cooked through. Remove from the grill and transfer to a clean work surface. Using a sharp knife, slice the chicken on an angle as thinly as you can. Place the chicken slices on the bottom half of each ciabatta, cover with the grilled pepper slices, and top with the mozzarella. Transfer to a cookie sheet and place the top halves of the ciabatta, cut-side up, on the cookie sheet.

Toast in the oven for 6 or 7 minutes or until the chicken is warm and the mozzarella has melted. Remove from the oven and top with the tomato slices and arugula. Spread the pesto on the top half of the ciabatta rolls, close the sandwiches, and serve immediately.

CHEF'S NOTES

You can grill the peppers and chicken a day ahead, if you wish.

Accompany the sandwiches with a small green salad and sliced seasonal fruit, if desired.

> I could make a meal out of grilled ciabatta bread simply spread with a good basil pesto.

NUTRITION FACTS —*1 sandwich*

560 calories	64G total carb.
17G total fat	7G sugars
6G saturated fat	900MG sodium
80MG cholesterol	39G protein

Southwest Turkey Burger with Chipotle Mayonnaise and Pico de Gallo

Yields 4 servings

Burgers have ridden a wave of popularity for the past decade that doesn't look to be letting up anytime soon. Turkey burgers, likewise, are popular due to the choice they give both in flavor and in healthiness. They are a great alternative for those limiting or avoiding red meat. The key here is spicing up the ground turkey so it's flavorful, complex, and leaves you wanting more — we want you to enjoy it. Giving it a Southwest twist comes naturally — after all, we are a Texas company with deep Texas roots. Finishing the sandwich with the flavors of chipotle and pico de gallo salsa keeps us true to that heritage.

FOR THE PICO DE GALLO SALSA

½	cup diced ripe plum tomatoes
1	tablespoon minced onion
1	teaspoon seeded and minced jalapeño
½	teaspoon minced garlic
1	teaspoon minced fresh cilantro leaves

FOR THE BURGERS

1½	pounds lean ground turkey
1	tablespoon blackening spice
1	tablespoon Worcestershire sauce
2	tablespoons olive oil *(optional)*
4	slices pepper Jack cheese, about 1 ounce each
4	soft brioche hamburger buns
½	cup Chipotle Mayonnaise *(page 228)*
4	Bibb or green leaf lettuce leaves
1	avocado, pitted, peeled, and cut into 16 thin slices

To prepare the pico de gallo salsa, combine the tomatoes, onion, jalapeño, garlic, and cilantro in a small mixing bowl. Cover and keep refrigerated.

To prepare the burgers, place the ground turkey in a mixing bowl and add the blackening spice and Worcestershire sauce. Gently mix the ingredients together, without overworking the ground turkey. Form into four patties about ½ inch thick. (If not cooking immediately, place on a plate, cover, and keep chilled until you are ready to grill; remove from the fridge about 15 minutes before cooking.)

Prepare the grill (or heat the olive oil in a sauté pan set over medium heat). Spray the grill rack with nonstick spray so the ingredients do not stick. Cook the turkey burgers for 3 or 4 minutes on each side or until the internal temperature reaches 165 degrees F. When the burgers are almost done, top with the pepper Jack cheese. Meanwhile, heat the burger buns on the grill or in a toaster oven.

To serve, spread the chipotle mayonnaise on the top half of each bun. On the bottom half, place a lettuce leaf and a tablespoon of pico de gallo. Top with the burger, avocado slices, and top half of the bun and serve immediately.

NUTRITION FACTS —*1 burger*

870 calories	**17G** saturated fat	**52G** total carbohydrate	**950MG** sodium
55G total fat	**210MG** cholesterol	**8G** sugars	**41G** protein

SUGGESTED WINE PAIRING

The Federalist Chardonnay

Grilled Cheese Sandwich with Gruyère, Sharp Cheddar, Gouda, and Tomato Jam

Yields 4 sandwiches and 1 cup tomato jam

How did something so simple get to become so popular? At first I felt a bit embarrassed to put a "grilled cheese" on our menus, but Anita Hirsch, our corporate chef, came up with a really upscale version that wowed me, and soon we were adding it to our restaurant repertoire across the country. You won't use all the jam, so save it for grilled chicken or fish, or fold it into your favorite mayo to make a great dip for fresh vegetables.

FOR THE TOMATO JAM

- 1½ pounds ripe plum tomatoes
- 1 tablespoon olive oil
- ½ cup finely diced white onion
- ½ tablespoon minced garlic
- ¼ cup light brown sugar
- 2 tablespoons balsamic vinegar
- ¼ teaspoon ground cinnamon
- 1 teaspoon kosher salt
- 1 teaspoon freshly ground black pepper
- 1 tablespoon fresh lemon juice

FOR THE SANDWICHES

- 8 slices artisan sourdough bread
- 8 slices good-quality Gouda cheese *(about 8 ounces)*
- 8 slices good-quality Gruyère cheese *(about 8 ounces)*
- 4 slices good-quality sharp cheddar cheese *(about 4 ounces)*
- 3 tablespoons softened unsalted butter

SUGGESTED WINE PAIRING

Marco Abella Mas Mallola Priorat Red Blend

To prepare the tomato jam, bring a large saucepan of water to a boil. With a paring knife, cut into the stem end of each tomato and remove the core. At the other end of the tomatoes, make a small X in the skin. Prepare a large bowl of ice water. Carefully drop the tomatoes into the boiling water and blanch for just 30 seconds. Remove the tomatoes with a slotted spoon and immediately transfer to the ice water to shock. When cool, peel the skin from the tomatoes. Cut the tomatoes in half lengthwise and gently squeeze out the seeds and discard. Coarsely chop the tomatoes and set aside. Heat the olive oil in a large sauté pan over medium-low heat. Add the onion and garlic. Sauté, stirring continuously, for 4 to 5 minutes, until translucent. Stir in the chopped tomatoes, brown sugar, balsamic vinegar, cinnamon, salt, and pepper. Stir well and turn down the heat to low. Simmer the tomato jam for about 30 minutes, stirring occasionally. When the jam has thickened, remove from the heat and stir in the lemon juice. Let the jam cool and then transfer to an airtight container; there should be about 1 cup of tomato jam. Keep in the refrigerator for up to 30 days.

For the sandwiches, lay out four slices of the bread on a clean work surface. Spread 1 tablespoon of tomato jam on a slice of bread and add a slice of Gouda and Gruyère. Spread 1 more tablespoon of the tomato jam on top of the cheese. Add a slice of cheddar and another slice of Gouda and Gruyère. Repeat with the remaining bread and cheese. Close the sandwiches. Heat a large griddle pan, sandwich press, or panini press. Evenly spread the softened butter on both the top and bottom slices of the bread. Griddle the sandwiches on low heat until brown and crispy on both sides, the centers of the sandwiches are warm, and the cheese has melted. Transfer the sandwiches to a cutting board. Let rest for 1 or 2 minutes so the cheese does not run when the sandwiches are cut in half. Cut the sandwiches and serve immediately.

NUTRITION FACTS —*1 sandwich*

760 calories	29G total carb.
52G total fat	0G sugars
33G saturated fat	1120MG sodium
175MG cholesterol	43G protein

NUTRITION FACTS —*tomato jam (about 2 tablespoons)*

45 calories	9G total carb.
1.5G total fat	7G sugars
0G saturated fat	150MG sodium
0MG cholesterol	1G protein

Grilled Flat Iron Steak Sandwich

Yields 4 servings

The flat iron steak has become very popular in the restaurant world over the past few years. The cut comes from the shoulder and the steak is cut on the thinner side to ensure a quick cooking time with optimum flavor. You can also use sirloin, strip loin, or tenderloin for this recipe. The ciabatta roll works really well because it helps soak up all the steak juices as they get released when eating.

FOR THE STEAK AND ONIONS

1   pound flat iron steak

2   tablespoons Worcestershire sauce

2   tablespoons plus 2 teaspoons olive oil

1   onion, thinly sliced

2   cloves garlic, minced

     Kosher salt and freshly ground black pepper

½   red onion, thinly sliced

FOR THE SANDWICHES

¼   cup sour cream

¼   cup mayonnaise

2   tablespoons Worcestershire sauce

1   teaspoon prepared horseradish

4   ciabatta rolls, about 3 inches square, cut in half, or 4 slices ciabatta loaf, 3 inches square

8   slices ripe tomato

1   cup baby arugula

SUGGESTED WINE PAIRING

Château Timberlay Rouge Bordeaux Blend

To prepare the steak, place the steak in a glass or ceramic dish. Mix together the Worcestershire sauce, 2 tablespoons of the olive oil, onion, and garlic in a bowl and pour over the steak. Cover the dish tightly and marinate the steak in the refrigerator for at least 6 hours or overnight, turning once or twice.

Prepare the grill. Bring the steak to room temperature and brush off the onions and garlic from the marinade. Season the steak with salt and pepper. Grill over medium-high heat for 4 minutes without moving the steak. Using tongs, move the steak one quarter turn and grill for 4 minutes longer. Meanwhile, on a plate, season the red onion with salt and pepper and sprinkle with 2 teaspoons of the olive oil. Transfer the red onion to the grill and brown over medium heat; do not let it burn. Remove the onion when cooked. Turn the steak over and cook for 8 minutes longer for medium-rare (125 to 130 degrees F.), or longer, depending on the thickness of the steak. Remove the steak from the grill and let rest on a clean cutting board for about 5 minutes. Slice the steak against the grain into ¼- to ½-inch slices.

To assemble the sandwiches, in a bowl, mix together the sour cream, mayonnaise, Worcestershire sauce, and horseradish and spread about 1 tablespoon of the mixture on both sides of each ciabatta. On the bottom half of each ciabatta, add the sliced steak, then the tomato slices, the grilled red onion, and finally the arugula. Close the sandwich with the top half of ciabatta. Serve immediately.

It's only fair to give you a heads-up: This sandwich is completely delicious, but may be a little messy to eat. So have plenty of napkins on hand!

NUTRITION FACTS —*1 sandwich*

790 calories	6G saturated fat	91G total carbohydrate	850MG sodium
24G total fat	115MG cholesterol	7G sugars	56G protein

Bistro Turkey Panini

Yields 4 servings

Panini have been the go-to sandwich of choice in Europe for many years. I remember my first trip abroad and driving down the *autoroutes* in France. I treasure the experience of taking breaks at the truck stops and sampling some fine *saucisson* (sausage) or *jambon* (ham) sandwiches. The saucisson variety were simply made with excellent salamis and softened butter, set inside an incredibly perfect baguette, then grilled in a panini press. The memory has never left me; to this day I want to go back and see if in fact those sandwiches are really as good as I remember. Enjoy making paninis with almost any sandwich — my feeling is that every sandwich is better if you use a panini press. This recipe is a great and classy way to use up leftover Thanksgiving turkey.

½	cup honey
¼	cup Dijon mustard
¼	cup mayonnaise *(optional)*
2	teaspoons olive oil
½	red onion, cut into ¼-inch slices
⅛	teaspoon kosher salt
⅛	teaspoon freshly ground black pepper
8	slices walnut or other nutty bread
8	ounces good-quality soft goat cheese
12	ounces turkey breast, thinly sliced
½	Granny Smith apple, quartered, cored, and sliced into half-moons
1	cup baby arugula

SUGGESTED WINE PAIRING

Luke Donald Viognier

In a bowl, mix together the honey and mustard. For a creamier and less pungent dressing, mix in the mayonnaise. Set aside.

Heat the olive oil in a sauté pan over medium heat. Sprinkle the onion with salt and pepper and sauté for about 5 minutes, until lightly browned. Heat a panini press or sandwich press to medium heat. Lay out four bread slices on a cutting board or clean work surface and spread with the goat cheese. Add the turkey breast, apple slices, grilled onion, arugula, and ½ tablespoon of the honey-mustard dressing to each. Top with the remaining bread slices.

Press down on the sandwiches and transfer to the panini press. Cook for about 3 minutes until the bread is toasted and the ingredients are warm inside.

CHEF'S NOTES

If you do not own a sandwich press you can use a flat griddle with a little butter or spray in the pan; press down on the sandwich with a metal spatula to slightly flatten.

We like to serve this with a simple spinach salad tossed with balsamic dressing.

NUTRITION FACTS *—1 sandwich*

590	calories	12G	saturated fat	48G	total carbohydrate	850MG	sodium
24G	total fat	115MG	cholesterol	14G	sugars	48G	protein

Salmon Burger with Red Cabbage Slaw and Roasted Jalapeño Aioli

Yields 4 servings

While the recipe is a bit involved, with grinding of the salmon to make smooth patties, it is one of the more popular sandwich recipes at Neiman Marcus and well worth the effort to put together at home. I suppose the acclaim and popularity has something to do with salmon's healthful qualities, but I like to think it's because our salmon patties taste so darn good! The crunchiness of the cabbage slaw makes it a great accompaniment.

FOR THE JALAPEÑO AIOLI

1	jalapeño
½	cup mayonnaise
1	clove garlic, smashed and minced
2	teaspoons fresh lemon juice
1	teaspoon kosher salt

FOR THE SALMON

1¼	pounds boneless, skinless salmon fillets *(about ½ inch thick)*, pin bones removed
1	large egg
2	tablespoons mayonnaise
2	tablespoons minced fresh dill
1	tablespoon minced shallot
1	tablespoon fresh lemon juice
½	tablespoon Dijon mustard
1	teaspoon Worcestershire sauce
2	teaspoons kosher salt
1	teaspoon freshly ground black pepper
½	cup dried bread crumbs
3	tablespoons butter

SUGGESTED WINE PAIRING

Sanford Santa Rita Hills Pinot Noir

FOR THE RED CABBAGE SLAW

2	cups julienned red cabbage
1	teaspoon apple cider vinegar
2	tablespoons olive oil
4	brioche buns, cut in half, or hamburger buns

To prepare the aioli, roast the jalapeño on a metal rack set over a gas flame until the skin is blistered and charred. Let cool, remove the stem and seeds, and finely mince. Transfer to a bowl and add the mayonnaise, garlic, lemon juice, and salt. Mix well and keep refrigerated in an airtight container for up to 5 days.

To prepare the salmon, cut it into large chunks and place in the bowl of a food processor fitted with a metal blade. Pulse the salmon about 12 times so it is minced but not pureed. Transfer to a bowl. In a separate bowl, mix the egg, mayonnaise, dill, shallot, lemon juice, mustard, Worcestershire sauce, salt, and pepper. Pour this mixture over the salmon and mix to incorporate. Add the bread crumbs and combine. Cover the salmon mixture tightly with plastic wrap and refrigerate for about 30 minutes.

Form the salmon into four 1-inch patties. Set a nonstick skillet over medium-low heat, add 2 tablespoons of the butter, and melt; do not let it brown. Add the salmon patties to the pan and cook for 3 or 4 minutes on each side. Transfer to a clean plate and cover loosely with foil.

To prepare the red cabbage slaw, in a mixing bowl, toss the cabbage with the vinegar and oil and season with salt and pepper. Wipe the nonstick skillet with a paper towel, melt the remaining 1 tablespoon butter, and toast the buns in the skillet. Spread the jalapeño aioli on the top halves of the buns. Place the salmon patties on the bottom halves and top with the cabbage slaw. Close the burgers and serve immediately.

NUTRITION FACTS —*1 burger*

990 calories	18G saturated fat	59G total carbohydrate	2320MG sodium
66G total fat	195MG cholesterol	8G sugars	39G protein

"The Cuban"

Yields 4 servings

Ask any local in South Florida where you can get the best Cubano sandwich and you'll get as many answers as people you ask. Our recipe follows the traditional style often found in and around the Miami and Coral Gables area. As the recipe migrates to our more northern cities, such as Boston and Chicago, we are sometimes expected to add a good Genoa salami, so feel free to adapt and change the recipe as you like. Keep in mind that a true Cuban sandwich does not have grooves in the toasted bread, which is why we call for a weight to press down the sandwich. A heavy-bottomed pan or skillet works well, as does a hamburger weight, which you can find in restaurant supply stores.

¼ cup Dijon mustard

¼ cup Roasted Garlic Aioli *(see variation to Simple Aioli, page 227),* or mayonnaise

4 Cuban bread rolls, or bolillo or telera rolls, found in Latin grocery stores

8 ounces thinly sliced grilled or roasted pork tenderloin

4 ounces thinly sliced ham

8 slices Swiss cheese *(about 8 ounces)*

16 dill pickle slices *(or your favorite pickle)*

2 tablespoons unsalted butter, melted

SUGGESTED PAIRING

Your favorite cold beer

In a bowl, mix together the mustard and aioli. Spread 1 tablespoon of this Dijon-aioli dip on the top half of each roll. On the bottom halves of the rolls, add a layer of sliced pork, then the ham, the cheese, and top with 4 pickle slices. Close with the top half of the bread.

Brush both sides of a panini or sandwich press with the butter or place the butter on a griddle. Press the sandwiches down and cook for 3 or 4 minutes over medium-low heat until the cheese has melted and the sandwiches are warm. (If you are using a griddle, weigh down the sandwiches using a heavy-bottomed pan, using a little pressure with your hands.) Remove the sandwiches, cut in half on an angle, and serve immediately.

CHEF'S NOTE

I usually buy the already marinated pork tenderloins in the meat department in the store. They grill fast and any of the marinades they come in will work with this sandwich.

A tall, chilled Red Stripe beer will add to the tropical mood set by "The Cuban."

NUTRITION FACTS —*1 sandwich*

480 calories	13G saturated fat	27G total carbohydrate	1660MG sodium
27G total fat	120MG cholesterol	3G sugars	32G protein

Smoked Salmon Finger Sandwiches

Yields 4 servings

Okay . . . so maybe finger sandwiches have never been on your radar, but let me just say that this recipe will really get the *wow!* reaction if you take the time to make them for your next luncheon. Making them requires some preparation beforehand, but once you're ready to build the sandwiches, the recipe comes together quickly. I recommend the suggestion of making and wrapping them the day before: This not only gives the sandwich filling time to meld together, but it also helps the sandwiches keep their shape and ensures a moist texture.

6	lengthwise slices pumpernickel bread, or your favorite bread, about ⅛ inch thick
½	cup cream cheese
6	ounces thinly sliced smoked salmon
½	cup thinly sliced red onion
½	head Bibb or butter lettuce
2	ripe tomatoes, thinly sliced
⅛	teaspoon kosher salt
⅛	teaspoon freshly ground black pepper

SUGGESTED WINE PAIRING

Nino Franco Rustico Prosecco

Place the bread slices on a clean work surface. Spread 1 tablespoon of the softened cream cheese over each slice. Top each of two slices with one-quarter of the smoked salmon, onion, a lettuce leaf, and tomato. Sprinkle with salt and pepper. Close this layer with two more slices of bread, cream cheese–side down. Spread another 1 tablespoon of cream cheese over each bread slice so it has cream cheese on both sides. Top with the remaining smoked salmon, tomato, and red onion and a lettuce leaf. Close the sandwiches with the remaining bread slices, cream cheese–side down. Press down firmly to seal the sandwiches. Wrap the sandwiches in a damp paper towel to cover entirely and then with plastic wrap. Refrigerate for at least 30 minutes and preferably for 2 hours or even overnight before serving.

When you are ready to serve, unwrap the sandwiches and place on a cutting board. With a sharp knife, trim the crusts away on all four sides and discard (or snack on them yourself!). Cut the sandwiches in half crosswise, and in half again crosswise two more times to get 16 equal-size finger sandwiches. Serve immediately.

CHEF'S NOTE

Seriously, take special care not to let the cut sandwiches to dry out. The biggest complaint about finger sandwiches is that they dry out quickly when exposed to the air. Keep them covered with the wrapping until the last minute.

NUTRITION FACTS —*4 finger sandwiches*

510 calories	12G saturated fat	44G total carbohydrate	1320MG sodium
26G total fat	85MG cholesterol	4G sugars	26G protein

Cucumber and Watercress Finger Sandwiches

Yields 4 servings

It does not get any more classic — or refined — than serving these sandwiches with afternoon tea here at Neiman Marcus. Visions of white gloves, delicate china teapots, fragrant loose teas, tempting pastries, and lots of bubbly Champagne — got the picture? Now all you have to do is make the sandwiches. Like the Smoked Salmon Finger Sandwiches on page 138, remember to keep them wrapped until the last minute.

4	tablespoons softened butter
⅛	teaspoon Dijon mustard
6	lengthwise slices marbled rye bread, about ⅛ inch thick
2	cucumbers, peeled, seeded, and thinly sliced crosswise
1	ripe tomato, thinly sliced
2	ounces Swiss cheese, thinly sliced
1	bunch watercress, washed and dried, stems trimmed

SUGGESTED WINE PAIRING

Berlucchi Cuvée 61 Rosé Sparkling Wine

In a small bowl, combine the softened butter with the mustard. Place the bread slices on a clean work surface and spread about ½ tablespoon of the butter mixture on each slice. Top each of two slices with one-quarter of the cucumber, tomato, cheese, and watercress. Top each with another slice of the bread, butter-side down. Spread ½ tablespoon of the butter mixture over each bread slice so both sides have butter. Top with the remaining cucumber, tomato, cheese, and watercress. Close the sandwiches with the remaining bread slices, butter-side down, and press down firmly to seal the sandwiches. Wrap each in a damp paper towel to cover entirely and then with plastic wrap. Keep in the refrigerator for at least 30 minutes and preferably for 2 hours or even overnight before serving.

When you are ready to serve, unwrap the sandwiches and place on a cutting board. With a sharp knife, trim the crusts away on all four sides and discard (or snack on them yourself!). Cut the sandwiches in half crosswise and then in half again crosswise two more times to get 16 equal size finger sandwiches. Serve immediately.

NUTRITION FACTS —*4 finger sandwiches*

590 calories	19G saturated fat	57G total carbohydrate	780MG sodium
34G total fat	90MG cholesterol	5G sugars	20G protein

I prefer a nice glass of
Bollinger Champagne
with my tea sandwiches.

The Duke of Windsor

Yields 4 servings

Much has been said about the Duke of Windsor sandwich over the years. It was named after the former King Edward VIII who became the Duke of Windsor following his abdication for personal reasons in 1937. His brother, George, became king and led the British nation through World War II. He was followed by his daughter and current monarch, Queen Elizabeth II. On one of the duke's visits to the United States in the 1950s, Helen Corbitt created this sandwich especially for his luncheon at Neiman Marcus. One thing is for sure: Anytime a royal travels abroad, you can usually expect a long note explaining exactly what the traveling dignitary wants to eat for every meal. For all we know, Helen threw out the note and came up with this sandwich! In any event, it's been a popular seller for the last 60 years.

2 cans pineapple rings, drained *(8 slices)*

8 slices egg bread or your favorite bread

½ cup store-bought cheddar cheese spread *(such as WisPride)*

1 pound smoked turkey, thinly sliced

4 tablespoons store-bought mango chutney *(such as Major Grey's)*

4 tablespoons butter

SUGGESTED WINE PAIRING

Loveblock Pinot Gris

Preheat the oven to 350 degrees F. Spray a cookie sheet with nonstick spray and place the pineapple rings on the sheet. Transfer to the oven and roast for about 20 minutes or until the rings are beginning to brown on the edges. Remove from the oven and let cool. Keep the oven on.

Place 4 slices of the bread on a clean work surface. Spread about 2 tablespoons of the cheese spread on each slice and add 4 ounces of the turkey and 2 slices of pineapple. Spread 1 tablespoon of the chutney on the remaining 4 bread slices and close the sandwiches, pressing gently to seal.

CHEF'S NOTE

Brioche or whole wheat bread also work well for this recipe.

Heat a griddle, large sauté pan, or panini press to high and when hot, add 1 tablespoon of butter (or use nonstick spray). When the butter has melted, carefully add a sandwich and cook until the bread slices are browned nicely on both sides. If using a griddle or pan, cook for 3 minutes, flip over, and cook for 3 or 4 minutes longer. If the center of the sandwich is not melted, place on a cookie sheet and finish heating through in the oven for about 5 minutes. (If they are cooked through, turn off the oven.) Repeat with the remaining butter and sandwiches. Cut each sandwich in half and serve immediately.

NUTRITION FACTS —*1 sandwich*

620 calories	4.5G saturated fat	88G total carbohydrate	1390MG sodium
16G total fat	100MG cholesterol	37G sugars	32G protein

5 ENTRÉE SALADS

ENTRÉE SALADS

This chapter represents the single most important menu category for Neiman Marcus restaurants. Our customers order more composed salads than any other menu item. As much as our customer base clearly loves salads, we take great pride and care in making them. Over the years our composed salad recipes have been reworked to support the changing eating habits of our customers. About four years ago we introduced our Go Figure Cuisine menu items and listed their complete nutritional values on our menus. The criteria for these dishes were that they contained no more than 560 calories and 960 milligrams of sodium. Along with the rollout of the Go Figure Cuisine, we included calorie counts for all our menu items. At first, a number of our customers were uneasy, knowing that some of their perennial favorites had more fat and calories than they had imagined; however, in a very short amount of time they not only began to appreciate the new information, but started asking more informed questions. Pretty soon, the Go Figure menu items shot up to the top of the sales list, outperforming some of our longtime bestsellers such as the Mandarin orange soufflé and the chicken salad!

The importance of composed salads is always a topic of conversation when a new chef comes on board for us. We need to let them know just how important salads are to us and how much our customers enjoy them. In the world of the professional kitchen, it's customary to put your entry-level cooks in the pantry where the composed salads are made, with your most experienced and talented cooks on the hot sauté line where the entrées are made. At Neiman Marcus, we have a different philosophy: I tell new chefs all the time that they need their strongest cooks in the pantry where all the action will be. Invariably they will take my suggestions lightly until they see the first big lunch day and learn for themselves that yes, the action is in the cold area of the kitchen and it's all hands on deck!

The question we are asked the most is, "What is the single best-selling menu item in your restaurants?" Hands down it's always the grilled shrimp salad in just about any format. People love shrimp, and we go through about 50,000 pounds of shrimp a year with no sign of this letting up. It's a good thing for us that the shrimp industry has come up with great new ways of providing us with already peeled and deveined shrimp, making our jobs less of a hassle than in the days when we needed to do this laborious work in our kitchens. Other menu items have also become more conveniently streamlined, such as pre-portioned salmon fillets that we buy from our vendor, Steve Connolly Seafood in Boston. Connolly is a family seafood company that has been around for more than 30 years; they supply all of our restaurants with fresh seafood, flying it in daily. Willie, our seafood guy, is probably the most knowledgeable person I know when it comes to fresh seafood, and we pride ourselves at Neiman Marcus in serving the freshest product we can buy.

So whether you're in the mood for fresh scallops, salmon, or shrimp, or a tender, flavorful cut of meat or poultry paired with fresh, crisp seasonal greens, chances are we have it and it's matched with your favorite salad dressing.

Seared Ahi Niçoise Salad

Yields 4 servings

Rare tuna has been the rage in our restaurants for a number of years now. I remember the days when people would never order a piece of rare fish, but then sushi restaurants took off in the United States and customers increasingly took to their fish — especially tuna — on the rarer side. Because we get most of our seafood flown in daily to our restaurants from New England, our line-caught tuna menu items have become very popular because our clientele knows that you can consume excellent tuna just off the boats at the Neiman Marcus restaurants.

8	fingerling potatoes, halved lengthwise
1	tablespoon chopped fresh Italian parsley
½	teaspoon fresh thyme leaves
1	teaspoon kosher salt
1	teaspoon freshly ground black pepper
6	ounces green beans
1	tablespoon olive oil
4	ahi tuna fillets, about 5 ounces each and 2 inches thick
2	heads Bibb lettuce, washed, dried, and quartered
8	heirloom cherry tomatoes, halved
4	hard-boiled eggs, peeled and quartered
3	ounces pitted Kalamata or Niçoise olives
½	cup Light Greek Vinaigrette *(page 212)*

SUGGESTED WINE PAIRING

M. Chapoutier Châteauneuf-du-Pape "La Bernardine" Rouge

Preheat the oven to 350 degrees F. Place the fingerling potatoes in a bowl, add the parsley, thyme, and ½ teaspoon each of the salt and pepper, and mix together. Spray a roasting pan with nonstick spray, transfer the potato mixture to the pan, and roast in the oven for 18 to 22 minutes or until the potatoes are cooked but not mushy. Remove from the oven and let cool.

Meanwhile, bring a saucepan of water to a boil and add the green beans. Return to a simmer over medium heat and cook for 4 or 5 minutes or until soft to the bite. Drain and rinse the beans under cold running water to "shock" the beans and stop the cooking process. Set aside.

Heat the olive oil in a sauté pan over high heat. Season the tuna on both sides with the remaining ½ teaspoon salt and pepper. When the oil is hot, sear the tuna for 1 minute on each side; the fillets should be rare. Remove the tuna from the pan and set aside.

Arrange 2 lettuce quarters in the middle of each salad plate in a crisscross pattern. Scatter the green beans decoratively on top of each lettuce quarter and arrange the tomato halves on each side. Place 2 egg quarters on each side of the lettuce and then the cooled potatoes and olives. Cut the tuna fillets against the grain into 5 slices each, and lean against the lettuce wedges. Drizzle the vinaigrette evenly around the salad and over the tuna, and serve immediately.

> **CHEF'S NOTE**
>
> Here at NM we sometimes sub out Little Gem lettuce for the classic Bibb lettuce. Little Gem is a smaller version of romaine but with the sweetness of Bibb. We also sometimes use the French greens beans called haricots verts (French for green beans) because they don't have any seeds or sinew, making them easier in some instances to eat.

NUTRITION FACTS —*1 serving*

580 calories	4G saturated fat	41G total carbohydrate	1160MG sodium
28G total fat	285MG cholesterol	2G sugars	43G protein

Bay of Fundy Salmon Salad with Hearts of Palm and Melting Goat Cheese

Yields 4 servings

This is not the forum for debating the pros and cons of wild-caught versus sustainable farm-raised salmon, or any other type of fish or seafood. Whichever side you're on, that's up to you. At Neiman Marcus restaurants, we believe that we're doing the fishing industry a service by supporting the sustainable farming methods of raising seafood in a healthful environment. The Bay of Fundy, located on the Canadian Atlantic seaboard between New Brunswick and Nova Scotia, is known for having the highest tidal range in the world. Because of this, some of the best farm-raised salmon in the world comes from the bay, because the fresh seawater is constantly being pushed through the ocean pens. This recipe is a perennial at Neiman Marcus and has been a customer favorite for years.

1½	tablespoons olive oil
4	skinless salmon fillets, about 5 ounces each
2	pinches of kosher salt
2	pinches of freshly ground black pepper
8	ounces goat cheese, cut into 8 slices
8	cups *(8 ounces)* mixed spring greens
1	cup bottled hearts of palm, sliced ½ inch thick on an angle
4	baby radishes, thinly sliced lengthwise
16	canned artichoke hearts packed in water
12	cherry tomatoes, halved
½	cup Light Balsamic Vinaigrette *(page 213)*

SUGGESTED WINE PAIRING

Château de Sancerre

Preheat the oven to 350 degrees F. Heat the olive oil in a large, nonstick, ovenproof sauté pan over medium heat. Season the salmon fillets with the salt and pepper and place top-side down in the pan. Sear the salmon for about 2 minutes on each side. Remove the pan from the heat and top each salmon fillet with 2 slices of the goat cheese. Transfer the pan to the oven and bake for 3 or 4 minutes longer, to the desired doneness.

Divide the mixed greens among 4 salad plates and arrange the hearts of palm, sliced radishes, artichokes, and cherry tomatoes around the greens. Drizzle each salad with vinaigrette, top with the salmon, and serve immediately.

NUTRITION FACTS —*1 serving*

730 calories	18G saturated fat	22G total carbohydrate	1490MG sodium
50G total fat	125MG cholesterol	8G sugars	48G protein

Our commitment to sustainable farm-raised seafood is more important now than ever.

Filet Mignon Caprese-Style Salad

Yields 4 servings

Here we have added steak to the classic salad in the style of Capri, the simple combination of mozzarella, tomatoes, and fresh basil. We serve it on a large platter, making for a big showy salad guaranteed to impress guests. This is one of those menu items that our regulars know to ask for if it's not printed on the menu. We learned early on that we needed to keep a nice cut of steak in the kitchens for our customers who craved a red meat fix, and pretty soon the filet mignon salad started taking off. I'm a big fan of a good steak salad and I think here at Neiman Marcus we have a real winner.

4	filet mignon steaks (about 6 ounces each), each cut crosswise into 2 medallions
1	teaspoon kosher salt
1	teaspoon freshly ground black pepper
1	large head iceberg lettuce, cut into 8 wedges
2	large beefsteak tomatoes, cut into 4 slices each
1	pound fresh mozzarella, cut into 8 slices
8	fresh basil leaves
½	cup Broken Balsamic Vinaigrette (page 212)

Prepare the grill. Place the steaks on a large plate, season on both sides with the salt and pepper, and bring to room temperature. Arrange the lettuce wedges on a platter in a row. Grill the medallions over medium-high heat for about 2½ minutes on each side for medium-rare, or to the desired doneness. Remove the medallions from the grill and let rest so the internal juices can reabsorb and keep the steak juicy.

To serve, shingle the beef, tomatoes, and mozzarella on the platter with each combination resting against a lettuce wedge. Tuck the basil leaves between each tomato and mozzarella slice. Drizzle the vinaigrette over and around the salad and serve immediately.

NUTRITION FACTS —*1 serving*

810 calories	23G saturated fat	13G total carbohydrate	1600MG sodium
50G total fat	230MG cholesterol	8G sugars	74G protein

SUGGESTED WINE PAIRING

Rutherford Hill Barrel Select Red Blend

I think our steak salad
is one of the best.

Bistro Salad with Roasted Chicken and Baby Spinach

Yields 4 servings

Day in and day out, this salad is a real menu "go-to" for us. We serve it at all kinds of catering events because it's very straightforward and people just plain love it. The chicken is roasted that morning and, when just cool enough, it's pulled from the bone and placed on top of the finished salad. Chicken just tastes better when it's freshly cooked. I'll bet that many of you will be making this salad for your luncheons for years to come.

FOR THE SPICED PECANS

1   cup pecan pieces *(about 4 ounces)*

2   tablespoons light corn syrup

1   tablespoon light brown sugar

2   pinches of kosher salt

2   pinches of cayenne

FOR THE SALAD

1   store-bought rotisserie chicken *(3 to 4 pounds)*

4   cups *(about 8 ounces)* baby spinach leaves, washed and dried

4   ounces mixed sun-dried fruit, such as raisins, cherries, and apricots *(about 1 cup)*

4   ounces crumbled blue cheese

1   Granny Smith apple, halved, cored, and sliced into 16 thin slices

½   cup Light Balsamic Vinaigrette *(page 213)*

SUGGESTED WINE PAIRING

Hanna Sauvignon Blanc

Preheat the oven to 325 degrees F. To prepare the pecans, mix together the pecan pieces, corn syrup, brown sugar, salt, and cayenne in a bowl. Spray a cookie sheet with nonstick spray and transfer the pecan mixture to the sheet. Bake in the oven for 10 to 12 minutes. Remove and let cool.

To prepare the salad, remove the skin from the rotisserie chicken. Using your fingers, pull away the breast meat and then the meat from all parts of the chicken; discard the bones. Check the pulled meat for any remaining small bones; cut the chicken meat into slices or 1-inch dice and set aside. Place the spinach, dried fruit, blue cheese, apple slices, and ½ cup of the spiced pecans in a mixing bowl. Add the vinaigrette and toss together to mix thoroughly. Divide the salad among 4 salad plates or salad bowls. Arrange the chicken so that it rests atop the salad, sprinkle the remaining pecans over each salad, and serve immediately.

> **CHEF'S NOTE**
>
> The spiced pecans make a great snack or gift, so make double the recipe — or more — if you like.

NUTRITION FACTS *—1 serving*

730 calories	9G saturated fat	54G total carbohydrate	740MG sodium
38G total fat	120MG cholesterol	36G sugars	46G protein

The perfect salad for
the perfect lunch.

Asian Chicken Salad

Yields 4 servings

We've been serving this salad for the last 20 years and it never seems to go out of favor with our guests. Turns out, this perennial favorite has a huge fan base. My guess is that the combination of flavors — soy sauce, chile garlic sauce, and sesame oil — with grilled chicken is the secret to its success. I'll leave you to make up your own mind but my prediction is that you'll enjoy this recipe for the next 20 years, I'll betcha!

¼   cup sweet garlic chile sauce
     (such as Mae Ploy)

3   tablespoons soy sauce

2   tablespoons sesame oil

12 ounces boneless, skinless chicken
     breast, cut into 4 portions

     Peanut, grapeseed, or canola oil, for
     deep-frying

1   package *(14 ounces)* frozen wonton
     wrappers, cut into triangles

1   head Napa cabbage, tender outer
     leaves only, thinly sliced *(julienne)*

1   cup grated carrot

1   red bell pepper, seeded and thinly
     sliced *(julienne)*

½   cup unsalted cashews

1   cup frozen shelled edamame,
     defrosted and drained

1   scallion, thinly sliced on an angle
     (white and green parts)

4   ounces Spicy Ginger and Sesame
     Vinaigrette with Lime *(page 222)*

4   fresh cilantro sprigs

SUGGESTED WINE PAIRING

Lapostolle Casa Sauvignon Blanc

In a mixing bowl, combine the sweet chile sauce, soy sauce, and sesame oil. Add the chicken breast and coat with the marinade. Let marinate in the refrigerator for at least 4 hours or overnight.

Prepare the grill. Remove the chicken from the marinade and grill over medium-high heat for about 3 minutes on each side, being careful not to let it burn. If the chicken is turning too dark, turn down the heat or place the chicken on a cooler part of the grill. Keep turning the chicken and cook until the internal temperature reaches 165 degrees F; it should take 10 to 15 minutes to cook depending on the thickness of the breast. Remove from the grill and let the chicken rest before cutting.

While the chicken is grilling, fry the wonton wrappers. Pour the peanut oil into a deep-fryer or a large, heavy-bottomed saucepan set over high heat; there should be at least 4 inches between the oil and the top of the pan as the oil will bubble up once you add the wonton strips. Heat the oil to 350 degrees F. and follow the directions on the wrapper package for frying spring rolls. The wrappers should be golden and crisp. Remove with a skimmer or slotted spoon and drain on paper towels.

Place the julienned Napa cabbage in a large bowl and add half of the carrots, bell pepper, cashews, edamame, and scallion; reserve the other half of these ingredients to sprinkle on top of the salad. Add the vinaigrette and mix thoroughly. Transfer the salad to a serving bowl and top with the reserved ingredients. Thinly slice the grilled chicken breast on an angle and place around the salad. Garnish with the fried wonton strips and cilantro sprigs.

Want the vinaigrette on the side? Want extra vinaigrette? Prefer beef or shrimp to the chicken? As with all our salads, you ask for it, we give it.

NUTRITION FACTS —*1 serving*

610 calories	7G saturated fat	26G total carbohydrate	800MG sodium
40G total fat	65MG cholesterol	10G sugars	36G protein

Grilled Shrimp and Quinoa Salad with Avocado, Grapefruit, and Toasted Almonds

Yields 4 servings ⧗ GO FIGURE

What a difference 10 years makes in the food scene in the United States! A decade ago, I would have never predicted that our grilled shrimp salad could outsell Neiman Marcus classics such as the chicken salad and tuna-pecan salad. But because it's a healthier dining alternative, it's become our number one best-seller. We also feature quinoa in the salad: It's been getting a lot of attention in the past couple of years because of its high nutritional value, with many calling it a "superfood." At first, our customers didn't quite know what to make of this salad ingredient when we introduced it, and many didn't know how to pronounce it (just in case, it's "keen-wah"). Now, you find it everywhere and it's appreciated by so many of our customers that it reincarnates in one of our recipes every season.

½	cup uncooked quinoa
1	pound colossal shrimp *(about 16)*, peeled and deveined *(tails on)*
1	tablespoon olive oil
⅛	teaspoon kosher salt
⅛	teaspoon freshly ground black pepper
8	cups *(8 ounces)* mixed spring greens
2	ounces crumbled goat cheese
1	avocado, halved, pitted, peeled, and cut into 4 wedges
1	ruby red grapefruit, peeled and divided into 8 segments
1	ounce toasted slivered almonds
½	cup Citrus Vinaigrette *(page 213)*

Prepare the grill. Using the directions on the package, cook the quinoa; there should be about 1 to 1½ cups cooked quinoa.

Place the shrimp and olive oil in a mixing bowl with the salt and pepper and toss together to coat. Grill the shrimp over medium-high heat for 2 to 3 minutes on each side or until cooked through and pink.

Divide the mixed greens among 4 salad bowls and top with the quinoa, goat cheese, avocado, grapefruit, and almonds. Drizzle each salad with the citrus vinaigrette, lay 4 shrimp around the sides, and serve immediately.

CHEF'S NOTE

Quinoa is also gluten free, a real plus to those with a gluten intolerance.

SUGGESTED WINE PAIRING

Sohm & Kracher Grüner Veltliner

NUTRITION FACTS —*1 serving*

470 calories	6G saturated fat	32G total carbohydrate	430MG sodium
26G total fat	230MG cholesterol	10G sugars	34G protein

Brussels Sprouts and Kale Salad

Yields 8 servings   ⧗ GO FIGURE

Who would have ever thought that the humble Brussels sprout would have its own recipe for a composed salad in our restaurants? The days of overboiled, mushy sprouts are over, especially in this recipe. In terms of popular acceptance, Brussels sprouts have come a long way over the last 25 years. Likewise, kale is "in" right now and with good reason — it's particularly healthful. I remember when corporate chef Anita Hirsch made this salad for the first time, the reaction from everyone who tried it was how delicious it was. Even back then, it was an early favorite for our next cookbook — and here it is. The secret to this recipe, besides the yummy greens, is the creamy and delicious Marcona almonds. Imported from Spain and found in specialty food stores, these almonds are to die for.

8	ounces Brussels sprouts, stem ends trimmed
2	cups kale leaves, washed, dried, and thinly sliced
1	head radicchio, washed, dried, cored, and thinly sliced
2	stalks celery, finely sliced on an angle
1	cup mixed sun-dried fruits, such as raisins, cranberries, and cherries
1	cup Marcona almonds *(see Chef's Note)*
1½	cups freshly grated Parmesan cheese
	Juice of 2 lemons *(about ¼ cup)*
1	cup olive oil
2	teaspoons kosher salt
2	teaspoons freshly ground black pepper

Using a food processor with a slicing blade, finely slice the Brussels sprouts without pushing them through too hard. Transfer to a large mixing bowl. Add the kale, radicchio, celery, dried fruits, almonds, and half of the Parmesan. Add the lemon juice, olive oil, salt, and pepper and gently toss the salad to thoroughly combine. Adjust the seasonings as necessary. Transfer the salad to a nice decorative bowl and arrange so that plenty of the garnishes are on top. Sprinkle with the remaining Parmesan.

CHEF'S NOTE

Spanish Marcona almonds, marketed as "the queen of almonds" are sweeter than most other types. They are round in shape and have a delicate, creamy texture. If unavailable, use regular almonds.

NUTRITION FACTS —*1 serving*

460	calories	11G	total carbohydrate
43G	total fat	3G	sugars
9G	saturated fat	890MG	sodium
20MG	cholesterol	15G	protein

SUGGESTED WINE PAIRING

Grace Lane Cabernet Sauvignon

> The secret to this recipe, besides the yummy greens, is the creamy and delicious Marcona almonds.

The Lenox Salad

Yields 4 servings

In our recipes that call for cooked or roasted chicken, I usually suggest using store-bought rotisserie chicken. It's a lot quicker, easier, and more convenient all around as well as cost effective. If you own a rotisserie and prefer preparing your own chicken, by all means do. When we reopened our Atlanta restaurants a number of years ago, we put in a rotisserie oven and soon became known for our excellent rotisserie chicken. In subsequent years we've put a few more of these ovens in our other restaurants, and in turn we've written menu items around the tasty birds. This salad, created at our store in Atlanta's Lenox Square Mall, is now served in many Neiman Marcus restaurants around the country, really putting Lenox Square on the map!

1	rotisserie chicken *(3 to 4 pounds)*
8	cups *(8 ounces)* mixed spring greens
1	avocado, halved, pitted, peeled, and cut into ½-inch dice
1	tomato, cored and cut into ½-inch dice
1	cup canned garbanzo beans, drained and rinsed
½	cup Kalamata olives, pitted and halved
4	ounces crumbled blue cheese
4	slices crispy cooked bacon, crumbled
¾	cup Red Wine Vinaigrette *(page 217)*

Remove the skin from the rotisserie chicken. Using your fingers, pull away the breast meat and then the meat from all parts of the chicken; discard the bones. Check the pulled meat for any remaining small bones; cut the chicken meat into 1-inch pieces and set aside.

Place the spring greens in a large mixing bowl and add the avocado, tomato, garbanzo beans, olives, blue cheese, and bacon. Add half of the pulled chicken meat and toss the salad with the vinaigrette. Transfer to a serving bowl, top with the rest of the pulled chicken, and serve immediately.

CHEF'S NOTE

It's easier to remove the rotisserie chicken skin and pull the meat when the chicken is still slightly warm; reheat it in a low oven for a few minutes, if necessary.

SUGGESTED WINE PAIRING

Greystone Chardonnay

NUTRITION FACTS *—1 serving*

1080 calories	13G saturated fat	24G total carbohydrate	2720MG sodium
61G total fat	325MG cholesterol	4G sugars	111G protein

Crab Louis Salad

Yields 4 servings

This salad is total indulgence, from the cost of the jumbo lump crabmeat to the calorie count of the Louis dressing. The message is "Indulge in moderation." At the Neiman Marcus restaurants, we like to think that a little (or a lot) of indulgence now and again makes life worthwhile, and the more people who follow that philosophy, the better. As the saying goes, "Seize the day!" At any rate, we pride ourselves on using only the best jumbo lump crabmeat, and the key to serving this precious ingredient is to handle it with care. You don't want to break up the crab by overhandling, so work gingerly — your guests will appreciate your efforts.

2   heads romaine lettuce, outer leaves discarded, washed and dried

1   pound jumbo lump crabmeat, picked through *(or Dungeness crabmeat)*

16   slices English cucumber *(¼-inch slices)*

12   heirloom cherry tomatoes, halved

4   hard-boiled eggs, peeled and sliced

1   cup Louis Dressing *(page 217)*

1   avocado, halved, pitted, peeled, and diced

1   cup baby watercress

SUGGESTED WINE PAIRING

Domaine Chanson Meursault

Cut the romaine heads in half lengthwise and place on 4 large salad plates, keeping the leaves together. Divide the crabmeat evenly on top of the romaine. Arrange the cucumber slices on one side of the romaine with the tomatoes next to the cucumbers to help prop them upright. On the other side of the romaine, fan out the slices from 1 egg. Drizzle the Louis dressing over the romaine and crabmeat. Top the crabmeat with the avocado and watercress. Serve extra Louis dressing at the table for your guests to enjoy!

NUTRITION FACTS *—1 serving*

520 calories	**7G** saturated fat	**23G** total carbohydrate	**1030MG** sodium
34G total fat	**290MG** cholesterol	**9G** sugars	**33G** protein

Ever since this salad was first served at our restaurant in San Francisco 25 years ago, it's proved a perennial favorite.

Pulled Rotisserie Chicken Salad with Hearts of Palm and Artichokes

Yields 4 servings

The flavors in this salad represent everything I like the most, so I can honestly say it's my single most favorite salad of all. I'm not alone; many of our catering requests call for the salad, and variations have been made by many of our chefs. Like all of our recipes, we anticipate that our restaurant guests may choose to modify their final menu selection so they get exactly as they please. We take pride that we never say no to any reasonable menu request.

12	ounces rotisserie chicken breast
4	hearts romaine lettuce *(about 8 cups)*, washed, dried, and chopped
1	cup bottled hearts of palm, cut on an angle into ½-inch pieces
8	large artichoke hearts, halved
1	avocado, halved, pitted, peeled, and cut into 4 wedges
4	ounces feta cheese
16	cherry or teardrop tomatoes, halved
8	cups *(8 ounces)* mixed salad greens
¾	cup Green Goddess Dressing or Light Green Goddess *(page 214)*

Remove the skin from the rotisserie chicken breast. Using your fingers, pull the meat apart so that it's shredded; cover and keep refrigerated.

CHEF'S NOTE

If you wish, warm the chicken through before adding to the salad.

Place the chopped romaine in a large salad bowl and add the hearts of palm, artichoke hearts, avocado, feta, tomatoes, and salad greens. Add the pulled chicken meat and the dressing and toss together gently to mix thoroughly.

NUTRITION FACTS —*1 serving*

510 calories	10G saturated fat	17G total carbohydrate	1040MG sodium
35G total fat	115MG cholesterol	6G sugars	34G protein

SUGGESTED WINE PAIRING

Tangley Oaks Chardonnay

> The flavors in this salad represent everything I like the most, so I can honestly say it's my single most favorite salad of all.

Seared Rare Sesame Ahi Tuna Salad

Yields 4 servings

We debated whether we needed two rare tuna salads in the book, but decided to go ahead as the Niçoise salad (page 147) is of French descent while this one is quite different, with Asian accents. This recipe has a huge following on the West Coast, but its popularity seems to be moving further East each year! The marinade has the perfect Asian flavor blend of soy, chile, garlic, and sesame that works so well with seafood and chicken in particular.

2	center-cut ahi tuna fillets, about 8 ounces each
2	tablespoons sweet chile garlic sauce *(such as Mae Ploy)*
2	tablespoons soy sauce
2	teaspoons sesame oil
2	teaspoons sesame seeds
⅛	teaspoon kosher salt
⅛	teaspoon freshly ground black pepper
3	cups cored and julienned Napa cabbage
4	cups *(4 ounces)* mixed spring greens
½	cup frozen shelled edamame, defrosted and blanched
½	cup julienned peeled carrots
¼	cup sliced blanched almonds
½	large cucumber, peeled, seeded, and cut into ½-inch half-moons
½	cup Spicy Ginger and Sesame Vinaigrette with Lime *(page 222)*

SUGGESTED WINE PAIRING

Santa Margherita Prosecco

Place the tuna in a glass or ceramic (nonreactive) dish and generously rub the sweet chile sauce and soy sauce all over. Cover tightly and let marinate in the refrigerator for at least 2 hours.

Remove the tuna from the refrigerator and bring to room temperature (about 30 minutes). Heat the sesame oil in a heavy-bottomed sauté pan over medium heat. Sprinkle the sesame seeds, salt, and pepper over the tuna to coat. When the oil is hot, add the tuna and sear for about 30 seconds on each side, including the ends. Let the tuna rest while assembling the salad.

> **CHEF'S NOTE**
>
> If you'd like the tuna to be more cooked, increase the cooking time on all sides by another 30 seconds or so.

In a mixing bowl, toss together the cabbage, spring greens, and half the edamame, carrots, almonds, cucumber, and vinaigrette. Divide the salad among 4 large plates, mounding it in the center of each plate. Take the remaining half of the vegetables and almonds and toss together in the mixing bowl you used to toss the salad so they absorb some of the dressing flavor. Transfer those ingredients to the tops of the salads. With a very sharp knife, cut the tuna into ½-inch slices and lean the slices against the sides of the greens. Drizzle the remaining vinaigrette around and on top of the salad and tuna.

NUTRITION FACTS —*1 serving*

410 calories	2G saturated fat	20G total carbohydrate	1060MG sodium
25G total fat	85MG cholesterol	11G sugars	27G protein

Roast Turkey Salad with Endive, Radicchio, and Frisée

Yields 4 servings   ⧗ GO FIGURE

We go through large amounts of freshly roasted turkey breast every day; it's the most popular meat on our menu after chicken. Usually there are three or four bone-in turkey breasts in our ovens each morning. We buy the breast only since the cumbersome turkey legs are for the State Fair rather than Neiman Marcus restaurants. We prefer our turkey breasts all-natural, with no added salt, and of course the skin is always removed, producing the best tasting meat that we dice, slice, or pull apart for many of our menu items.

2	heads Belgian endive *(preferably 1 red and 1 white)*, cored, washed, and dried
2	cups cored frisée lettuce, washed and dried
1	head radicchio, cored, washed, dried, and leaves torn into large pieces
12	ounces *(4 cups)* diced cooked turkey breast
3	ounces crumbled Gorgonzola
2	ounces sun-dried apricots, sliced
½	cup walnut pieces
	Pinch of kosher salt
2	cups Orange-Yogurt-Parsley Dressing *(page 221)*

Cut each endive head lengthwise into quarters. Separate the leaves and place in a mixing bowl. Place the frisée and radicchio leaves in a salad spinner and gently spin to remove any excess water. Transfer the frisée and radicchio to the mixing bowl. Setting aside a little of each ingredient for garnish, add the turkey, gorgonzola, apricots, and walnuts. Add the salt and drizzle with 1 cup of the yogurt dressing. Gently toss the salad to mix well and transfer to a nice serving bowl. Garnish the salad with the reserved turkey, Gorgonzola, apricots, and walnuts and serve immediately with the remaining dressing on the side.

This is a great recipe for leftover turkey, or use store-bought.

NUTRITION FACTS —*1 serving*

450 calories	**9G** saturated fat	**25G** total carbohydrate	**640MG** sodium
23G total fat	**105MG** cholesterol	**12G** sugars	**42G** protein

SUGGESTED WINE PAIRING

Rutherford Hill Sauvignon Blanc

6 ENTRÉES

ENTRÉES

For any chef, one of the most frequently asked questions is, "What is your favorite thing to cook?" Many professionals have a certain genre or cooking philosophy or concept that has made them successful, and I would imagine for many chefs, this question can be answered fairly easily. When people ask me that question my answer is usually that my favorite thing to cook is whatever is freshest and seasonally available at the time. When the temperature outside is chilly you can expect something cooked long and slow, either in a large Staub with a tight-fitting lid, or in our crock pot. Usually, in the winter, it's a piece of beef brisket or shoulder of pork that requires hours of cooking; in the warmer months I can be found outside tending my Lynx grill, cooking a nice piece of fish or all-natural chicken.

The other question I frequently get asked is, "Who does the cooking at home, you or your wife?" Well that's easy to answer — my wife, Jody, does the cooking during the week, but on the weekends, I take over. Usually we're at our East Texas house and I've brought along a couple of good meals from the Zodiac kitchen that I'm trying out for a new menu. Sometimes I test a recipe myself in home kitchen surroundings. Oh, and I should mention that I usually bring along a great bottle or two of wine that might find their way onto a Neiman Marcus menu some-where, depending on how well they're liked at my house.

Whether it's writing a menu for a special event or simply creating a dinner for myself, my family, or friends, my starting point is usually making a decision on what we'll eat as the entrée. This decision will then dictate the planning for the rest of the meal. For many of our events, the

> My favorite thing to cook is whatever is freshest and seasonally available at the time.

safest bet is having a piece of red meat for the entrée, which works best with a big red wine, which many people prefer. Then, to start, we'll typically feature a small salad, perhaps with a shrimp or scallop garnish to start off a fancy meal. When we have guests over at our house, we'll typi-cally serve a piece of salmon as the entrée or a nice steak along with a pinot noir or merlot wine. I advise you to make your entrée decision based on your personal preference and then round out the menu how it best makes sense. If I'm really at a loss on what the entrée should be, I'll go to the butcher shop first, see what looks best, and then build the menu. This can be dangerous sometimes because you could wind up spending too much money if you went to the store without a list — something I try to avoid when-ever possible. The other thing I try to avoid is going to the store hungry — boy, do I overspend and wind up getting way too much food!

Bay of Fundy Salmon with Brussels Sprouts and Farro

Yields 4 servings   ⧗ GO FIGURE

This dish never goes out of favor with our customers; my guess is it's because of the salmon and the farro. Farro, a type of wheat, is the oldest cultivated grain in the world, dating back to Biblical times. Talk about staying power! You'll notice in this recipe that the final cooking process comes together in the sauté pan you used to sear the fish. When I cook, I like to capture lots of layers of flavor that are left in a sauté pan used to sear the main protein in the recipe. We use Nova Scotia salmon, farm-raised in the Bay of Fundy — I love that name. The tide movement there ensures the healthfulness of the fish and I appreciate the sustainable way in which the fishery is managed.

FOR THE FARRO

1   tablespoon olive oil

1   shallot, minced

1   cup farro

     Pinch of kosher salt and freshly ground black pepper

FOR THE SALMON

2   cups cleaned and quartered shiitake mushrooms *(about 6 ounces)*

1   tablespoon olive oil

2   teaspoons chopped fresh thyme

     Kosher salt and freshly ground black pepper

24   Brussels sprouts *(about 1 pound)*, stem ends trimmed and halved

1   tablespoon extra-virgin olive oil

4   skinless salmon fillets, 5 ounces each

½   cup low-sodium prepared chicken broth or vegetable broth

2   cups baby spinach leaves

4   tablespoons Red Bell Pepper Vinaigrette *(page 216)*

SUGGESTED WINE PAIRING

Terlato Family Vineyards Pinot Noir

To prepare the farro, heat the olive oil in a heavy medium skillet over medium heat. Add the shallot and sauté until soft, about 2 minutes. Add the farro and sauté until lightly toasted, about 3 minutes. Add 2 cups water and the salt and pepper, and bring to a simmer. Cook, covered, over medium-low heat until the water is absorbed and the farro is tender but still a little al dente, 35 to 40 minutes. Drain the farro and lay out on a baking sheet or in a large roasting pan to cool. (The cooked farro will keep in an airtight container for up to 3 days in the refrigerator.)

Preheat the oven to 450 degrees F. and line a cookie sheet with parchment paper. To prepare the salmon, toss the shiitake mushrooms with the olive oil and thyme in a bowl and sprinkle with a pinch each salt and pepper. Transfer to the prepared cookie sheet and roast in the oven for 5 minutes. Remove and set aside.

Turn down the oven to 350 degrees F. Place the Brussels sprouts in a bowl, add the extra-virgin olive oil, and toss together. Transfer to a roasting pan and roast in the oven for 30 minutes. Remove and set aside; leave the oven on. Spray a large nonstick skillet with nonstick spray and set over medium heat. Place the salmon fillets in the hot pan and sauté for 2 minutes on each side.

Transfer the fillets to a cookie sheet or roasting pan and roast in the oven for 5 minutes longer.

Add the chicken broth and mushrooms to the same skillet you used for the salmon and add the cooked farro and the Brussels sprouts. Add the spinach and cook until heated through and the spinach has wilted. Season to taste with salt and pepper and divide the farro mixture among 4 serving plates. Place the salmon fillets on top of the farro and drizzle 1 tablespoon of the vinaigrette around each plate.

NUTRITION FACTS —*1 serving*

550 calories	5G saturated fat	40G total carbohydrate	260MG sodium
26G total fat	80MG cholesterol	5G sugars	40G protein

Chicken Paillard Milanese, Israeli Couscous, and Tomato-Basil Sauce

Yields 4 servings **GO FIGURE**

In this popular Go Figure dish we have taken a traditional Italian recipe and given it a healthier twist. The tomato-basil sauce is a great, easy recipe I use for many different dishes, like a simple pasta or baked chicken with some good mozzarella.

FOR THE TOMATO-BASIL SAUCE

1   tablespoon olive oil

2   cloves garlic, minced

1   small onion, finely diced

1   *(22-ounce)* can plum tomatoes *(preferably San Marzano)*, pureed

4   fresh basil leaves, torn

    Pinch of kosher salt and freshly ground black pepper

FOR THE CHICKEN

12 portions chicken breast *(3 ounces each)*, thinly pounded into scaloppini

3   egg whites, beaten

½   cup plain bread crumbs

5   tablespoons grated Parmesan cheese

1   tablespoon all-purpose flour

2   teaspoons olive oil

1   tablespoon minced shallot

1   cup sliced shiitake mushrooms *(about 4 ounces)*

1¼ cups cooked Israeli couscous *(follow the cooking directions on the package)*

1   cup prepared low-sodium chicken broth

2   tablespoons chopped fresh Italian parsley

2   cups baby arugula or baby watercress *(about 2 ounces)*

½   teaspoon fresh lemon juice

SUGGESTED WINE PAIRING

Rutherford Hill Chardonnay

To prepare the tomato-basil sauce, heat the olive oil in a saucepan over medium heat. Add the garlic and onion, and sauté for 3 minutes or until the onion is translucent. Add the pureed tomatoes, basil, salt, and pepper. Simmer for 30 minutes.

To prepare the chicken, preheat the oven to 350 degrees F. Pat the chicken dry with paper towels. Place the egg whites in a bowl. Place the bread crumbs, 3 tablespoons of the Parmesan, and the flour in another bowl and mix together. With one hand, take a chicken breast and dip it in the egg whites. With the same hand, place it in the bread crumb mixture. With the other hand, coat the chicken with the bread crumbs and place it on a clean plate. Repeat this process for all the chicken pieces. (You can do this step up to 1 day in advance; if so, wrap tightly and keep in refrigerator.) To cook the chicken, spray a large nonstick pan with nonstick spray and set over medium heat. Add the chicken, being careful not to crowd the pan; cook for 2 minutes on each side, taking care not to burn the bread crumbs. If the chicken appears to be getting too dark, turn down the heat. Transfer the chicken to a roasting pan, and finish cooking in the oven for 5 to 6 minutes longer or until the chicken is cooked through and reaches 165 degrees F. on a meat thermometer.

Add 1 teaspoon of the olive oil to the same pan in which the chicken was sautéed. Add the shallot and sauté for about 45 seconds. Add the shiitake mushrooms and cook for 1 minute longer. Add the cooked couscous, chicken broth, and parsley, season with salt and pepper, and heat through.

To serve, ladle ¼ cup of the tomato-basil sauce into each of 4 wide soup bowl or plates. Spoon the couscous mixture in the center of the sauce. Top with the chicken paillards. In a bowl, toss the arugula with the remaining olive oil, the lemon juice, and a pinch of salt and pepper. Top each of the chicken paillards with the arugula and sprinkle with the remaining Parmesan.

NUTRITION FACTS —*1 serving*

| 480 calories | 3.5G saturated fat | 24G total carbohydrate | 960MG sodium |
| 12G total fat | 175MG cholesterol | 4G sugars | 67G protein |

Braised Flat Iron with Mashed Potatoes and Corn

Yields 6 to 8 servings

The cut of meat termed "flat iron" has become more popular the past few years because of the terrific marbling found in this shoulder roast. We like it because it cooks more quickly than the traditional pot roast meats like chuck roast or bottom round, yet tastes better because of the marbling. If ever there was a dish that says "make this on a cold day to warm the soul," this is the dish. My wife, Jody, is excited about including this dish in the book because the mashed potatoes and corn recipe here is her all-time favorite food.

FOR THE STEAK

2½ pounds flat iron steak, at least 1½ to 2 inches thick *(or beef pot roast)*

Kosher salt and freshly ground black pepper

1½ tablespoons olive oil

¼ cup all-purpose flour

1 large white onion, diced

1 large carrot, peeled and diced

1 stalk celery, diced

3 cloves garlic, minced

2 cups dry red wine

1½ cups canned crushed tomatoes

2 cups prepared beef broth

6 sprigs fresh thyme

FOR THE MASHED POTATOES AND CORN

2 pounds Yukon Gold potatoes, peeled and cut into large dice

1½ cups heavy cream

3 tablespoons unsalted butter

1 tablespoon minced shallot

2 ears fresh corn, husks and silks removed

1¼ teaspoons kosher salt

¼ teaspoon freshly ground white pepper

1 teaspoon minced fresh thyme leaves

SUGGESTED WINE PAIRING

GALAXY Red Blend

To prepare the steak, preheat the oven to 325 degrees F. Season the steak with salt and pepper. Heat the oil in a large, heavy-bottomed, ovenproof saucepan (with a tight-fitting lid) over medium-high heat. Dust the steak with the flour and carefully place in the pan. Sear for 3 minutes on each side or until nicely browned. Remove the steak and set aside on a clean platter. Add the onion, carrot, celery, and garlic to the pan and continue to sauté for 8 to 10 minutes. Add the red wine and deglaze the pan, using a wooden spoon to scrape any solids off the bottom. Reduce the liquid by half, and then add the crushed tomatoes. Reduce for another minute. Add the beef broth and thyme, and return the cooked steak to the pan.

Cover the pan with the lid and place in the oven for about 2½ hours or until the meat is fork-tender.

To prepare the mashed potatoes and corn, place the potatoes in a saucepan and cover completely with salted water. Bring the water to a boil and then turn down the heat to a gentle simmer and cook for 15 to 20 minutes or until the potatoes are fork-tender. While the potatoes are cooking, heat the cream in a small saucepan and keep warm. Place 2 tablespoons of the butter in a large saucepan set over medium heat. Add the shallot and sauté for about 3 minutes. Cut the corn kernels from the cobs and add to the shallot; continue to sauté for 6 to 8 minutes longer, stirring occasionally. Season with the salt, white pepper, and fresh thyme. Set aside and keep warm.

Drain the potatoes in a colander and transfer to the bowl of an electric mixer fitted with a whisk. Whip the potatoes on high speed for 1 minute and scrape down the sides of the bowl. Add the remaining 1 tablespoon butter and whip for 1 minute longer. Reduce the speed to low and pour in the warm cream.

Continue to mix until the potatoes are smooth and fluffy. Fold in the corn mixture with a spatula and adjust the seasonings. Keep warm.

Transfer the steak to a clean platter, and loosely place some foil over the steak. Remove the thyme stems. Slowly reduce the sauce over medium heat for about 15 minutes until thickened. Cut the steak into 4 portions and serve with the mashed potatoes and corn mixture. Drizzle the pan sauce over the meat.

Make this on a cold day to warm the soul.

NUTRITION FACTS —*1 serving*

640 calories	**25G** total carbohydrate
22G total fat	**7G** sugars
8G saturated fat	**890MG** sodium
190MG cholesterol	**69G** protein

Grilled New York Steak with Chimichurri Sauce

Yields 4 servings

I like to use my outdoor Lynx grill as often as I can and nothing is better than searing a nice New York steak at 500 to 600 degrees F. Once both sides are seared I move the steak to a cooler part of the grill to finish cooking. It's that outside crispy char that I strive for all the time. Using Falk salt gives you a nice crunchy saltiness with every bite. Be sure you "relax" the steaks by letting them rest for about 5 minutes before serving.

4	New York sirloin steaks, about 8 ounces each *(preferably Certified Black Angus or USDA prime)*
1¼	pounds fingerling potatoes, halved lengthwise
3	tablespoons olive oil
2	tablespoons Falk salt
1	tablespoon plus 1 teaspoon freshly ground black pepper
1	white onion, julienned
1	cup seeded and julienned red bell pepper
2	cloves garlic, chopped
1	teaspoon smoked paprika
2	tablespoons chopped fresh Italian parsley
½	tablespoon chopped fresh thyme leaves
½	teaspoon kosher salt
2	ounces feta cheese *(about ⅓ cup)*
1½	cups Chimichurri *(page 226)*

SUGGESTED WINE PAIRING

Chimney Rock Stags Leap District Cabernet Sauvignon

NUTRITION FACTS —*1 serving*

770	calories	45G	total carbohydrate
43G	total fat	4G	sugars
45G	saturated fat	4550MG	sodium
165MG	cholesterol	56G	protein

Preheat the oven to 350 degrees F. and prepare the grill to maximum heat (at least 500 degrees F.). Remove the steaks from the refrigerator and bring to room temperature.

Place the potatoes in a bowl and toss with 1 tablespoon of the olive oil. Transfer to a roasting pan and roast in the oven for 20 minutes or until a knife pulls out easily when inserted into a potato. Remove from the oven and set aside.

Season the steaks with the Falk salt and 1 tablespoon of the pepper and grill over high heat on the first side for 3 minutes. Move the steaks one quarter turn and cook for 3 minutes longer. Turn the steaks over and continue to cook for 3 minutes, then give another quarter turn and cook for 3 minutes longer. Depending on your grill and the thickness of the steak, the steaks should be medium-rare to medium. When the steaks are at the desired doneness, remove them from the grill and let them rest on a clean platter.

Heat the remaining 2 tablespoons oil in a large, nonstick sauté pan over medium-high heat. Add the onion and bell pepper and sauté for about 4 minutes or until they begin to brown. Add the garlic and sauté for 1 minute longer. Remove the vegetables and set aside. Add the roasted potatoes to the pan and sprinkle with the paprika. Sauté for about 4 minutes longer or until the potatoes begin to brown and then return the onion and bell pepper to the pan. Add the parsley, thyme, kosher salt, and remaining 1 teaspoon black pepper and cook for about 3 minutes longer, until the flavors meld together.

> **CHEF'S NOTE**
>
> Falk salt is a specialty sea salt from Sweden used mostly for finishing dishes. The attractive, soft, conically triangular sea salt flakes are harvested from the Mediterranean sea in Cyprus. Because the salt is harvested naturally, the salt flakes aren't washed as much as normal salt, leaving trace elements and minerals intact.

Transfer the steaks to a cutting board and cut on an angle into ½-inch-thick slices. Divide the steak among 4 serving plates and arrange the potatoes and vegetables next to the meat. Sprinkle with the feta cheese and drizzle the chimichurri over the steaks. Serve extra chimichurri on the side.

Cauliflower Steak with Sautéed Garlic Spinach and Gremolata

Yields 4 servings ⏳ GO FIGURE

I first tasted this vegetarian dish at our Bergdorf Goodman restaurant, BG, in New York. It was created by our Chef, Marybeth Boller, and I loved the overall simplicity of the seared cauliflower, which is then smothered in the rest of the ingredients. This dish has become a "go-to" recipe for me at home when I have vegetarians coming for dinner. I like to make the dish with organic cauliflower not only for health reasons but also because the cauliflower heads feel much tighter and you seem to get a better-looking steak.

FOR THE GREMOLATA

1 cup fresh bread crumbs *(not too fine)*

Zest of 1 lemon

1 clove garlic, minced

½ cup minced fresh Italian parsley

⅛ teaspoon kosher salt

½ teaspoon freshly ground black pepper

FOR THE CAULIFLOWER

2 ounces pine nuts *(about ⅓ cup)*

2 large heads cauliflower

1 tablespoon unsalted butter

2 tablespoons olive oil

1 teaspoon minced garlic

1 tablespoon minced shallot

8 ounces spinach leaves, washed and dried

⅛ teaspoon kosher salt

⅛ teaspoon freshly ground black pepper

½ cup store-bought roasted red bell peppers

10 cherry tomatoes, halved

5 tablespoons prepared bread crumbs

2 tablespoons freshly grated Parmesan cheese

½ cup Roasted Tomato Vinaigrette *(page 219)*

SUGGESTED WINE PAIRING

Markham Merlot

To prepare the gremolata, place all the ingredients in a small bowl and mix with a fork to evenly distribute. Transfer to an airtight container and keep refrigerated for up to 3 days.

To prepare the cauliflower, preheat the oven to 325 degrees F. Place the pine nuts on a small cookie sheet and toast in the oven for 10 minutes or until slightly brown. Remove from the oven and let cool. Remove any outer leaves from the cauliflower heads. Carefully lay the cauliflowers on their side and cut 2 slices, 1½ inches thick, from each. Heat the butter and 1 tablespoon of the oil in a large, nonstick skillet over medium heat. When the butter has melted, gently add a cauliflower steak, taking care not to break it. Sear the cauliflower for 4 to 5 minutes on each side or until golden brown. Transfer to a roasting pan and repeat for the remaining cauliflower; you may need to add a little more butter and oil. Place the pan with the cauliflower in the preheated oven and bake for 20 minutes. In the same sauté pan you used for the cauliflower, heat the remaining 1 tablespoon olive oil over low heat. Add the garlic and shallot and sauté for 1 minute. Add the spinach leaves, season with the salt and pepper, and sauté for 1 to 2 minutes until wilted. Add the roasted red bell pepper and cook for 3 minutes longer. Turn off the heat and add the cherry tomatoes. Drain any excess water from the spinach mixture.

Remove the pan containing the cauliflower from the oven and divide the spinach mixture on top of the cauliflower. Add the prepared bread crumbs on top of the spinach and sprinkle the Parmesan on top of the bread crumbs. Return the cauliflower to the oven and bake for about 5 minutes longer. Carefully remove the steaks from the roasting pan and place on serving plates. Sprinkle a little gremolata on top of the bread crumbs, then the toasted pine nuts. Drizzle 2 tablespoons of the tomato vinaigrette around the cauliflower on each plate.

NUTRITION FACTS —*1 serving*

430 calories	**4.5G** saturated fat	**49G** total carbohydrate	**960MG** sodium
22G total fat	**10MG** cholesterol	**11G** sugars	**15G** protein

Holiday-Style Roasted Stuffed Turkey with Sausage Stuffing, Pan Gravy, Butternut Squash, and Basmati–Wild Rice Salad

Yields 8 servings

I recently completed another Thanksgiving turkey feast at my house and changed up some of the original recipes that I included in our last cookbook, *Neiman Marcus Taste*. Now that my son, Patrick, is in his early twenties he's become a big help with the early morning prep so we can get out of the kitchen more quickly and tend to more fun things like log splitting or burning a big Thanksgiving bonfire. In the original turkey recipe I wrote that I did not favor fresh turkeys because they had a tendency to be drier than processed frozen turkeys; but I'm here to tell you that I've changed my mind. There seems to be more turkey farmers out there who are doing an excellent job at fattening up their birds, and prices for fresh turkeys seem to be more in line with their frozen cousins. Sure you can still get a "Free Bird" (no relation to that great Lynyrd Skynyrd song) if you purchase enough at the grocery store to accompany the meal, but maybe you're ready to try that fresh turkey this year? At any rate, I've included a great dry rub recipe along with a brining method to help add flavor and moisture to the bird before cooking. Either recipe can be used — or not at all. If you're the one cooking the turkey this year I hope I've explained enough to make it the best that your guests have ever eaten!

FOR THE TURKEY BRINE *(OPTIONAL)*

2 cups soy sauce

2 cups apple juice

2 cups pineapple juice

1 head garlic, papery skin removed and cloves minced

1 onion, cut into large dice

3 jalapeños, stemmed, split, and seeded

2 lemons, quartered

6 sprigs fresh thyme

6 sprigs fresh rosemary

FOR THE TURKEY DRY RUB *(OPTIONAL)*

1 tablespoon Falk salt or other flaked salt

1 tablespoon light brown sugar

2 teaspoons coarsely ground black pepper

2 teaspoons dried thyme

1 teaspoon poultry seasoning

1 teaspoon paprika

½ teaspoon onion powder

½ teaspoon garlic powder

FOR THE SAUSAGE STUFFING

½ cup unsalted butter

1 onion, finely diced

2 cloves garlic, minced

2 stalks celery, finely diced

2 pounds Italian sausage, loose *(not in casings)*

2 large eggs

4 cups milk

1 cup prepared low-sodium chicken broth

6 cups day-old, dried-out bread cubes *(1-inch dice)*

1 tablespoon poultry seasoning

¼ teaspoon kosher salt

¼ teaspoon freshly ground black pepper

FOR THE BASTING LIQUID

8 to 10 cups low-sodium prepared chicken stock

1 cup diced onion *(1 onion)*

1 cup diced carrots *(about 2 carrots)*

1 cup diced celery *(about 5 stalks)*

4 sprigs fresh thyme

FOR THE TURKEY

1 turkey *(about 18 pounds)*

Kosher salt and freshly ground black pepper

2 cups diced onions *(2 onions)*

1 cup diced celery *(about 5 stalks)*

2 cups diced carrots *(about 4 carrots)*

8 cloves garlic, minced

6 sprigs fresh thyme

¼ cup olive oil

½ cup unsalted butter, melted

2 teaspoons Falk salt, or other flaked salt

2 teaspoons coarsely ground black pepper

FOR THE GRAVY

2 cups water

1 cup all-purpose flour

FOR THE BASMATI-WILD RICE AND BUTTERNUT SQUASH SALAD

2 cups sliced shiitake mushrooms, or cremini or button mushrooms

1 cup Citrus Vinaigrette *(page 213)*

½ cup walnut pieces

2 cups diced butternut squash *(1 large squash)*

1 tablespoon olive oil

1 teaspoon fresh thyme leaves

Kosher salt and freshly ground black pepper

1½ cups cooked basmati rice *(follow the cooking directions on the package)*

1½ cups cooked wild rice *(follow the cooking directions on the package)*

1 large head frisée, washed, dried, cored, and coarsely chopped

---

SUGGESTED WINE PAIRING

M. Chapoutier Côtes-du-Rhône
Belleruche Rosé

NUTRITION FACTS —*1 serving roasted turkey*

| 600 calories | 20G saturated fat | 6G total carbohydrate | 1180MG sodium |
| 63G total fat | 760MG cholesterol | 2G sugars | 195G protein |

NUTRITION FACTS —*1 serving stuffing*

| 290 calories | 9G saturated fat | 17G total carbohydrate | 680MG sodium |
| 17G total fat | 75MG cholesterol | 5G sugars | 17G protein |

NUTRITION FACTS —*1 serving rice salad*

| 110 calories | 0.5G saturated fat | 15G total carbohydrate | 600MG sodium |
| 4.5G total fat | 0MG cholesterol | 3G sugars | 2G protein |

NUTRITION FACTS —*1 serving gravy*

| 770 calories | 3.5G saturated fat | 132G total carbohydrate | 1030MG sodium |
| 8G total fat | 35MG cholesterol | 21G sugars | 35G protein |

THE DAY BEFORE If brining the turkey, start by preparing the brine the day before you are cooking. Place all the brining ingredients with 10 cups water in a large saucepan and bring to a boil. Turn down the heat to low and simmer for 10 minutes. Remove from the stove and set aside to cool. Brine the turkey following the directions below.

Alternatively, in a bowl, mix together the dry rub ingredients and dry-rub the bird following the directions below.

THE DAY OF To prepare the sausage stuffing, melt the butter in a large skillet over medium heat. Add the onion, garlic, and celery and sauté for 3 to 5 minutes or until the vegetables are softened and lightly browned. Remove from the skillet and set aside. In the same skillet, place the sausage and pat down so the sausage is flat in the pan. Cook over medium-low heat for about 10 minutes until the underside of the sausage is nicely browned. Turn the sausage over with a spatula and break up the sausage into small pieces. Cook for 5 to 7 minutes longer until completely cooked. Drain the sausage in a colander and make sure the pieces are bite-size. Set aside.

TALKING TURKEY

CHEF'S NOTES

This stuffing recipe is enough for an 18-pound bird with about 5 cups left over to be baked separately in a small loaf pan. Bake at 350 degrees F. for about 25 minutes.

This dry rub recipe will make enough to dry rub an 18- to 22-pound turkey. If you cook a smaller bird, use the leftovers for seasoning any type of poultry.

My wife, Jody, usually buys our turkey the Tuesday before Thanksgiving, and we allow it to defrost in a large insulated cooler bag in our kitchen area. I must admit it's a bit unorthodox, but it's worked for us for many years so we stick with it.

There are a couple of things you'll need to do if you decide to brine or rub your turkey:

If you brine: The day before cooking the bird you'll need to remove the packaging and remove all the innards that come packed inside the bird; set them aside for later use in the basting liquid. Place the brine in a large stockpot or clean bucket and submerge the turkey in the brine. Keep refrigerated overnight. The same morning you're going to cook the bird, remove the turkey from the brine and allow it to air-dry for 1 or 2 hours in the refrigerator.

If you dry rub: The day before roasting the turkey you'll need to remove the bird from the packaging and remove all the innards that come packed in the bird; set them aside for later use in the basting liquid. Rub the outside of the bird with the dry rub and sprinkle a generous amount in the cavity of the turkey. Let sit in the refrigerator overnight, preferably uncovered (this will make for crispier skin).

If you don't brine or dry rub: The day of roasting the turkey you'll need to remove the turkey from the packaging and remove all the innards that come packed in the bird; set them aside for later use.

Following any of these techniques, the turkey is now ready for the oven.

In a large mixing bowl, whisk together the eggs and the milk and add the chicken broth. In another bowl, mix the sautéed vegetables, cooked sausage, and diced bread. Stir in the poultry seasoning, salt, and pepper and add the milk mixture. Mix well to form a smooth consistency.

To prepare the basting liquid, place all the ingredients in a large saucepan and bring to a boil over high heat then reduce the heat to medium-low. Let the liquid simmer for at least an hour while you roast the turkey.

To roast the turkey, preheat the oven to 375 degrees F. Sprinkle the inside and outside with salt and pepper and loosely fill the cavity of the bird with the sausage stuffing. Place the turkey on a wire rack in a roasting pan. Scatter the onion, celery, carrots, garlic, and thyme around the turkey. Pour the olive oil and butter over the bird and season with the salt and pepper.

Place the turkey in the oven and roast for 1 hour, uncovered (allow an additional 30 minutes for a larger turkey). Carefully pull the turkey out of the oven and check to see how browned the turkey is. If the turkey is sufficiently browned, pour half of the warm basting liquid over it, cover tightly with aluminum foil, and return to the oven. Turn the oven down to 350 degrees F. and roast for 3½ hours longer.

Remove the turkey from the oven and place a meat thermometer into the turkey breast, just above the spot where the wings attach; at this point, the turkey should be just under the finished target temperature of 165 degrees F. At the same time, pour the remaining basting liquid over the turkey and place the bird back in the oven. At this point you can choose to uncover the bird for the last 30 to 45 minutes of cooking or keep it wrapped in foil. By uncovering you will crisp up the skin (keep in mind this may encourage your guests to request that you pull off the crispy skin, leaving your bird a bit naked for the grand display before carving!).

Once the internal temperature reaches 165 degrees F., remove the bird from the oven and carefully transfer to a large serving platter. Loosely "tent" the bird in the aluminum foil it was cooked in and let it rest for 20 minutes before carving.

To prepare the gravy, place the turkey roasting pan on the stove, straddling two burners set on medium-low heat. Bring the liquid in the pan to a boil and turn down the heat to a simmer, removing any grease that rises to the top of the liquid. In a bowl, whisk together the water and flour (creating a "slurry," in professional chef terms). Slowly whisk half of the slurry into the pan. The gravy will begin to thicken; add as much or as little of the remaining slurry as you want, to get the desired thickness of gravy. My preference is not to strain or do anything further with the gravy; usually there is no need to adjust any seasonings since the flavor from the turkey is sufficient.

To prepare the rice salad (which can be prepared up to 3 hours in advance), marinate the sliced mushrooms in ½ cup of the Citrus Vinaigrette for 1 hour. Preheat the oven to 325 degrees F. Place the walnuts on a small cookie sheet and toast in the oven for 10 minutes or until slightly brown. Remove from the oven and let cool. Turn up the oven temperature to 375 degrees F. Place the butternut squash in a bowl and toss with the olive oil, thyme, and a pinch each salt and pepper. Transfer to a roasting pan lined with parchment paper and roast in the oven for 8 to 10 minutes or until the squash is al dente. Place the cooked rices, marinated mushrooms, and roasted butternut squash in a large bowl. Add the frisée, walnuts, remaining Citrus Vinaigrette, and 1 teaspoon salt to the bowl. Toss together and let marinate for about 30 minutes.

To carve the turkey, remove the breast from the carcass by cutting down through the top of the bird, following the breast blade all the way down to where the wing meets the breast. Lay the boneless breast on a cutting board and carefully slice crosswise. Using your fingers, remove the drumsticks and thighs in one piece and then separate into two portions with a knife. Usually the dark meat falls off the bone, making this process easier. Remove the stuffing and place in a serving bowl. Serve the turkey meat with the stuffing, gravy, and rice salad.

CHEF'S NOTES

I recently made a great discovery for roasting a turkey and making the best gravy when I bought a stainless-steel-lined copper roasting pan. In the past I've used everything from nonstick-coated pans to grocery-store-bought aluminum pans, but my stainless-steel-lined copper pan is perfect for turkey. The stainless lining allows for great caramelization to happen when the vegetables start to brown during the roasting process. The end result is a gravy with a deep, rich, brown color that everyone loves.

During the holiday season, butternut squash typically can be found already peeled and diced in many grocery stores.

Garvin Family New Year's Eve Lobster Fest with Grilled Garlic Bread and Wild Mushroom Risotto

Yields an intimate dinner for 2

Before coming to Neiman Marcus in my current position, I was a working chef for 16 years after graduating from the Culinary Institute of America in 1978. As a chef this meant that you worked every holiday, and one of the busiest holidays was always New Year's Eve. So when I took the job here at Neiman's I found myself with time off on New Year's Eve for the first time in my culinary career. My wife, Jody (who also worked in restaurants for over 20 years before we were married), and I found ourselves sitting at home feeling excited that we both had this super-busy restaurant night off! Now what to do? We never considered going out to a restaurant since we always called New Year's Eve "Amateur Night Out" and the last place we wanted to be was in a scene at a restaurant on one of the busiest nights of the year. So with a young baby at home we decided to create our own New Year's Eve tradition: The Lobster Fest was born!

FOR THE LOBSTERS

2   lobsters, about 2 pounds each

½   cup unsalted butter, melted

FOR THE WILD MUSHROOM RISOTTO

6   cups prepared chicken broth

3   tablespoons olive oil

2   cloves garlic, minced

3   cups mixed wild mushrooms, washed and finely sliced

1   cup Arborio rice

1   cup grated Parmesan cheese

2   tablespoons unsalted butter

1   cup heavy cream

⅛   teaspoon kosher salt

⅛   teaspoon freshly ground black pepper

FOR THE GARLIC BREAD

½   cup unsalted butter, melted

4   cloves garlic, minced

1   large loaf French- or Italian-style bread, split in half lengthwise

SUGGESTED WINE PAIRING

Terlato Family Vineyards Chardonnay

To prepare the lobsters, bring a stockpot of water to a boil. Be sure to leave the rubber bands on the lobster claws unless you want to possibly lose a finger or two. Plunge the lobsters headfirst into the boiling water and close the lid. Set a timer for 10 minutes and then remove the lobsters with a sturdy set of tongs; they will be a bright red color. Transfer the lobsters to the sink and rinse under cold running water for 10 seconds; this will remove any white scum that may have appeared in the boiling liquid. (I usually have a kitchen towel in each hand while handling the lobsters since they are hot.) Keeping the lobsters in the sink, break away the tail from the upper body with a twisting motion and with a similar twisting motion, break away both claws. Have a cutting board handy next to the sink, and with your chef knife, split the lobster tail in half lengthwise. Place the lobster claws on the cutting board and with your chef knife make a few cracks on the shells with the back side of the knife. Serve each person one split tail and two claws. Be sure you have an extra bowl on the table for the empty shells. Serve with the melted butter alongside.

To prepare the wild mushroom risotto, pour the chicken broth into a saucepan and bring to a simmer. Heat the olive oil in a separate saucepan over medium-high heat. Add the garlic and sauté for 1 minute. Add the wild mushrooms and sauté for 5 minutes longer or until the mushrooms start to brown on the edges. Add the rice, stir well to mix with the mushrooms, and turn down the heat to low. Using a ladle, add 1 ladle of the simmering chicken broth to the rice while stirring with a wooden spoon, allowing the rice to absorb the liquid. When absorbed, add another ladle of broth and continue this process until all the chicken broth is absorbed or until the rice is al dente. Turn off the heat and add the Parmesan cheese, butter, and cream; stir well to incorporate and season with the salt and pepper.

To prepare the garlic bread, preheat the oven to 350 degrees F. Mix the butter and garlic and smear on the bread. Wrap the bread in foil, place on a cookie sheet in the oven, and bake for 10 minutes. Unwrap the bread and open it up to expose both halves. Set the oven to broil and brown the bread for 30 seconds. Serve immediately.

NUTRITION FACTS —*1 lobster*

560 calories	32G saturated fat	0G total carbohydrate	900MG sodium
46G total fat	390MG cholesterol	0G sugars	35G protein

NUTRITION FACTS —*1 serving risotto*

270 calories	5G saturated fat	35G total carbohydrate	400MG sodium
9G total fat	25MG cholesterol	1G sugars	11G protein

NUTRITION FACTS —*1 serving garlic bread*

150 calories	5G saturated fat	15G total carbohydrate	250MG sodium
9G total fat	20MG cholesterol	0G sugars	3G protein

CHEF'S NOTES

I like 2-pound lobsters because I believe they yield the perfect amount of lobster meat for a dinner portion. You'll need a very large pot with a lid that will hold both lobsters at the same time while cooking.

Laksa Seafood Curry, Brown Rice Stir-Fry

Yields 4 servings

This dish was first served at our Mariposa restaurant in Honolulu's Ala Moana Center. Our version of Laksa took the classic spicy noodle soup, added loads of fresh seafood, and gave it a curry flavor. Since then it's become so popular that it's impossible to take it off the menu because of the loyal following of customers. I suppose this is the type of dish that invokes comfort and a sense of a complete meal in a bowl. There's something to be said about really fresh seafood and a warm coconut curry sauce; the combination seems to warm the soul every time. You can also heat it up by adding more red curry to really spice things up.

FOR THE LAKSA CURRY SAUCE

- 1 tablespoon olive oil
- 1 tablespoon peeled and chopped fresh ginger
- 2 cloves garlic, minced
- 1 shallot, minced
- 2 stalks lemongrass, trimmed and crushed
- 2 teaspoons red curry paste
- 2 cups prepared lobster broth or seafood stock
- 1 (13.5-ounce) can coconut milk
- ½ cup chopped fresh cilantro leaves
- 4 kaffir lime leaves
- 2 teaspoons kosher salt

FOR THE BROWN RICE STIR-FRY

- 2 tablespoons plus 1 teaspoon sesame oil
- 2 teaspoons minced garlic
- ½ teaspoon peeled and minced ginger
- 1 cup shelled edamame
- 3 large eggs, lightly beaten
- 1 cup bean sprouts
- 4 cups cooked brown rice (*follow the cooking directions on the package*)
- 3 tablespoons low-sodium soy sauce
- 2 scallions, cut on an angle into 1-inch lengths

FOR THE SEAFOOD CURRY

- 2 tablespoons olive oil
- 8 jumbo u-15 shrimp (*about 8 ounces*), peeled, deveined, and tails removed
- 8 large u-10 sea scallops (*about 12 ounces*), halved
- 8 ounces snapper or other firm-fleshed fish, such as halibut, swordfish, or tuna, cut into 2-inch pieces
- ⅛ teaspoon kosher salt
- ⅛ teaspoon freshly ground black pepper
- 16 littleneck clams, scrubbed
- ½ cup seeded and finely sliced red bell pepper
- ½ cup seeded and finely sliced yellow bell pepper
- 1 cup finely sliced white onion
- ½ teaspoon minced garlic
- 1 cup peeled and cubed eggplant (*1-inch dice*)
- ¼ cup roughly chopped fresh cilantro leaves

SUGGESTED WINE PAIRING

Chimney Rock Elevage Blanc White Blend

CHEF'S NOTES

Searing the seafood separately helps prevent overcooking the fish that take less time than others. It also helps retain moisture and gives you a more tender product.

You can substitute the scallops with other shellfish like mussels if you prefer.

This is a meal in a bowl, great couch food . . .

To prepare the Laksa curry sauce, heat the oil in a saucepan over medium heat. Add the ginger, garlic, shallot, and lemongrass and sauté, stirring continuously, for about 3 minutes. Add the curry paste and sauté for 1 minute longer. Add the broth, stir well to blend the flavors, and reduce for 5 minutes. Add the coconut milk, cilantro leaves, kaffir lime leaves, and salt. Cook the sauce for 20 minutes longer at a low simmer. Strain the sauce through a fine sieve, and set aside. (You can make this sauce up to 2 days in advance and keep refrigerated in an airtight container for up to 4 days.)

To prepare the brown rice stir-fry, heat a heavy-duty wok or nonstick skillet over medium-high heat. Add 2 tablespoons of the sesame oil and heat until just smoking. Add the garlic and ginger and stir-fry with a wooden spoon for 1 minute, taking care that they do not burn. Add the edamame and cook for 1 minute longer. Remove the vegetables from the pan and set aside. Add the remaining 1 teaspoon sesame oil to the wok and when hot add the eggs. Let the egg mixture solidify for 30 to 45 seconds and then flip over and cook on the other side for 30 seconds longer. Remove from the pan and set aside. Return the stir-fried vegetables to the wok, add the bean sprouts, and stir-fry for 10 seconds. Add the cooked egg and the cooked brown rice. Stir well to break up the egg and to distribute throughout the rice, and cook until the rice is hot. Mix in the soy sauce and when the mixture is warm enough to serve, turn off heat and fold in the scallions. Adjust the seasonings by adding more soy sauce if desired and serve in a bowl at the table.

To prepare the seafood curry, heat the oil in a large sauté pan over medium-high heat. Season the shrimp, scallops, and snapper with salt and black pepper. Begin by searing the snapper for about 1 minute on each side without moving the fish around. Remove from the pan and set aside. Add the scallops to the pan and sear for 2 minutes on each side until browned. Remove from the pan and set aside. Add the clams to the pan with the red and yellow bell peppers, onion, garlic, and eggplant and continue to cook until the clams open (you may need to coax the clams to open by deglazing the pan with a little broth or white wine). Remove the mixture from the pan and set aside. Add the shrimp to the pan and sauté for 6 to 8 minutes or until cooked through. Remove from the pan and set aside. Add the Laksa curry sauce to the pan and bring to a boil. Carefully add back all the seafood and vegetables and cook at a simmer for 3 or 4 minutes or just long enough to reheat all the seafood. Turn off the heat and add the cilantro leaves. Divide the curry among 4 soup bowls and serve with a side of stir-fried brown rice.

NUTRITION FACTS —1 serving

770 calories	57G total carbohydrate
42G total fat	11G sugars
24G saturated fat	2200MG sodium
175MG cholesterol	45G protein

Family Meal Roast Chicken

Yields 6 servings

After this recipe appeared in our last cookbook, *Neiman Marcus Taste*, I heard that it's become a favorite recipe for quite a few of our customers. Recently, there's been a wave of cookbooks based on restaurant employee meals, and it's no secret that some great food gets prepared at these "family meals." Typically, there's a cook who's responsible for the all-important staff meal and it's a very important role, as you can imagine. I created this recipe years ago when I was the staff cook. I was running out of both ideas and time as the 10:30 a.m. dead-line approached, before lunch service. So I threw the "kitchen sink" of the spice shelf at the chicken and discov-ered that the spiciness and zestiness of the roasted chicken was a big hit.

½	cup extra-virgin olive oil
2	teaspoons paprika
2	teaspoons garlic powder
2	teaspoons dried thyme
⅛	teaspoon cayenne
¼	teaspoon crushed fennel seeds
1	tablespoon kosher salt
¼	teaspoon freshly ground black pepper
2	chicken breasts, skin on, bone-in, about 1 pound each
2	chicken legs, skin on, bone-in, split to separate thighs and drumsticks
10	new potatoes (*about 1½ pounds*), halved
½	cup dry white wine
2	tablespoons unsalted butter

SUGGESTED WINE PAIRING

Wairau River Sauvignon Blanc

Preheat the oven to 375 degrees F. Place the oil in a large mixing bowl (large enough to hold all the ingredients) and add the paprika, garlic powder, thyme, cayenne, fennel, salt, and pepper. Mix well, add the chicken and potatoes, and toss to evenly coat. Transfer all of the chicken pieces, skin-side-up, and potatoes to a large roasting pan. Roast in the oven for 20 minutes; check the chicken breasts and if cooked through, remove and keep warm. When all the chicken pieces and the potatoes are finished roasting (this should take a total of 30 to 40 minutes), keep warm by turning down the oven to 250 degrees F., placing the chicken and potatoes in a clean roasting pan, and covering with foil.

Place the roasting pan used for the chicken on the stove top over medium heat. Add the wine and deglaze the pan by loosening the remaining solids left on the bottom of the pan using a wooden spoon. Let the wine simmer for about 30 seconds and add the butter, stirring until it melts. Return the chicken pieces to the pan along with any juices that have collected in the pan. Coat the chicken pieces with the sauce and serve with the potatoes.

CHEF'S NOTE

If you have time to let the cooked, wrapped chicken marinate in the flavors for an hour, you'll be even happier with the outcome. I like mine crispy, and if you do too, move up the heat by 10 degrees F. but be careful to not burn the chicken and smoke out your kitchen.

NUTRITION FACTS —*1 serving*

410	calories	11G	total carbohydrate
27G	total fat	0G	sugars
6G	saturated fat	1390MG	sodium
115MG	cholesterol	26G	protein

Creamed Chicken à la King in a Popover

Yields 6 servings

Nothing "Go Figure" about this dish. One thing I told our customers when I rolled out the Go Figure concept is that they'll still have every opportunity to splurge with the calories on our menus at Neiman Marcus — and this recipe splurges really well. It's not often we get to enjoy a cream sauce, so when the time comes, I see this recipe as the perfect choice for a cold winter's day and suggest you go for it. Nothing says splurge like heavy cream and butter. And you get to eat a popover while you're at it!

3	tablespoons unsalted butter
1	large onion, minced
1	cup sliced cremini mushrooms
1	large green bell pepper, minced
1	large red bell pepper, minced
2	tablespoons all-purpose flour
1	quart heavy cream
2	chicken bouillon cubes
4	cups diced cooked chicken or rotisserie chicken
3	sprigs fresh tarragon
2	sprigs fresh thyme
½	teaspoon kosher salt
¼	teaspoon freshly ground black pepper
6	Neiman Marcus Popovers *(page 16)*
½	cup sliced canned pimentos
2	tablespoons chopped fresh Italian parsley

SUGGESTED WINE PAIRING

Rochioli Chardonnay

Preheat the oven to 350 degrees F.

Melt the butter in a large sauté pan over medium heat and add the onion, mushrooms, and green and red bell peppers. Sauté for 3 to 4 minutes or until the vegetables are softened. Add the flour, mix well with a wooden spoon, and cook the mixture for 2 minutes longer. Add the cream, bring to a simmer, and let thicken for about 1 minute. Add the bouillon cubes and diced chicken and turn down the heat to barely a simmer, allowing the cream mixture to warm the chicken. Stir in the tarragon, thyme, salt, and black pepper. Remove the pan from the stove and keep warm.

When ready to serve, heat the popovers in the oven for about 2 minutes. Remove from the oven and make a slit down the center of each popover. Ladle the hot creamed chicken into the popovers and arrange the sliced pimentos over the chicken. Sprinkle the parsley over the chicken and serve.

Nothing "Go Figure" about this dish!

NUTRITION FACTS —*1 serving*

1040 calories	44G saturated fat	49G total carbohydrate	1490MG sodium
74G total fat	415MG cholesterol	8G sugars	44G protein

Sea Scallops Fra Diavolo with Basil Linguine

Yields 4 servings

A literal translation of *Fra Diavolo* is "Brother Devil," so named because of the spicy naughtiness provided by the crushed red pepper. We put this dish on the menu of our NM Café in Natick, Massachusetts, and it just took off. The local jumbo sea scallops that we get fresh daily are sweet and milky and just soak up the richness of the Fra Diavolo sauce. I love the way the arugula and Parmesan finish this dish, very authentic Italian-style. *Mangia bene!*

FOR THE FRA DIAVOLO SAUCE

- 1 (*28-ounce*) can whole plum tomatoes (*preferably San Marzano*)
- 2 tablespoons olive oil
- 1 white onion, finely diced
- 2 cloves garlic, chopped
- ½ teaspoon crushed red pepper flakes
- ½ teaspoon dried oregano
- ⅛ teaspoon kosher salt

FOR THE PASTA AND SCALLOPS

- 2 tablespoons plus 2 teaspoons kosher salt
- 12 ounces dry or fresh linguine
- 1 tablespoon olive oil
- 16 large sea scallops, cleaned
- ⅛ teaspoon freshly ground black pepper
- 2 tablespoons chopped fresh Italian parsley
- 4 fresh basil leaves, gently torn
- 4 cups baby arugula, washed and dried
- 2 teaspoons extra-virgin olive oil
  Pinch of kosher salt
- 2 tablespoons freshly grated Parmesan cheese

SUGGESTED WINE PAIRING

Santa Margherita Pinot Grigio

To prepare the Fra Diavolo sauce, place the tomatoes in a bowl and break them up with your hands. Heat the olive oil in a saucepan over medium-high heat. Add the onion, garlic, red pepper flakes, and oregano and sauté for about 3 minutes or until the onions are translucent. Turn down the heat to low and add the hand-crushed tomatoes. Simmer the sauce for about 30 minutes and then add the salt.

To prepare the pasta and scallops, heat a large saucepan of water and add 2 tablespoons of the salt. Bring to a boil and add the pasta; cook until al dente. Meanwhile, preheat the oven to 200 degrees F. Heat the olive oil in a large skillet over medium-high heat. Pat the scallops dry with a paper towel and season with the remaining 2 teaspoons salt and the pepper. Cook the scallops in two batches so you do not overcrowd the skillet: When the skillet is hot, carefully add half of the scallops and sauté for 1 to 2 minutes on each side, until they are caramelized. Transfer the first batch of scallops to a cookie sheet or roasting pan, and keep warm in the oven. Repeat for the second batch of scallops.

In the same pan you cooked the scallops, add the Fra Diavolo sauce and warm through. As soon as the pasta is done, drain and add the pasta to the sauce. Carefully toss the pasta in the sauce and add the parsley and basil. Divide the pasta among 4 large pasta bowls. Arrange 4 scallops around each serving of pasta. Place the arugula in a bowl and toss with the extra-virgin olive oil and a pinch of salt. Top each serving of pasta with the arugula salad and Parmesan.

CHEF'S NOTE

You can serve either fresh or dried pasta, as long as it's al dente when cooked. Nothing is worse than over- or under-cooked pasta! My suggestion is to stay by the saucepan when cooking pasta and have your colander ready in the sink because when it's time to drain the pasta you need to move quickly.

The sauce can be made up to two days ahead and kept in an air-tight container in the refrigerator. If you make it ahead, you will need to reheat it first.

NUTRITION FACTS —*1 serving*

610 calories	3G saturated fat	86G total carbohydrate	2010MG sodium
18G total fat	30MG cholesterol	14G sugars	28G protein

Turkey Meatloaf with Cream Gravy

Yields 4 servings

I once made this dish for Chef Georges Perrier (owner of Le Bec-Fin in Philadelphia) at his La Mère restaurant outside Philadelphia when I was a guest chef at the Book and the Cook symposium. He told me that this was the best meatloaf he had ever tasted, quite a compliment coming from one of the finest French chefs in the United States. This recipe was originally published in our first cookbook here at Neiman Marcus. I had just returned from our Troy, Michigan, restaurant where the chef at the time showed me a recipe that he had worked on for quite a while. I have to say it's the most moist meatloaf I have ever eaten; I imagine the reduced cream has something to do with that. At any rate, the entire dish is perfectly showcased with the mushroom gravy and creamy polenta.

FOR THE MEATLOAF

1   tablespoon extra-virgin olive oil

1   tablespoon unsalted butter

1½ cups minced onion

1   tablespoon minced garlic

¼   teaspoon dried thyme

¼   teaspoon dried oregano

¼   teaspoon ground allspice

¾   cup heavy cream

1½ pounds ground turkey

1   cup plain bread crumbs

2   large eggs, lightly beaten

¼   cup minced fresh Italian parsley

3   tablespoons tomato ketchup

1½ tablespoons kosher salt

1½ teaspoons freshly ground black pepper

SUGGESTED WINE PAIRING

Rutherford Hill Merlot

FOR THE CREAM GRAVY

¼   cup unsalted butter

3   tablespoons minced shallots

¼   cup all-purpose flour

4   cups heavy cream

2   teaspoons chicken bouillon

½   teaspoon Tabasco sauce

½   teaspoon Worcestershire sauce

¼   teaspoon dried thyme

¼   teaspoon kosher salt

Preheat the oven to 350 degrees F. Spray a 1½-quart loaf pan measuring 8½ inches long by 4½ inches wide and 2½ inches deep with nonstick spray.

To prepare the meatloaf, heat the oil and butter in a large, heavy-bottomed saucepan over medium heat. When the butter has melted, add the onion and garlic and sauté for 6 to 8 minutes or until translucent. Add the thyme, oregano, allspice, and heavy cream and bring to a simmer. Continue to simmer, stirring frequently, for 8 to 10 minutes, until the liquid has reduced by one-third and has the consistency of cooked oatmeal. Transfer to a large mixing bowl and let cool. When cool, add the turkey, bread crumbs, eggs, parsley, ketchup, salt, and pepper and mix well. Form a small (2-ounce) patty in your hands and place on a microwavable plate. Cook in the microwave for about 1 minute or until the patty is cooked through. Let the patty cool a little and then taste; adjust the seasonings accordingly.

Transfer the turkey mixture to the prepared pan and pat down with the back of a large spoon to form a smooth top to the meatloaf. Bake the meatloaf in the oven for about 1 hour or until the internal temperature reaches 165 degrees F.

While the meatloaf is cooking prepare the cream gravy. In a heavy-bottomed saucepan, melt the butter over medium heat, add the shallots, and sauté for 1 minute. Add the flour and stir with a wooden spoon to form a roux. Sauté the roux, stirring continuously, for 1 minute. Add the cream, bouillon, Tabasco sauce, Worcestershire sauce, thyme, and salt and bring to a simmer, using a wire whisk to help the roux thicken.

Continue to simmer for 5 minutes, making sure the cream does not boil over (see Chef's Notes). When the cream has thickened to the consistency of a thin oatmeal, remove from the stove. If you prefer a thinner gravy, stir in a little warm water.

Cut the meatloaf into 2-inch-thick slices, transfer to serving plates, and cover with the cream gravy.

CHEF'S NOTES

It's important to taste the meatloaf mixture before assembling. When I make this for a group of people, I prepare it the previous day so the flavors can marry overnight. Then the next day I'll microwave a small portion and taste it: Invariably, I add more of the spices to heighten the flavor.

Pay attention when bringing cream to a simmer because it has a habit of boiling over the sides of the pan. I can't tell you how many times I have seen this happen in professional kitchens, and believe me, it makes a big mess all over the stove.

NUTRITION FACTS —*1 serving*

1080 calories	**30G** total carbohydrate
95G total fat	**5G** sugars
54G saturated fat	**2810MG** sodium
430MG cholesterol	**31G** protein

Grilled Filet Mignon Carpetbagger Style with Crisp Oysters and Béarnaise Sauce

Yields 4 servings

The derivation of the term "carpetbagger style" is open to some debate, and most likely the name refers to the combination of opulent steak and decadent fresh oysters, just as the carpetbags brought by the Northerners who came South during reconstruction after the Civil War contained their personal items, cash, and valuables.

Some recipes call for oyster-stuffed steaks, so the steaks are literally containing a rich bounty. Certainly, the combination of filet mignon and oysters suggests a lush affluence, especially paired with a velvety Béarnaise sauce. This is a special occasion dish that will get rave reviews every time you serve it.

FOR THE BÉARNAISE SAUCE

1   teaspoon minced shallot

¼   cup white wine vinegar
     or Champagne vinegar

1   cup unsalted butter

4   large egg yolks

2   tablespoons fresh lemon juice

1   tablespoon minced fresh tarragon

2   drops Tabasco sauce

⅛   teaspoon Falk salt

⅛   teaspoon freshly ground black pepper

FOR THE STEAK AND OYSTERS

4   center-cut filet mignon steaks, about
     8 ounces each

⅛   teaspoon kosher salt

⅛   teaspoon freshly ground black pepper
     Vegetable oil, for deep-frying

16   shucked oysters, drained

1   cup buttermilk

1   cup all-purpose flour

FOR THE GARNISH

4   small bunches watercress

2   teaspoons olive oil

⅛   teaspoon Falk salt

SUGGESTED WINE PAIRING

Two Hands Sexy Beast Cabernet Sauvignon

To prepare the sauce, place the shallot and vinegar in a small saucepan. Reduce the liquid by half over high heat, until about 2 tablespoons of liquid are left. Set aside to cool. About 30 minutes before you are ready to cook the steaks, melt the butter in the microwave or in a saucepan and keep warm. Place the egg yolks in a small stainless-steel bowl and set on top of a small saucepan of simmering water, making sure the bowl does not touch the water. Add 1 tablespoon of lukewarm water to the eggs and begin whisking the egg yolks with a wire whisk. After 3 or 4 minutes, the egg yolks should become pale in color and thicken. Remove the bowl from the saucepan and set on a slightly damp dish towel so the bowl does not move. In a very slow, steady stream, begin to drizzle the melted butter into the yolks while whisking; do not add the butter too fast or else the Béarnaise will break.

CHEF'S NOTE

There's a lot of talk out there about different grades of meat and the best place to buy it; here's my take on the subject. At Neiman Marcus we always purchase Prime beef. Whether it's a Prime Filet or Prime New York Steak, you can be assured that the end result will be well received by our customers. For our hamburgers, we specify All-Natural from our suppliers. While the term All-Natural simply means minimally processed, we take it many steps forward and only make hamburgers from beef that is fresh, free of hormones, and in many cases raised exclusively on grass. For our other beef menu items such as Filet Mignon and New York Steak, we specify choice cuts of meat that when cooked correctly are also enthusiastically received by our customers. My personal feeling about your selection of beef is that it should fit your budget and then you should take the time and effort to season and cook it correctly. There's a time and place for Prime and there's a time and place for the rest of the grades of meats. It all depends on your wallet that day!

When half of the butter has been added, add 1 tablespoon of the lemon juice. Slowly add the rest of the butter and then add the reserved shallot and vinegar mixture. Stir in the tarragon and season with the Tabasco, salt, and pepper. Add the remaining 1 tablespoon lemon juice. Cover the Béarnaise with a towel and keep in a very warm place (on the stove top not over direct heat, or in a low oven) so it does not get cold and solidify.

Prepare the grill. To prepare the filet mignon, dry the steaks with a paper towel and bring them to room temperature. Season the steaks on both sides with salt and pepper. Transfer to the grill and cook on the first side for 3 to 4 minutes over medium-high heat. Using tongs, move the steaks a quarter turn and cook on the same side for 3 to 4 minutes longer. Turn the steaks over and cook for 3 to 4 minutes before moving them a quarter turn and then cooking for 3 to 4 minutes longer. If the steaks are at least 2 inches thick, they should take about 12 minutes in total to reach an internal temperature of 120 degrees F. for rare; 14 to 16 minutes for medium-rare (125 to 130 degrees F.), and another few minutes for medium (135 to 140 degrees F.). Remove the steaks from the grill and let them rest on a clean cutting board or plate.

To prepare the oysters, preheat the oil in a deep-fryer to 350 degrees F. Place the oysters in a bowl and cover with the buttermilk. Place the flour on a large plate. Remove the oysters from the buttermilk and place in the flour. Dredge the oysters in the flour and make sure they are completely covered. Shake off the excess flour and carefully place the oysters in the deep-fryer basket. Lower the oysters into the oil and fry for 1 minute, until golden brown. Transfer to a plate lined with paper towels and season lightly with salt and pepper.

To serve, place a steak on each serving plate. Place 4 oysters on each filet and top with Béarnaise sauce. In a bowl, toss the watercress with the oil, sprinkle with the Falk salt, and serve next to the steak.

NUTRITION FACTS —*1 serving*

| 1270 calories | 48G saturated fat | 32G total carbohydrate | 620MG sodium |
| 94G total fat | 525MG cholesterol | 4G sugars | 71G protein |

Vegetarian Gluten-Free Pasta

Yields 4 servings ⏳ GO FIGURE

Whatever your reason for avoiding gluten, you don't have to miss your favorite wheat recipes anymore, especially pasta recipes. So many new brands of wheat-free pastas are hitting the market every day, and they keep getting better and better. We started identifying gluten-free menu items a few years back and really had to be careful about using the term since our kitchens are truly not gluten-free. While the recipe items are indeed gluten-free, we still have to deal with the possibility of cross-contamination from other preparations, and this is a serious business for us here in the Neiman Marcus kitchens. We train our serving staff to explain this to our guests and leave it up to them to order gluten-free, or not.

1	pound gluten-free pasta *(linguine or your favorite gluten-free noodle)*
1½	tablespoons olive oil
1	clove garlic, minced
8	spears asparagus *(tough part of stems removed)*, cut into 1-inch pieces on a angle
1	cup bottled artichoke hearts, quartered
1	cup prepared vegetable broth
1	cup halved cherry tomatoes
6	ounces fresh mozzarella, diced
1	tablespoon chopped fresh Italian parsley
6	fresh basil leaves, torn
½	teaspoon kosher salt
½	teaspoon freshly ground black pepper
½	cup freshly grated Parmesan cheese
1	tablespoon extra-virgin olive oil, for serving *(optional)*

SUGGESTED WINE PAIRING

Il Poggione Rosso di Montalcino

Cook the pasta according to the directions on the package. (If using fresh pasta note the cooking times, as fresh gluten-free pasta cooks differently than fresh pasta.) Prepare the remaining ingredients while the pasta is cooking. Heat the oil in a large sauté pan over medium heat. Add the garlic and asparagus and sauté for 1 or 2 minutes, stirring continuously so the garlic does not burn. Add the artichokes and sauté for 3 minutes longer. Add the vegetable broth and bring to a simmer. When the pasta is done, drain in a colander but do not rinse. Add the cooked pasta immediately to the pan with the artichokes and asparagus and toss together so the pasta absorbs the broth. Transfer the pasta to a large serving bowl. Add the cherry tomatoes, mozzarella, parsley, basil, salt, and pepper. Toss together with tongs to mix well. Top the pasta with the grated Parmesan and serve immediately. If desired, drizzle a finishing tablespoon of extra-virgin olive oil on top of the pasta.

CHEF'S NOTE

There's always the question of whether or not to rinse your pasta after boiling. Here's my take: If you have to wait on serving the pasta that you've just cooked, then rinse it and cool it down to hold for service. If you go directly from cooking and draining the pasta to serving with the sauce, then there's no need to rinse the pasta.

NUTRITION FACTS —*1 serving*

460	calories	50G	total carbohydrate
21G	total fat	2G	sugars
10G	saturated fat	1110MG	sodium
50MG	cholesterol	22G	protein

Grilled Ahi Steak Provençal with Eggplant and Mushrooms

Yields 4 servings

The key to the success of this dish is to serve the fresh tuna steak perfectly rare. A lot of factors will play into the complexity of this dish — for example, the freshness of the tuna, the type of pan in which you cook the tuna, and how soon after cooking you serve the tuna steak. Basically what I'm telling you is typical of the thought process for all chefs today; timing is key as well as the freshness of ingredients and using the correct tools of your trade.

4   center-cut ahi tuna steaks, about 6 ounces each and at least 1 inch thick

1   cup small white baby potatoes

     Falk salt and freshly ground black pepper

2   tablespoons olive oil

2   cloves garlic, minced

1   cup finely sliced red onion

1   cup diced peeled eggplant

1   cup mushrooms, cleaned and halved

½   cup pitted Kalamata or Niçoise olives

¼   to ½ cup prepared chicken broth or vegetable broth

1   cup halved cherry tomatoes

1   anchovy, diced *(optional)*

     Juice of 1 lemon

2   tablespoons fresh basil leaves

1   tablespoon fresh oregano leaves

1   tablespoon extra-virgin olive oil

Remove the tuna from the refrigerator 30 minutes before cooking to bring to room temperature. Meanwhile, for the potatoes, bring 2 cups water to a boil in a small saucepan. Add the potatoes, turn the heat down to medium, and cover with a lid. Simmer for 10 minutes and drain. When cool enough to handle, cut the potatoes in half and set aside. Season the tuna steaks with ½ teaspoon each of salt and pepper. Heat 1 tablespoon of the oil a large, heavy-bottomed sauté pan over medium-high heat. When the oil is hot, add the tuna and sear for 1 to 2 minutes on each side depending on the desired doneness. Remove from the pan and transfer to a clean platter.

Using the same pan, add the remaining 1 tablespoon olive oil. Add the garlic and onion and sauté for 6 to 8 minutes. Add the eggplant and mushrooms and sauté for 3 minutes longer. Add the reserved blanched potatoes and the olives and sauté for another 2 to 3 minutes. Deglaze the pan by adding the broth and stirring to dislodge any solids. Add the cherry tomatoes and anchovy (if using) and simmer for 1 minute. Add the lemon juice, season to taste with salt and pepper, and fold in the basil and oregano.

CHEF'S NOTE

I usually don't rinse potatoes under cold running water after blanching since I don't want them to absorb any more water.

On a clean cutting board, slice the tuna steaks in half, on an angle. Place half the vegetables on a platter, top with the tuna, and then add the rest of the vegetables over the tuna. Drizzle with the extra-virgin olive oil and serve the platter at the table, family style.

The rarer the better when it comes to fresh ahi tuna.

NUTRITION FACTS —*1 serving*

430 calories	16G total carbohydrate
20G total fat	4G sugars
3G saturated fat	660MG sodium
65MG cholesterol	44G protein

Neiman Marcus Cassoulet

Yields 6 servings

If there was such a thing as a perfect food, this would be it for me. We've taken this very classic French dish and made it fit into our Neiman's world in a modern way, combining many favorite foods and some convenient foods as well. Some might ask "Why use canned beans in such a great classic dish?" and I'd reply, "Why not?" There are some incredible prepared beans on the market today, and I'm never shy about utilizing a product that's both convenient and great-tasting. This is where I get to show off my Staub cookware at its best. I especially like to bring the Staub to the table and open the lid in front of my guests, releasing the wonderful aromas to add to the effect. Be sure to have some good, crusty French bread available to soak up the delicious sauce!

3	tablespoons olive oil
2	pounds pork shoulder, cut into 6 pieces
4	duck legs
6	ounces Andouille or lamb sausage *(preferably merguez)*
4	chicken thighs
1	tablespoon plus ⅛ teaspoon kosher salt
1	tablespoon plus ⅛ teaspoon freshly ground black pepper
½	cup diced bacon or pancetta
2	cups diced white onion
1½	tablespoons minced garlic *(4 or 5 cloves)*
3	tablespoons tomato paste
1	cup dry white wine
1	*(14.5-ounce)* can crushed tomatoes
4	cups prepared chicken broth
2	dried bay leaves
3	sprigs fresh thyme, tied with butcher string
2	*(15-ounce)* cans white beans, rinsed and drained

Preheat the oven to 325 degrees F. Heat the oil in a large, heavy-bottomed casserole dish (preferably Staub) over medium-high heat. Season the pork, duck, sausage, and chicken with 1 tablespoon each of the salt and pepper. Sear in batches: first the pork, then the duck, next the sausage, and finally the chicken. When each is seared, set aside on a platter. Add the bacon to the casserole and cook until almost crisp. Remove the bacon and add the onion and garlic. Season with the remaining ⅛ teaspoon each of salt and pepper and sauté for about 8 minutes or until the onions are brown and almost caramelized. Add the tomato paste and stir to incorporate. Deglaze with the white wine while stirring with a wooden spoon to dislodge any solids sticking to the bottom of the casserole, and reduce the liquid by half. Add the crushed tomatoes, broth, bay leaves, and thyme.

Return the pork, duck, sausage, chicken, and bacon to the casserole and add more broth if necessary to cover the meat. Cover the pan with a lid and bake in the oven for about 3 hours or until all the meats are fork-tender. (See Chef's Note regarding skimming any fat.) In the last 30 minutes of cooking add the beans and return to the oven. Discard the bay leaves and thyme sprigs. Divide up the meats among serving bowls and spoon the sauce and beans over the meat.

CHEF'S NOTE

Because of the fat content of the sausage and chicken, a fair amount of fat will be released during the cooking process. You'll need to pull the casserole dish from the oven two or three times during the cooking process to skim off the grease that collects on the surface. If you are not serving the cassoulet until the next day, then there's no need to drain off the fat during cooking. Just allow the cassoulet to cool overnight and skim off the layer of fat in the morning, before reheating.

SUGGESTED WINE PAIRING

EPISODE Red Blend

NUTRITION FACTS —*1 serving*

990 calories	8G saturated fat	42G total carbohydrate	2780MG sodium
30G total fat	140MG cholesterol	8G sugars	74G protein

Sea Bass with Parsnip Puree

Yields 4 servings

Black sea bass is a favorite of many chefs, especially along the Eastern Seaboard of the United States. This is another fish that is commonly raised sustainably in ocean pens. Whenever we serve parsnip puree we often get asked, "What is that?" because when people see white puree, they expect to taste mashed potatoes. Usually, the parsnip puree gets high marks from first-timers. This recipe calls for browning the butter, and I'll never forget the first time I made brown butter, with a chef instructor. I thought he was setting me up for a practical joke when he asked me to burn the butter. Little did I know what that nutty flavor would add to the finished sauce.

FOR THE PARSNIP PUREE

1	pound parsnips, peeled and cut into 2-inch pieces
2	cups heavy cream
2	tablespoons unsalted butter
2	teaspoons kosher salt
⅛	teaspoon freshly ground white pepper

FOR THE SEA BASS AND VEGETABLES

4	cups *(about 8 ounces)* kale, stems removed, washed
16	baby carrots, peeled, tops trimmed
3	tablespoons unsalted butter
1	tablespoon olive oil
4	black sea bass fillets, about 7 ounces each
½	teaspoon Falk salt
¼	teaspoon freshly ground white pepper
1	tablespoon minced shallot
½	cup chopped fresh Italian parsley
3	tablespoons fresh lemon juice

SUGGESTED WINE PAIRING

Mischief & Mayhem Meursault

To prepare the parsnip puree, place the parsnips in a saucepan and add the cream. Bring to a boil and cook at a high simmer for 30 minutes or until the parsnips are fork-tender. Remove the parsnips with a slotted spoon and transfer to the bowl of an electric mixer fitted with a whisk attachment. Add the butter, salt, and pepper and slowly add the hot cream from the pan while mixing at low speed. Once all the liquid has been added, increase the speed to medium and mix until smooth. Keep warm until ready to serve.

To prepare the sea bass and vegetables, preheat the oven to 350 degrees F. Half-fill a large saucepan with salted water and bring to a boil. Add the kale, cover the pan, and cook over medium heat for 3 minutes. Drain the kale and set aside. In a separate pan, blanch the carrots in boiling salted water for 2 minutes; drain and set aside.

Place 1 tablespoon butter and the oil in a large sauté pan over high heat. Season the bass with Falk salt and white pepper and sear, skin-side down, for 2 to 3 minutes or until the skin is crispy. Carefully turn over and sear for 1 minute longer. Transfer to a roasting pan and bake for 4 or 5 minutes longer, depending on the thickness of the fish.

In the same sauté pan, cook the blanched kale for about 3 minutes over medium heat to just heat through. Remove the kale from the pan and set aside. Melt the remaining 2 tablespoons butter in the pan and sauté the shallot for 1 minute over medium heat. Turn up the heat to medium-high, add the blanched carrots, and let the butter become nutty and brown. Remove from the heat and add the parsley.

To serve, spoon the parsnip puree onto serving plates. Arrange the kale next to the puree and place the bass on top of the kale. Scatter the carrots over the fish and drizzle the browned butter over the fish and around the kale. Drizzle the lemon juice over the fish and serve immediately.

NUTRITION FACTS —*1 serving*

1050 calories	39G saturated fat	61G total carbohydrate	1780MG sodium
71G total fat	340MG cholesterol	15G sugars	53G protein

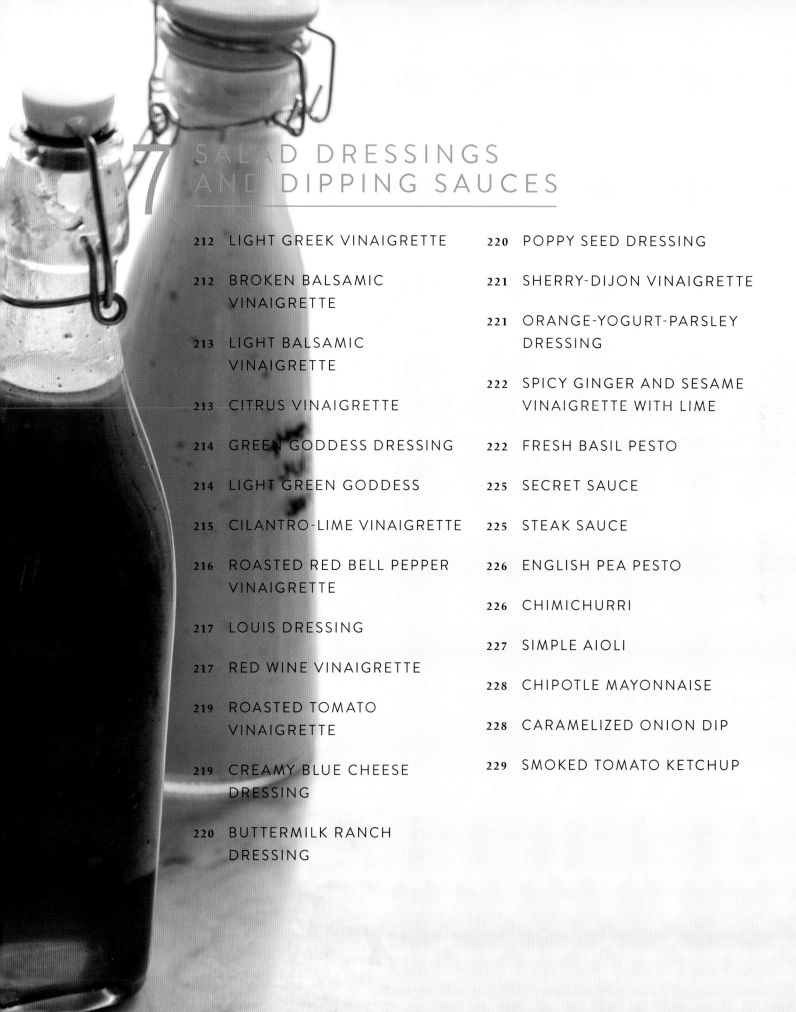

7 SALAD DRESSINGS AND DIPPING SAUCES

SALAD DRESSINGS
AND DIPPING SAUCES

When customers ask us, "How come when I make the same thing, yours always tastes better than mine?" I tell them the difference is flavor. Adding flavor comes in a variety of ways. An experienced chef is not afraid to season with more salt, herbs, or spices, always tasting before serving the finished dish. I guess it's all that tasting that led to the saying, "Never trust a skinny chef!" One of the major challenges when operating a restaurant group as large as ours at Neiman Marcus is ensuring that our chefs and cooks reproduce the flavors of the recipes we created. One of the trade secrets for adding flavor to food is utilizing salad dressings, vinaigrettes, and chilled sauces as flavor enhancers. These flavor enhancers can work with all types of proteins, either before (as a marinade) or after cooking. From a chicken breast to a piece of swordfish or a center-cut filet mignon, these dressings, vinaigrettes, and chilled sauces will definitely add flavor to your finished dish.

Years ago when I was studying at the Culinary Institute of America, the sauce class was strictly confined to hot sauces, and a lone chilled sauce — mayonnaise. I must admit I'm a big fan of extra-heavy mayonnaise; I like to lather it on my sandwiches, not just use a light schmear. Never enough when it comes to mayo! But here at Neiman Marcus, we take a lighter approach, and many times we will make our own mayonnaise-based aiolis and add certain flavors such as spinach or roasted garlic to use in sandwiches. Sometimes, we'll rub a flavored aioli on a piece of fish after roasting. The other versatile element in these chilled sauces is that they work great for dips, whether you're dipping French fries or veggies or even a grilled cheese sandwich. Be creative, and add flavor the professional chef way.

Here are some tricks of the trade to guide you through the basics:

MIXING

We prefer to emulsify or mix together our salad dressings by using small blenders, food processors, immersion blenders, or thin-blade whips. Sometimes we use jars or plastic bottles fitted with pour spouts that you just shake. If you've ever watched infomercials, you probably know about the Magic Bullet, which I can attest is the easiest way to mix a dressing or vinaigrette. One thing I love about the Magic Bullet is that the containers have lids so it is really easy to keep the finished product in the refrigerator.

OIL AND SALAD DRESSINGS

At Neiman Marcus, we use a variety of different oils; each one has a unique flavor and desired end result. Extra-virgin olive oil (EVOO), the most expensive type, is preferred for splashing over a piece of fish or chicken for finishing. We also use it when customers request olive oil at their table as it's also excellent for dipping with a good, crusty bread. As far as the importance of the country of origin, I've tasted excellent EVOO from Greece, Spain, Italy, Portugal, and the United States and all have had certain characteristics that I've really loved. Be aware that using straight-up EVOO in certain dressings may give a bitter or pungent flavor due to its high acid content. This is why we call for other types of oil in some of the following recipes that we feel work best. We prefer virgin olive oil for recipes in which we want to add flavor but want to limit the powerful punch of EVOO — for example, in Asian dressings with soy and chile. Pure olive oil has a less acidic finish and pungency and is good for mixing with many of our dressing recipes. It's less expensive but still good quality, and I like to use it for sautéing as it has a high smoking point. Olive oil refers to blended olive oil with little or no acidic flavor. It's less expensive and is also a good sautéing oil.

VINEGARS

Vinegars have become increasingly popular as flavor enhancers over the last twenty years or so. When I first started at Neiman Marcus, we used three types of vinegar in our restaurants: distilled (clear), red wine (for most salad dressings), and apple cider (used in our chicken salad). Today, the selection at Neiman Marcus restaurants is infinite. Most vinegars have a harsh acidic flavor that needs to be neutralized by sweetness for salad dressings; typically, we would use a good-quality honey. Vinegars add acidity to a dish and enhance the flavor. When you taste the final version of your dish and you think there's something lacking, try adding a squeeze of lemon or lime juice or a splash of vinegar. It really does bring the true flavor of the food to the front of your taste buds.

With balsamic vinegars becoming more and more popular, you don't need as much sweetness added to the recipe. Years ago, we held a Festa d'Italia event here at our Dallas flagship store, and we received a large shipment of 75-year-old balsamic vinegar aged in oak casks. We used it primarily on fresh berries as a sweet dessert sauce for the fruit! Here are some guidelines for using vinegar: Aged balsamic vinegar is made with white grapes aged in wood casks, with the premium types coming from Modena in Italy. Balsamic vinegar aged more than five years should be consumed in its own pure form. Here at Neiman Marcus, we serve an aged balsamic vinegar with our EVOO whenever customers ask for simple oil and vinegar on the side with a salad. The better wine vinegars, made from red or white grapes, such as sherry or Champagne vinegar, will be aged in wood barrels for a couple of years. Fruit vinegars are typically made from fruit wines like apple and raspberry or rice wine in the case of Asian cuisine. Other flavorings are used for these fruit wines such as figs or other spices and fresh herbs such as tarragon.

TERMINOLOGY

*A note on why I differentiate between the terms
vinaigrette, dressing, and cold sauce:*

VINAIGRETTES are oil-and-vinegar-based recipes that
have not been thickened by emulsification. We are looking
for a broken-style end result that needs to be shaken or
stirred each time the vinaigrette is used. These types of
vinaigrettes "nappe" to salad greens in a much lighter
fashion than dressings. In turn, **DRESSINGS** are usually
held together with a dairy based ingredient such as sour
cream, mayonnaise, or a small amount of milk, cream, or
buttermilk. We use dressings when the recipes call for a
thicker consistency to cover and coat the salad or final recipe.
CHILLED SAUCES and **DIPS** are used as accompaniments
to main course dishes. Many times, these recipes are served
with side dishes or offered as dips on the table for guests to
serve themselves.

Light Greek Vinaigrette

Yields 1¾ cups

The mustard and sugar in this recipe cut the acidity and smooth out the finish. We use this vinaigrette for our Greek salad; it also makes a great marinade for poultry and pork.

1	cup olive oil
½	cup red wine vinegar
2	tablespoons fresh lemon juice
½	tablespoon Dijon mustard
1	tablespoon sugar
1	tablespoon fresh oregano leaves
½	teaspoon minced garlic
½	tablespoon onion powder
1	teaspoon kosher salt
½	teaspoon freshly ground black pepper

Place all the ingredients in a blender and blend for 30 seconds. Keep in an airtight container in the refrigerator; the vinaigrette will last for up to 2 weeks. When using again, shake well to mix the ingredients.

NUTRITION FACTS —*2 tablespoons*

150	calories	2G	total carbohydrate
16G	total fat	1G	sugars
2G	saturated fat	160MG	sodium
0MG	cholesterol	0G	protein

Broken Balsamic Vinaigrette

Yields 1⅔ cups

We use the term "broken" because of the way this vinaigrette separates soon after it's mixed. By using a blender or some other type of electric mixer, the vinaigrette will stay together longer than if you whisk it by hand. Keep in mind that hand-mixing the vinaigrette will make it thinner so it will more lightly coat the salad. It also makes a great marinade for grilled vegetables and a tasty dip for a good crusty bread.

1	cup olive oil
⅓	cup balsamic vinegar
2	tablespoons honey
1	tablespoon Dijon mustard
2	tablespoons minced Italian parsley
1	teaspoon minced shallot
½	teaspoon minced garlic
1½	teaspoons kosher salt
½	teaspoon freshly ground black pepper

Place all the ingredients in a bowl and stir with a whisk until incorporated. Alternatively, place all the ingredients in a clean glass jar, cover with lid, and shake vigorously for 10 seconds or until incorporated. Because the dressing will "break," shake the dressing well before serving to recombine. Keep in an airtight container in the refrigerator for up to 2 weeks.

NUTRITION FACTS —*2 tablespoons*

170	calories	4G	total carbohydrate
17G	total fat	4G	sugars
2.5G	saturated fat	260MG	sodium
0MG	cholesterol	0G	protein

CHEF'S NOTE

Adding ¼ cup of mayonnaise when using an electric mixer will emulsify the dressing and keep it from breaking, as long as you keep the dressing in the refrigerator.

Light Balsamic Vinaigrette

Yields 2½ cups   GO FIGURE

In helping to reduce the calories, we've removed the honey from our Broken Balsamic Vinaigrette and lightened up on the olive oil. As a result, this dressing will have a tart edge in the final taste. It makes a good accompaniment to an aged cheese as it counteracts the sharpness.

1	cup balsamic vinegar
¾	cup olive oil
2	tablespoons minced fresh Italian parsley
2	tablespoons minced shallot
2	teaspoons Dijon mustard
1	teaspoon minced garlic
1	tablespoon kosher salt
½	tablespoon freshly ground black pepper

Place all the ingredients in a bowl with ½ cup water and whisk vigorously until incorporated. Alternatively, place all the ingredients in a clean glass jar, cover with a lid, and shake vigorously for 10 seconds or until incorporated. Keep in an airtight container in the refrigerator for up to 2 weeks.

NUTRITION FACTS —*2 tablespoons*

90	calories	3G	total carbohydrate
8G	total fat	2G	sugars
1G	saturated fat	310MG	sodium
0MG	cholesterol	0G	protein

Citrus Vinaigrette

Yields 2½ cups   GO FIGURE

In this all-purpose recipe, we use only citrus juice as the acid rather than vinegar. Ginger is the secret to bringing out the unique flavor that best enhances poultry and seafood. It makes a superb drizzle over cooked scallops and shrimp.

1	cup fresh orange juice
⅔	cup fresh grapefruit juice
¼	cup fresh lemon juice
2	tablespoons olive oil
2	tablespoons honey
2	tablespoons Dijon mustard
2	teaspoons kosher salt
1	teaspoon peeled and grated fresh ginger

Place all the ingredients in a blender and blend for 30 seconds or until smooth. Keep in an airtight container in the refrigerator; the vinaigrette will last for up to 1 week.

CHEF'S NOTE

Fresh basil, Italian parsley, or tarragon make interesting flavor variations for this vinaigrette.

NUTRITION FACTS —*2 tablespoons*

30	calories	4G	total carbohydrate
1.5G	total fat	4G	sugars
0G	saturated fat	230MG	sodium
0MG	cholesterol	0G	protein

Green Goddess Dressing

Yields 3 cups

The name of this dressing can be traced back to the early 1900s when restaurants across the country started getting serious about their cuisine and began naming dishes after famous people or events of the times. In this case it was a play called *The Green Goddess* in San Francisco. More than likely, the chef at the time had some French training and took creative liberty with the French *sauce vert* ("green sauce"). It's interesting that even way back then, chefs knew the importance of being creative! We love this sauce for its vibrant green color and use it as a bold-tasting dressing or dip for all types of seafood, chicken dishes, and salads.

1	cup mayonnaise
¼	cup buttermilk
¼	cup apple cider vinegar
1	cup spinach leaves
3	tablespoons roughly chopped fresh Italian parsley
2	tablespoons roughly chopped fresh tarragon leaves

4	scallions, chopped *(green part only)*
2	cloves garlic, minced
2	anchovy fillets
1	teaspoon kosher salt
1	teaspoon freshly ground black pepper
1	teaspoon Worcestershire sauce
1	cup sour cream

Place all the ingredients except the sour cream in a blender. Blend for 1 minute and then fold in the sour cream. Keep in an airtight container in the refrigerator for up to 1 week.

NUTRITION FACTS —*2 tablespoons*

100	calories	1G	total carbohydrate
10G	total fat	1G	sugars
2.5G	saturated fat	170MG	sodium
10MG	cholesterol	1G	protein

Light Green Goddess

Yields 3 cups   ⏳ GO FIGURE

This lighter version of the Green Goddess was created because over the last few years many of our customers let us know they wanted to enjoy our great salads but with reduced calories and fat. This recipe provides that while maintaining the flavors of the original.

CHEF'S NOTE

This also makes a great low-calorie dip or sauce for salmon and other seafood or chicken.

1	cup low-fat plain Greek yogurt
1	cup light mayonnaise
¼	cup apple cider vinegar
1	cup spinach leaves
½	cup roughly chopped fresh Italian parsley
2	tablespoons roughly chopped fresh tarragon

1	tablespoon chopped scallion *(green part only)*
1	clove garlic, minced
1	anchovy fillet
1	teaspoon freshly ground black pepper
	Pinch of kosher salt

Place all the ingredients in a blender with ¼ cup water and blend for 1 minute. Keep in an airtight container in the refrigerator for up to 3 days.

NUTRITION FACTS —*2 tablespoons*

35	calories	2G	total carbohydrate
2.5G	total fat	1G	sugars
0.5G	saturated fat	105MG	sodium
0MG	cholesterol	1G	protein

Cilantro-Lime Vinaigrette

Yields 2 cups

We use this vinaigrette exclusively for our Asian-style salads. It also works really well as a coleslaw dressing with shaved cabbage, and in Tex-Mex cuisine as it packs a punch and marries well with spicy flavors.

1   cup olive oil

½   cup fresh lime juice

¼   cup Japanese rice vinegar

2   tablespoons honey

3   tablespoons chopped fresh cilantro

½   tablespoon kosher salt

1   teaspoon freshly ground black pepper

Place all the ingredients in a blender and blend for 1 minute or until completely smooth. Keep in an airtight container in the refrigerator for up to 1 week.

NUTRITION FACTS —*2 tablespoons*

130 calories	**4G** total carbohydrate
2G total fat	**3G** sugars
0G saturated fat	**160MG** sodium
0MG cholesterol	**0G** protein

Roasted Red Bell Pepper Vinaigrette

Yields 4 cups GO FIGURE

The idea behind this recipe was to create a colorful vinaigrette with complex flavor. You often see vinaigrettes drizzled around a plate, and this one will impress every time with its deep red color and taste.

1 *(28-ounce)* can roasted red bell peppers, drained

¼ cup olive oil

¼ cup white balsamic vinegar or Champagne vinegar

2 tablespoons fresh lemon juice

Place all ingredients in a blender. Blend for 1 minute and strain through a fine strainer into an airtight container. The vinaigrette will keep for up to 1 week in the refrigerator.

NUTRITION FACTS —*2 tablespoons*

20 calories	**1G** total carbohydrate
2G total fat	**0G** sugars
0G saturated fat	**60MG** sodium
0MG cholesterol	**0G** protein

CHEF'S NOTE

This recipe yields plenty of vinaigrette, which is useful because it makes a versatile and delicious accompaniment to all kinds of proteins.

Louis Dressing

Yields 2½ cups

While the origin of the name of this dressing is disputed, there's no debate that the flavor is out-standing. We usually serve it with a seafood salad. It makes a great dip and a spread for ham-and-cheese or corned beef sandwiches.

1   cup Hellman's or Best Foods mayonnaise

½   cup Heinz chile sauce

½   cup sour cream

2   tablespoons fresh lemon juice

½   tablespoon prepared horseradish

3   tablespoons seeded and minced green bell pepper

2   tablespoons chopped scallion *(white and green parts)*

1   teaspoon celery salt

1   teaspoon kosher salt

½   teaspoon freshly ground white pepper

Place all the ingredients in a bowl and whisk until well incorporated. Keep in an airtight container in the refrigerator for up to 1 week. Shake well before using.

NUTRITION FACTS —*2 tablespoons*

110 calories	3G total carbohydrate
10G total fat	2G sugars
2G saturated fat	320MG sodium
10MG cholesterol	0G protein

Red Wine Vinaigrette

Yields 2½ cups

This recipe is a workhorse in our kitchens: It's a good marinade for all types of meat and seafood, especially tuna, and a flavorful dressing for pasta salads, as well as for all types of vegetable salads. We include a small amount of balsamic vinegar and canola oil to help lower the acidity of the vinaigrette.

½   cup red wine vinegar

2   tablespoons balsamic vinegar

1   tablespoon Dijon mustard

¼   cup chopped mixed fresh herbs, such as oregano, Italian parsley, and thyme

1   tablespoon sugar

1   teaspoon minced shallot

1   teaspoon minced garlic

1   tablespoon kosher salt

1   teaspoon freshly ground black pepper

1   cup olive oil

½   cup canola oil

Place the red wine vinegar and balsamic vinegar in a blender and add the mustard, herbs, sugar, shallot, garlic, salt, and pepper. Blend together while slowly pouring in the olive oil and canola oil. Adjust the seasonings as necessary. Keep in an airtight container in the refrigerator for up to 3 days.

CHEF'S NOTE

You can eliminate the sugar if you prefer by substituting 1 tablespoon pure honey.

NUTRITION FACTS —*2 tablespoons*

160 calories	2G total carbohydrate
17G total fat	1G sugars
2G saturated fat	310MG sodium
0MG cholesterol	0G protein

Roasted Tomato Vinaigrette

Yields 2½ cups   ⧗ GO FIGURE

I remember the first time I tasted a roasted tomato and thought *WOW! What an intense tomato flavor!* While this recipe calls for roasting in an oven, try roasting on your wood or charcoal grill some time and see what the wonderful smoky flavor adds to the vinaigrette. Depending on your grill temperature you'll need to keep an eye on the tomatoes. You can also roast slices of heirloom tomatoes in the same way.

6	ripe plum tomatoes, halved and seeded
2	cloves garlic, minced
	Kosher salt and freshly ground black pepper
¾	cup plus 1 tablespoon olive oil
2	tablespoons honey
2	tablespoons red wine vinegar
3	fresh basil leaves

Preheat the oven to 300 degrees F. Place the tomatoes, garlic, and 2 pinches each of salt and black pepper in a mixing bowl. Add 1 tablespoon of the olive oil and toss together. Transfer to a roasting pan with the tomatoes cut-side up. Roast in the oven for 45 minutes. Remove from the oven and let cool.

Transfer the tomato mixture to a blender and add the honey, vinegar, basil, and 1 teaspoon salt. Add black pepper to taste and slowly add the remaining olive oil. Blend for 1 minute or until completely smooth. Strain through a large-hole strainer; if you want the vinaigrette to have a little texture, leave unstrained. Keep in an airtight container in the refrigerator for up to 1 week.

NUTRITION FACTS —*2 tablespoons*

80	calories	2G	total carbohydrate
9G	total fat	2G	sugars
1G	saturated fat	25MG	sodium
0MG	cholesterol	0G	protein

Creamy Blue Cheese Dressing

Yields about 4½ cups

This is my favorite dressing for a variety of reasons. First and foremost, I'm a real lover of all blue cheeses, especially the Maytag blue we use here. The sharper the blue, the better. Some people put ranch dressing on everything, but I prefer using blue cheese dressing on everything from roast chicken and grilled fish to fresh vegetables. Of course it also works on a big pile of crisp greens like iceberg lettuce and as a simple dipping sauce for hot chicken wings or freshly cut vegetables.

3	tablespoons olive oil	½	tablespoon minced shallot
3	tablespoons apple cider vinegar	1	teaspoon kosher salt
1½	cups mayonnaise	½	teaspoon freshly ground black pepper
1	cup sour cream		
½	cup buttermilk	8	ounces Maytag blue or imported blue cheese, crumbled
	Dash of Tabasco sauce		
1	teaspoon Worcestershire sauce		

Place the olive oil and vinegar in a mixing bowl and add the mayonnaise, sour cream, buttermilk, Tabasco, Worcestershire sauce, shallot, salt, and pepper. Whisk together until thoroughly incorporated and then whisk in the blue cheese. If the dressing becomes too thick, add a few drops of water. Add more blue cheese if desired. Keep in an airtight container in the refrigerator for up to 1 week.

CHEF'S NOTE

This dressing is best made the day before it is served so the flavors really marry together.

NUTRITION FACTS
—*2 tablespoons*

120 calories
12G total fat
3.5G saturated fat
15MG cholesterol
1G total carbohydrate
0G sugars
210MG sodium
2G protein

Buttermilk Ranch Dressing

Yields 2¾ cups

At my house, this dressing goes on everything from pizza to potato chips! Ranch is probably the most popular American salad dressing, and it dates back to the 1950s and a dude ranch in Santa Barbara named Hidden Valley Ranch. Over the years, our customers constantly asked for ranch dressing so instead of saying, "No, we don't serve it at Neiman Marcus," we decided to come up with our own version. After all, good customer service is all about saying "yes" to reasonable requests.

3 tablespoons apple cider vinegar

1 teaspoon Worcestershire sauce

1 clove garlic, minced

2 tablespoons minced scallion *(white and green parts)*

2 tablespoons minced fresh Italian parsley

1 tablespoon minced fresh dill

1 cup buttermilk

1 cup mayonnaise

½ cup sour cream

1½ teaspoons kosher salt

½ teaspoon freshly ground white pepper

Place the vinegar and Worcestershire sauce in a mixing bowl, add the garlic, scallion, parsley, and dill, and whisk together. Whisk in the buttermilk, mayonnaise, and sour cream and season with the salt and pepper. Keep in an airtight container in the refrigerator for up to 5 days.

NUTRITION FACTS —*2 tablespoons*

90 calories	1G total carbohydrate
9G total fat	1G sugars
2G saturated fat	200MG sodium
10MG cholesterol	1G protein

Poppy Seed Dressing

Yields 4 cups

This is one of Helen Corbitt's recipes and a Neiman Marcus staple for the last 60 years or so. As well as a standout salad dressing, it makes a great dip for all kinds of fruit — we have a couple of generations of customers who don't know how to eat fruit without it!

1 cup sugar

¾ cup white vinegar

2 teaspoons dried mustard powder

2 teaspoons kosher salt

3 tablespoons grated onion *(plus the juice released from grating)*

2 cups canola oil

3 tablespoons poppy seeds

Place the sugar, vinegar, mustard, and salt in the bowl of an electric mixer. Add the grated onion and onion juice and mix on low speed. Turn the mixer to high speed and gradually add the oil in a slow, steady stream until well incorporated. Continue to mix on high speed for 10 minutes longer until the dressing is very thick. Stir in the poppy seeds. Transfer to an airtight container and keep refrigerated for up to 3 weeks.

NUTRITION FACTS —*2 tablespoons*

160 calories	7G total carbohydrate
15G total fat	7G sugars
1G saturated fat	150MG sodium
0MG cholesterol	0G protein

Sherry-Dijon Vinaigrette

Yields 2½ cups

Sherry vinegar and honey give this vinaigrette a sweetness that works really well with roasted pork loin or chicken and any meat salad, as it cuts through the richness. It's also delicious on a plain salad.

1½ cups olive oil

⅓ cup plus 2 tablespoons sherry vinegar

3 tablespoons Dijon mustard

2 tablespoons honey

2 tablespoons finely minced fresh Italian parsley

1 teaspoon minced shallot

2 teaspoons kosher salt

1 teaspoon freshly ground black pepper

Place all the ingredients in a blender with 3 tablespoons water and blend together for 30 seconds. Transfer to an airtight container and keep refrigerated for up to 2 weeks.

NUTRITION FACTS —*2 tablespoons*

160	calories	3G	total carbohydrate
17G	total fat	2G	sugars
2.5G	saturated fat	290MG	sodium
0MG	cholesterol	0G	protein

Orange-Yogurt-Parsley Dressing

Yields 5¼ cups

We use this dressing for our Roast Turkey Salad (page 165). You can also use it for a roasted pork salad or side salads accompanying poultry or pork.

4 cups low-fat plain yogurt

¼ cup apple cider vinegar

1 tablespoon orange zest

½ cup fresh orange juice *(from 2 oranges)*

¼ cup minced fresh Italian parsley

1 tablespoon minced shallot

Pinch of kosher salt

Pinch of freshly ground black pepper

Place all the ingredients in a bowl and whisk until thoroughly incorporated. The dressing will keep in an airtight container in the refrigerator for up to 2 weeks.

NUTRITION FACTS —*2 tablespoons*

20	calories	2G	total carbohydrate
0G	total fat	2G	sugars
0G	saturated fat	25MG	sodium
0MG	cholesterol	1G	protein

Spicy Ginger and Sesame Vinaigrette with Lime

Yields 2¾ cups

This vinaigrette packs a punch with spiciness from sweet chile sauce and crushed red pepper flakes. It makes a great flavor enhancer at the end of the cooking process — try drizzling it on grilled salmon, grilled shrimp, or fish tacos. A little goes a long way, so use it sparingly.

1½ cups virgin olive oil

¼   cup soy sauce

¼   cup rice wine vinegar

¼   cup sesame oil

¼   cup honey

¼   cup sweet chile garlic sauce *(such as Mae Ploy)*
    Juice of 2 limes

3   tablespoons chopped fresh cilantro

1   tablespoon peeled and minced fresh ginger

¼   teaspoon crushed red pepper flakes
    Kosher salt

Place all the ingredients in a blender and blend for 1 minute or until thoroughly incorporated. Keep in an airtight container in the refrigerator for up to 1 week.

NUTRITION FACTS *—2 tablespoons*

180 calories	**5G** total carbohydrate
18G total fat	**4G** sugars
1.5G saturated fat	**190MG** sodium
0MG cholesterol	**0G** protein

Fresh Basil Pesto

Yields 1¾ cups

Most people know what pesto sauce is, but fewer know that the origin of the Italian word describes the crushing or pounding of ingredients in a mortar with a pestle. Instead of using the traditional tools, most chefs today use a food processor fitted with a sharp metal blade. Pesto comes in many variations, but by far the most common is basil pesto, which has many uses — as pizza topping, pasta sauce, sandwich spread, or a wonderful marinade for seafood and chicken. You can also use a schmear as a great way to finish these proteins after cooking.

¼   cup pine nuts

2   cups packed fresh basil leaves

2   cloves garlic, chopped

¾   cup freshly grated
     Parmesan cheese

¾   cup olive oil

¼   teaspoon kosher salt
     Freshly ground black pepper

CHEF'S NOTE

Other nuts such as walnuts or pecans can be used.

Preheat the oven to 325 degrees F. Place the pine nuts on a small cookie sheet and toast in the oven for 10 minutes or until slightly brown. Remove from the oven and let cool. Transfer the pine nuts to a food processor or blender. Add the basil, garlic, and Parmesan, and process well. With the motor running, slowly add the olive oil in a steady stream and continue to process for 1 minute. Season with salt and pepper. Transfer to an airtight container and keep refrigerated for up to 2 weeks, or freeze immediately.

NUTRITION FACTS *—2 tablespoons*

160 calories	**1G** total carb.
17G total fat	**0G** sugars
3.5G saturated fat	**160MG** sodium
5MG cholesterol	**3G** protein

Secret Sauce

Yields 2½ cups

Oops! I guess this recipe is less of a secret now that we've published it! I suppose you can still let your inquisitive guests know that your recipe does have secret ingredients — the smoked paprika and Sriracha sauce — that you cannot divulge. Really this is just a "fancied-up" ketchup that many of our customers have come to love. It's the ideal condiment with just about anything grilled — from burgers to steaks to chicken — and it's also great with French fries.

1   cup mayonnaise
½   cup tomato ketchup
½   cup sour cream
½   cup dill pickle relish
1   tablespoon Worcestershire sauce
½   tablespoon smoked paprika
1   teaspoon Sriracha sauce
1   teaspoon garlic salt
1   teaspoon onion salt
½   teaspoon freshly ground black pepper

Place all the ingredients in a mixing bowl and thoroughly combine with a whisk. Transfer to an airtight container and keep refrigerated for up to 2 weeks.

NUTRITION FACTS —*2 tablespoons*

100 calories	2G total carbohydrate
10G total fat	2G sugars
2G saturated fat	320MG sodium
10MG cholesterol	0G protein

Steak Sauce

Yields 2 cups

I must admit I'm addicted to steak sauce. I realize chefs are held to a higher standard when it comes to eating our own food, but please leave me alone when you see me adding this sauce to my steak. After all, to each their own when it comes to favorite foods and dining!

1   cup tomato ketchup
¾   cup Worcestershire sauce
2   teaspoons garlic salt
1   teaspoon onion salt
1   teaspoon freshly ground black pepper

Place all the ingredients in mixing bowl and thoroughly combine with a whisk. Transfer to an airtight container and keep refrigerated for up to 2 weeks.

NUTRITION FACTS —*2 tablespoons*

25 calories	6G total carbohydrate
0G total fat	5G sugars
0G saturated fat	520MG sodium
0MG cholesterol	0G protein

English Pea Pesto

Yields 3¾ cups

This version of the classic pesto began as a way of using a lot of fresh peas we had bought in the height of the summer season. The color and flavor of the peas make a perfect match for the fresh ricotta and the traditional pesto ingredients. Use this recipe the same way you would use basil pesto.

¼ cup pine nuts	½ cup fresh ricotta
1½ cups frozen peas	1½ cups olive oil
1 clove garlic, minced	1 teaspoon kosher salt
¼ cup fresh basil leaves	⅛ teaspoon freshly ground black pepper
Juice of 1 lemon	
1 cup Pecorino Romano or Parmesan cheese	

Preheat the oven to 325 degrees F. Place the pine nuts on a small cookie sheet and toast in the oven for 10 minutes or until slightly brown. Remove from the oven and let cool.

Place the peas in a food processor and let defrost for 30 minutes. Add the garlic, basil, lemon juice, Pecorino, ricotta, and pine nuts and process for 30 seconds. Slowly add the olive oil in a steady stream and process until smooth. Season with salt and pepper. Transfer to an airtight container and keep refrigerated for up to 1 week.

CHEF'S NOTE

For an even smoother puree, use a blender. If the pesto is too thick, add a little more oil.

NUTRITION FACTS
—2 tablespoons

140 calories
14G total fat
3G saturated fat
5MG cholesterol
2G total carbohydrate
0G sugars
140MG sodium
3G protein

Chimichurri

Yields 2 cups

Here's a great sauce for grilling, either marinating beforehand or finishing meats or vegetables as they come off your grill. Chimichurri is a classic recipe originating in Argentina, where they're known for excellent cuts of meat cooked on large wood-fired grills. I also like basting simple seafood skewers with a touch of this sauce right when I take them from the grill. Because of the vinegar content, a little goes a long way.

1 bunch fresh Italian parsley, most of the stems removed
1 bunch fresh cilantro, most of the stems removed
¼ cup fresh oregano leaves
1 tablespoon chopped red onion
4 cloves garlic, chopped
1½ cups olive oil
2 tablespoons sherry vinegar
1 tablespoon fresh lemon juice
1 tablespoon kosher salt
Pinch of crushed red pepper flakes

Place all the ingredients in a blender and blend until smooth. If you prefer a more chunky consistency, pulse while blending. Transfer to an airtight container and keep refrigerated for up to 1 week.

NUTRITION FACTS *—2 tablespoons*

170 calories	1G total carbohydrate
21G total fat	0G sugars
3G saturated fat	310MG sodium
0MG cholesterol	0G protein

Simple Aioli

Yields 2 cups

Years ago when I was still a full-time chef in the kitchen, I used to test the cooks applying for a job by having them make me an aioli. I would then ask them to flavor the aioli and explain how the aioli matched up to certain foods. This is a good basic recipe that can be varied endlessly. If you want it spicy, add Tabasco or Sriracha sauce; if you want to give it an Asian twist, add some soy sauce. If you want to add depth, blend with anchovy.

4   large egg yolks

1½ teaspoons Dijon mustard

2   cloves garlic, chopped

1   cup olive oil

4   teaspoons fresh lemon juice *(1 large lemon)*

1   teaspoon kosher salt

    Pinch of freshly ground white pepper

Place the egg yolks in a food processor and add the mustard and garlic. With the motor running, slowly add ½ cup of the olive oil in a steady stream. Add the lemon juice and then the rest of the oil and season with salt and pepper. Scrape down the sides of the bowl and process for a few seconds more. Transfer to an airtight container and keep refrigerated for up to 1 week.

For the Roasted Garlic Aioli that accompanies the Truffle Fries on page 43 and "The Cuban" on page 137, first roast 1 whole bulb of garlic: Preheat the oven to 300 degrees F. With a sharp knife, carefully cut off about ¼ inch from the top (pointy) part of the garlic cloves. Place the bulb on a large sheet of aluminum foil (about 12 inches square), drizzle with 1 tablespoon olive oil, and sprinkle with a few pinches of salt. Wrap tightly in the foil and place in a small roasting pan or on a cookie sheet. Roast in the oven for 45 to 50 minutes or until soft. Remove from the oven and let cool. With your fingers, squeeze the entire bulb from the bottom to release the softened roasted garlic. Add to the Simple Aioli and mix thoroughly. Transfer to an airtight container and keep refrigerated for up to 1 week.

CHEF'S NOTE

If you only have a large, 4-quart or 5-quart food processor, it may be too large to properly blend the yolks and oil without breaking the mixture. A blender would be a better choice.

NUTRITION FACTS —*2 tablespoons*

180 calories	1G total carbohydrate
19G total fat	0G sugars
3G saturated fat	180MG sodium
60MG cholesterol	1G protein

Chipotle Mayonnaise

Yields 1¼ cups

Chipotles are dried and smoked jalapeños and most likely, you will find them in the Mexican section of your grocery store packaged in adobo sauce. Adobo sauce is a combination of spices, most notably paprika, garlic, and oregano, with a vinegar base. A little goes a very long way so after opening the canned chipotles, it's best to freeze the remainder for the next use. You can also use chipotles in stews and soups where you want that deep, rich, spicy taste.

2   tablespoons canned chipotle chiles in adobo sauce
1   cup mayonnaise or Simple Aioli *(page 227)*
     Juice of 1 lime

In a food processor, puree the chipotles in abodo until smooth. Transfer to a small bowl, add the mayonnaise and lime juice, and mix with a whisk until incorporated. Transfer to an airtight container and keep refrigerated for up to 1 week.

NUTRITION FACTS —*2 tablespoons*

200 calories	**0G** total carbohydrate
22G total fat	**0G** sugars
3G saturated fat	**160MG** sodium
10MG cholesterol	**0G** protein

Caramelized Onion Dip

Yields 3 cups

This is a great dip to accompany any crisp food — raw vegetables, new potatoes, or French fries. It also makes a great topping for steak.

1   tablespoon unsalted butter
1   tablespoon olive oil
2   large white onions, peeled and thinly sliced *(julienne)*
⅛   teaspoon kosher salt
⅛   teaspoon freshly ground black pepper
1   teaspoon garlic salt
1   tablespoon light brown sugar
1   tablespoon balsamic vinegar
1½   cups sour cream
2   teaspoons Worcestershire sauce

Set a large, heavy-bottomed sauté pan over medium heat. Add the butter and olive oil and when the butter has melted, add the onions, salt, and pepper. Turn down the heat to medium-low and cook the onions, without stirring, for about 5 minutes; do not let them burn. Add the garlic salt and when the onions start to brown, stir occasionally so they caramelize evenly. When the onions have browned consistently, stir in the brown sugar and then deglaze the pan with the balsamic vinegar. Continue cooking the onions for about 2 minutes longer until they are a deeply caramelized color. Transfer the onions to a large plate or cookie sheet, spread out evenly, and let cool.

Transfer the cooled onions to a food processor fitted with a metal blade. Pulse the onions about 15 times but do not totally puree them. Transfer to a mixing bowl and add the sour cream and Worcestershire sauce. Mix together and adjust the seasonings to taste. The dip will keep in an airtight container in the refrigerator for up to 3 days.

NUTRITION FACTS —*2 tablespoons*

45 calories	**2G** total carbohydrate
4G total fat	**2G** sugars
2G saturated fat	**105MG** sodium
10MG cholesterol	**2G** protein

Smoked Tomato Ketchup

Yields 3½ cups

Not everyone has a backyard smoker, so here we offer a stovetop smoking technique. Needless to say, you'll need to use a grill if you have indoor smoke detectors. You can use the smoking method for other ingredients when you want that attractively smoky flavor. Be sure to store the ketchup in an airtight container or everything in your fridge will take on a smoky essence.

3   cups mesquite wood chips

6   plum tomatoes, halved lengthwise

1   white onion, quartered

4   large cloves garlic, peeled

2   tablespoons olive oil

½   cup tomato paste

3   tablespoons Worcestershire sauce

½   cup light brown sugar

¼   cup molasses

¼   cup apple cider vinegar

½   teaspoon salt

½   teaspoon freshly ground black pepper

In a large bowl, let the wood chips soak in 2 cups water for 20 minutes. Remove the wood chips from the water and place in a stainless-steel roasting pan off to one side. Place a wire rack over the pan. Place the tomatoes, onion, and garlic on the wire rack and cover with a lid big enough so the smoke does not escape. Place the pan over a very low flame. Smoke the tomatoes, onion, and garlic for about 30 minutes or until they absorb a smoky essence and flavor. If you own a backyard smoker, follow the manufacturer's instructions and smoke the ingredients for 30 to 45 minutes.

Heat the oil in a saucepan and add the smoked onion, tomatoes, and garlic. Sauté over medium-high heat for about 3 minutes. Add the tomato paste and sauté for 3 minutes more, then stir in the Worcestershire sauce. Add the sugar and stir to dissolve. Stir in the molasses, vinegar, salt, pepper, and 2 cups of water and bring to a gentle simmer; continue to simmer for about 45 minutes. If the ketchup looks like it is getting too thick, add a little more water.

Transfer the ketchup mixture to a blender large enough to hold the ingredients, or blend in batches. Carefully pulse the blender while holding the lid so the ingredients do not escape. Turn the blender to the puree setting and blend for 1 minute or until completely emulsified. Adjust the seasonings as necessary. The ketchup will keep in an airtight container in the refrigerator for up to 2 weeks.

NUTRITION FACTS —*2 tablespoons*

60 calories	0G saturated fat	11G total carbohydrate	90MG sodium
1.5G total fat	0MG cholesterol	10G sugars	0G protein

8 DESSERTS AND COOKIES

DESSERTS AND COOKIES

Dessert has always been a tough sell at lunchtime in the Neiman Marcus restaurants. People have a tendency to eat lighter during the day and selling desserts can be a real chore for our servers and chefs! So over the years we've had to improvise and come up with smaller types of desserts that our customers can feel less guilty about eating at lunch. In this chapter you will find great dessert recipes that can be made in a large or smaller format and that will also work well for a small catered affair in your home. One of the more popular features of our downtown Dallas restaurant is the Holiday Buffet that takes place in the Zodiac Room from Thanksgiving through New Year's Eve. While the buffet is being served we take special care with our dessert selection and serve them in a miniature style so our guests can nibble and sample all the holiday dessert treats. You'll find many of these recipes here — such as the lollipop cheesecakes, white and dark chocolate mousse cups, and the tiramisu, which we serve in smaller glasses during the holiday time.

One of the fun parts of my job is I get to eat for a living, and it's especially fun when eating dessert samples. Over the years I've been sent dessert tastings ranging from a cookie someone baked in their home and then wrapped and shipped to my office in their own Tupperware container, to exquisite cakes sent by famous concert pianist Dino Kartsonakis — which, incidentally, were some of the best cakes I've ever tasted. I think it's important here at Neiman Marcus restaurants that we give our customers a broad range of offerings; purchasing finished desserts from some of the best dessert makers in each city is good for the customer and good for the business. Among the dessert vendors we feature at our stores are Sweet Lady Jane cakes in Los Angeles and Lady M Confections in New York.

Cookies are another popular dessert offering here at Neiman Marcus. We've come up with our signature small cookie box that people love to share at the table or that they can take home in the cute little jewelry boxes that we get from our Precious Jewelry salons. I can't begin to tell you how many cookies we sell yearly in all of our restaurants but I will say that since the Internet made famous the urban myth of the Neiman Marcus Chocolate Chip Cookie (see page 19), it has become so popular that we've gone headfirst into cookie production. Hey — as the old saying goes, "make cookies while the sun shines." And BTW, I'm a big fan of Fig Newtons, and not the low-fat type! Check out the Gristmill Grahams on page 250 — my play on the classic Fig Newton.

Chocolate Velvet Cake

Yields 10 servings

I have loved this cake from the first time I tried it. It's another old Helen Corbitt recipe, brought back to life here at Neiman Marcus. This is for the chocolate cake lovers who are looking for that "something special" cake with a different twist. I especially love the chocolate frosting. With the addition of the dark corn syrup it will form almost a chocolate crust once the cake has time to set up. This makes it ideal for traveling, knowing the frosting won't smudge or melt on the way to a friend's house for dinner. Be sure to invest in a nice cake plate with a cover. Trade secret number one: Cakes are best eaten at room temperature.

FOR THE CAKE

1½ cups cake flour, plus some
      for dusting the pans

½   cup cocoa powder

2   teaspoons baking powder

1½ teaspoons baking soda

1   teaspoon salt

1¼ cups granulated sugar

1   cup sour cream

¼   cup milk

⅓   cup vegetable oil

2   tablespoons vegetable shortening

1   teaspoon vanilla extract

2   large eggs

FOR THE FROSTING

1¾ cups heavy cream

⅓   cup dark corn syrup

1   pound semisweet chocolate chips

Preheat the oven to 350 degrees F. Spray two 8-inch cake pans with nonstick cooking spray and lightly flour it, shaking off any flour that does not stick. To prepare the cake, sift together the flour, cocoa, baking powder, baking soda, and salt into a bowl and set aside. Combine the sugar, sour cream, and milk in a bowl of an electric mixer fitted with the paddle attachment and add the oil, shortening, and vanilla. Mix on low speed for 2 minutes until thoroughly incorporated and smooth. Using a spatula, scrape down the sides of the bowl and add the eggs, one at a time, on low speed. Scrape down the sides of the bowl again and add the flour and cocoa mixture in one-third increments, waiting for each amount to mix in well and scraping down the sides of the bowl after each addition. Transfer the mixture to the prepared cake pans and bake for 25 to 30 minutes or until a toothpick inserted into the middle of the cake comes out clean. Let the cake cool for 10 minutes and then turn out onto a wire rack to cool completely.

While the cake is baking, prepare the frosting. Place the cream and syrup in a saucepan and bring to a boil. Place the chocolate chips in a mixing bowl and pour the boiling cream mixture over them, whisking until smooth. Let the mixture cool and then transfer to the bowl of an electric mixer fitted with the paddle attachment. Beat for 4 minutes, until fluffy.

Spread the frosting between the two layers, then frost the top and sides of the cake.

NUTRITION FACTS —*1 serving*

750 calories	**22G** saturated fat	**84G** total carbohydrate	**550MG** sodium
44G total fat	**110MG** cholesterol	**61G** sugars	**9G** protein

Italian Cream Cake

Yields 10 servings

This cake was famous at Neiman Marcus back in the 1950s, and still today we get requests to make it for birthdays and other special events and celebrations in our customers' lives. In fact, it's so popular, we sell more whole cakes than slices!

FOR THE CAKE

2   cups sweetened coconut flakes

½   cup walnuts

½   cup unsalted butter

½   cup vegetable shortening

1½ cups plus ⅓ cup granulated sugar

4   large eggs, separated

1   teaspoon vanilla extract

2   cups cake flour, plus some for the pans

1   teaspoon baking soda

½   cup buttermilk

FOR THE PASTRY CREAM FILLING

6   large egg yolks

½   cup granulated sugar

¼   cup all-purpose flour

2   tablespoons cornstarch

2   cups milk

1½ teaspoons vanilla extract

FOR THE BUTTER–CREAM CHEESE FROSTING

4   tablespoons unsalted butter

¾   cup *(6 ounces)* cream cheese

2   cups confectioners' sugar

1   teaspoon vanilla extract

1   teaspoon fresh lemon juice

SUGGESTED WINE PAIRING

Tiramisú Italian Liqueur

Preheat the oven to 350 degrees F. To prepare the cake, spread the coconut flakes evenly on an ungreased cookie sheet and transfer to the oven. Toast for 3 or 4 minutes, watching carefully, until nicely browned. Remove, let cool, and set aside. Place the walnuts in a single layer on the cookie sheet and toast in the oven for about 10 minutes, until fragrant, shaking or stirring the nuts once or twice. Remove, let cool, and set aside.

Turn down the oven to 325 degrees F. Place the butter, shortening, and 1½ cups of the sugar in the work bowl of an electric mixer fitted with the paddle attachment. Beat at medium speed for about 30 seconds, until the mixture is fluffy. Turn down the speed to low and beat in the egg yolks and vanilla, stopping to scrape down the sides of the bowl with a spatula. In a bowl, sift together the cake flour and the baking soda and then add to the bowl of the mixer. Beat on slow speed for about 15 seconds, stopping once to scrape down the sides of the bowl. Add the buttermilk, ½ cup of the toasted coconut, and the toasted walnuts, and beat for about 15 seconds, stopping again to scrape down the sides of the bowl. Transfer the batter mixture to a clean mixing bowl. Clean and dry the work bowl of the mixer and fit with a whisk attachment. Add the egg whites and the remaining ⅓ cup sugar, and using the whisk attachment, beat on high speed for about 1½ minutes, until stiff peaks form. Fold the egg white mixture into the batter and mix well with a spatula.

Spray two 9-inch cake pans with nonstick spray and flour the bottom of the pans, discarding any flour that does not stick to the pans. Divide the cake batter evenly between the two pans, transfer to the oven, and bake for about 30 minutes or until a toothpick inserted in the middle of the cake comes out clean. Cool the pans on a wire rack, and when cool, run a knife around the edge of the cake pans to loosen and invert the cakes on plates to release.

To prepare the pastry cream filling, place the egg yolks and sugar in a mixing bowl and whisk with a wire whisk until pale yellow in color and ribbons form. In a separate bowl, sift together the flour and cornstarch and beat into the egg yolk mixture. Pour the milk and vanilla into a small heavy-bottomed saucepan and bring to a simmer over medium heat. Slowly add the hot milk mixture to the egg yolk mixture and whisk continuously to temper and prevent curdling. Pour the tempered mixture into the saucepan and continue cooking over low heat, whisking continuously, until almost boiling and thickened (if lumps form, whisk harder). Remove the pan from the heat

and whisk for 1 minute longer. Transfer to a clean bowl, cover the surface of the pastry cream with plastic wrap, and refrigerate for 2 hours or until set.

To prepare the butter–cream cheese frosting, place the butter and cream cheese in the work bowl of an electric mixer fitted with the paddle attachment. Beat on medium speed for about 30 seconds, until fluffy. Add the confectioners' sugar, vanilla, and lemon juice, and beat for 30 seconds longer, until the mixture is completely incorporated.

Using a long, clean bread knife, cut the cakes in half horizontally (giving you four sections). Reserve one of the bottom-half sections. Top each of the remaining three sections with one-third of the pastry cream, using a spatula to evenly spread the pastry cream over the surface. Place the three cake sections on top of one another with the pastry cream facing up. Place the reserved cake section upside-down on top of the other three sections, so the bottom side faces up. Using a metal spatula, evenly cover the top and sides of the cake with the frosting. Once the cake is frosted, lift it up, holding the cake from the bottom, and press some of the remaining coconut flakes into the sides of the cake. Transfer the cake to a serving platter and top with the remaining coconut flakes.

NUTRITION FACTS —*1 serving*

870 calories	108G total carb.
44G total fat	80G sugars
23G saturated fat	290MG sodium
245MG cholesterol	12G protein

Tiramisu in a Glass

Yields 10 servings

Tiramisu means "pick-me-up" in Italian and in this version we build it in a glass, giving your guests a visual clue of all the recipe components. And literally, they will then "pick up" the glass filled with the tiramisu. The ladyfingers are meant to be eaten with your fingers as a vehicle to scoop the wonderful mascarpone filling from the glass.

7	large eggs
1	cup granulated sugar
1	cup heavy cream
3	cups mascarpone cheese
1½	cups miniature chocolate chips
½	cup instant espresso powder, or 1 cup brewed espresso
½	cup light brown sugar
2	tablespoons cocoa powder, plus ⅛ teaspoon for dusting
½	cup Kahlúa or other coffee liqueur
30	ladyfingers *(see Chef's Notes)*
¾	cup shaved dark chocolate

SUGGESTED WINE PAIRING

Tiramisú Italian Liqueur

Place the eggs and granulated sugar in a stainless-steel bowl and mix to combine. Prepare a double boiler by bringing a saucepan with 2 inches of water to a simmer and placing the bowl with the egg mixture on top, making sure the bottom of the bowl does not touch the water. Whisk the mixture for about 6 minutes until it forms thick ribbons and triples in size. Transfer the mixture to the bowl of an electric mixer fitted with the whisk attachment and beat on medium speed for about 5 minutes. In a separate bowl, whip the heavy cream until soft peaks form. Fold half of the mascarpone into the egg mixture and then fold in half of the whipped cream. Fold in the rest of the mascarpone and then the rest of the whipped cream. Fold in the chocolate chips and keep refrigerated.

Bring 4 cups water to a boil in a saucepan. Add the espresso powder, brown sugar, cocoa powder, and Kahlúa and mix until the sugar is dissolved. Remove from the stove and set aside to cool.

Assemble ten glasses (large, stemmed wine glasses work well) and divide the mascarpone filling among the glasses. (If you're so inclined, fill a pastry bag with the filling and use it to fill each glass evenly.) Line each glass with four ladyfingers and drizzle each glass with the Kahlúa sauce. Add a couple shavings of chocolate to each glass, dust with the remaining cocoa powder, and serve.

CHEF'S NOTES

For the ladyfingers, use a good-quality Italian brand — they're worth it.

Use a vegetable peeler to shave the chocolate.

Well worth the effort – and the calories.

NUTRITION FACTS —*1 serving*

760 calories	**28G** saturated fat	**74G** total carbohydrate	**135MG** sodium
47G total fat	**300MG** cholesterol	**48G** sugars	**12G** protein

Rice Pudding Crème Brûlée

Yields 22 servings

This is a special-occasion dessert my mom used to make. Every time we serve this at my house, it ushers in shared memories of when we all first tasted rice pudding. When we make it at home, we get creative by using a different type of alcohol each time: From rum, to brandy, to Scotch, to amaretto. It's whatever strikes your fancy and what works best for the time of year.

1	cup raisins
¼	cup dark rum
5	cups milk
1½	cups plus 2 tablespoons granulated sugar
¼	teaspoon kosher salt
1	vanilla bean, split and seeds scraped, or 1 teaspoon vanilla extract
1	cup long-grain white rice
1	cup heavy cream
3	large eggs
½	teaspoon ground cinnamon

SUGGESTED WINE PAIRING

Seven Daughters Moscato

Preheat the oven to 375 degrees F. Spray eight 6-ounce ramekins with nonstick spray and set aside. Put the raisins in a bowl, add the rum, and let the raisins soak while you cook the rice.

Pour the milk into a saucepan and add 1½ cups of the sugar, the salt, vanilla bean (or extract), and rice. Bring to a boil over medium heat. Reduce the heat to low, cover the pan, and cook, stirring often, for about 35 minutes, or until the rice is tender. Turn off the heat and let cool.

Bring about 4 cups water to a boil in a saucepan. Meanwhile, in a bowl, whisk together the cream and eggs. When the rice is cool, remove the vanilla bean and stir in the egg mixture, the cinnamon, and the marinated raisins (add any leftover rum from the bowl, if you wish). Pour the rice mixture into the prepared ramekins.

Place the ramekins in a small roasting pan, transfer to the oven, and pour the boiling water into the pan so it comes halfway up the sides of the ramekins. Bake for about 30 minutes or until the custard is set. Remove from the oven and let cool. Sprinkle the remaining sugar over each custard and burn the tops with a kitchen torch until the sugar is dissolved and browned. Serve warm, at room temperature, or chilled.

CHEF'S NOTE

This recipe yields a large amount, so choose what you feel represents a nice size portion. We decided on about ½ cup per guest for a nice finish to a dinner party. But don't worry— leftovers will never go to waste here!

NUTRITION FACTS —*½ cup*

200	calories	6G	saturated fat	23G	total carbohydrate	75MG	sodium
11G	total fat	65MG	cholesterol	11G	sugars	5G	protein

CHEF'S NOTES

Keep all the mixing bowls and whisks you use chilled.

Use a vegetable peeler to "shave" the chocolate.

White and Dark Chocolate Mousse Cups

Yields 8 servings

A good mousse recipe is a must for your repertoire. Many adaptations to this recipe work — from cake fillings with mousse or a filling for cream puffs — but here we kept it simple with a color contrast in a martini-style glass, with a simple garnish.

1   cup white chocolate chips

3   large egg whites

6   tablespoons granulated sugar

⅛   teaspoon cream of tartar

¾   cup heavy cream

2   cups semisweet chocolate bar cut into small chunks

½   cup unsalted butter, diced

1   tablespoon instant espresso power

3   tablespoons hot water

2   cups heavy cream

6   large eggs, separated

2   tablespoons granulated sugar

¾   cup shaved dark chocolate, for garnish

24   raspberries, for garnish

NUTRITION FACTS —*1 serving dark mousse*

690 calories	45G total carb.
56G total fat	36G sugars
34G saturated fat	85MG sodium
270MG cholesterol	9G protein

NUTRITION FACTS —*1 serving white mousse*

260 calories	23G total carb.
18G total fat	22G sugars
11G saturated fat	50MG sodium
45MG cholesterol	3G protein

To prepare the white chocolate mousse, place the white chocolate chips in a stainless-steel bowl. Prepare a double boiler by bringing a saucepan with 2 inches of water to a simmer and placing the bowl with the chocolate on top, making sure the bottom of the bowl does not touch the water. Melt the chocolate, stirring occasionally. Place the egg whites in the bowl of an electric mixer fitted with the wire whisk. Begin whisking until foamy. In a saucepan, combine the sugar, cream of tartar, and 3 tablespoons water. Bring the syrup to a boil (or until a candy thermometer reaches 238 degrees F.). Remove from the heat and pour the hot syrup in a thin, steady stream over the whisked egg whites to form a meringue. Whisk the meringue until stiff peaks form. Carefully fold one-quarter of the meringue into the melted chocolate. Then fold this mixture back into the rest of the meringue mixture, and let cool.

In a bowl, whip the cream to soft peaks. Stir one-quarter of the whipped cream into the meringue mixture to lighten it. Then fold in the remaining whipped cream and thoroughly combine. Keep refrigerated until ready to serve.

To prepare the dark chocolate mousse, place the chocolate and butter in a stainless-steel bowl. In a cup, mix the espresso powder with the hot water, stir to dissolve, and add to the chocolate. Prepare a double boiler by bringing a saucepan with 2 inches of water to a simmer and placing the bowl with the chocolate mixture on top, making sure the bottom of the bowl does not touch the water. Melt the chocolate mixture, stirring occasionally. Remove from the heat and let cool until slightly warm (about 90 degrees F.).

In a bowl, whip the cream to soft peaks and set aside in the refrigerator. In a clean bowl, whisk the egg whites with the sugar until soft peaks form. Once the chocolate mixture is cooled, gently whisk in the egg yolks. Using a rubber spatula, fold in half of the chilled whipped cream and then fold in the egg whites in two increments. Fold in the rest of the whipped cream.

Divide both mousses evenly among the serving glasses, with the dark chocolate mousse on the bottom and the white on top. Garnish each serving with shaved chocolate and 3 raspberries.

"Sock It to Me" Cake

Yield 10 servings

This breakfast cake is a favorite in my house; I like to make it on weekend mornings to go with coffee or brunch. It's always gone before dinnertime! The recipe originated way back, with a member of my kitchen crew at the Adolphus Hotel in Dallas. His version was based on a Southern recipe that seems to vary from one baker to the next.

3½ cups all-purpose flour

1 teaspoon baking soda

1 teaspoon kosher salt

1 cup unsalted butter

2 cups granulated sugar

½ cup light brown sugar

6 large eggs

1 cup sour cream

1 teaspoon vanilla extract

1 tablespoon ground cinnamon

½ cup chopped pecans

2 tablespoons confectioners' sugar, for dusting

SUGGESTED WINE PAIRING

Fizz 56 Sparkling Moscato d'Asti

Preheat the oven to 350 degrees F. Generously spray a 10-inch Bundt pan or tubular baking pan with nonstick spray and dust with ½ cup of the flour, discarding any flour that does not stick to the pan. In a mixing bowl, sift together the remaining 3 cups flour, the baking soda, and salt and set aside. Place the butter, granulated sugar, and brown sugar in the bowl of an electric mixer fitted with the paddle attachment and beat together on low speed for 2 minutes or until fluffy. Add the eggs, one at a time, and mix on medium speed for 3 minutes. Add the sour cream, vanilla, and cinnamon and then mix in the flour mixture in three increments, waiting for each amount to mix in and scraping down the sides of the bowl each time with a spatula. Fold in the pecans and mix until incorporated.

Transfer the mixture to the prepared pan and bake for about 1 hour or until a toothpick inserted in the center comes out clean. Let the cake cool for 15 minutes and then turn out onto a serving platter. Sprinkle with the confectioners' sugar and serve warm.

This breakfast cake is a favorite in my house.

NUTRITION FACTS —*1 serving*

580 calories	**10G** saturated fat	**89G** total carbohydrate	**450MG** sodium
20G total fat	**150MG** cholesterol	**54G** sugars	**10G** protein

Butterscotch–Macadamia Nut Pie

Yield 10 servings

We can't take this scrumptious dessert off the menu at our Mariposa restaurant in Honolulu. It's been there since we opened in 1997. At some point, I guess we'll have to move the recipe to the Neiman Marcus "Classics" section! This pie is decadent, super rich, and a real treat.

FOR THE PIE SHELL

1¼ cups all-purpose flour

½ cup unsalted butter

1 tablespoon granulated sugar

⅛ teaspoon salt

¼ cup ice water

**FOR THE BUTTERSCOTCH–
MACADAMIA NUT FILLING**

1½ cups chopped macadamia nuts

1¼ cups milk

½ teaspoon vanilla extract

½ cup unsalted butter

1⅓ cups light brown sugar

⅓ cup all-purpose flour

1 teaspoon salt

7 large egg yolks

1 cup heavy cream

1 teaspoon granulated sugar

SUGGESTED WINE PAIRING

Kracher Trockenbeeren Auslese NV

To prepare the pie shell, place the flour in the work bowl of an electric mixer fitted with the paddle attachment and add the butter, granulated sugar, and salt. Beat the mixture on low speed for about 2½ minutes or until the dough has a mealy consistency. Add the ice water and continue to beat on low speed for 15 seconds longer, or until the dough pulls away from the sides of the bowl. Remove the dough from the bowl and form into a smooth ball. Wrap with plastic wrap and refrigerate for at least 4 hours.

Unwrap the dough and place on a lightly floured work surface. Using a rolling pin, roll the dough into a 15-inch circle, about ⅛ inch thick. Carefully transfer the dough to a 10-inch removeable-bottom tart ring and press gently into the bottom and against the sides. Using a small paring knife, trim away the excess dough. Refrigerate the pie shell for 30 minutes.

Preheat the oven to 350 degrees F. Remove the pie shell from the refrigerator and pierce the bottom of the dough with a fork ("docking" the dough). Cover the empty pie shell with parchment paper or a coffee filter and cover that with pastry weights or dried beans. Transfer to the oven and bake for 20 minutes, until golden brown. Transfer to a wire rack to cool. Keep the oven on.

To prepare the butterscotch–macadamia nut filling, place the macadamia nuts in a single layer on a cookie sheet and toast in the oven for about 10 minutes, until fragrant, shaking or stirring the nuts once or twice. Remove, let cool, and set aside.

This Macadamia nut pie is fast becoming a Neiman Marcus classic!

Pour the milk and vanilla into a small saucepan and bring almost to a boil over medium heat. Remove and set aside. Meanwhile, melt the butter in a heavy-bottomed saucepan over medium heat and cook for about 2 minutes until it begins to brown. Add the brown sugar to the butter and cook for 1 minute. Add the flour and salt and stir vigorously with a wooden spoon until well incorporated. Remove from the heat.

In a mixing bowl, whisk the egg yolks until pale yellow in color and ribbons form. Slowly add the hot milk mixture to the yolks, tempering slowly while whisking continuously. Slowly add this mixture to the butter and flour mixture over medium-low heat, and whisk continuously for about 1 minute, until very thick. Immediately pour the custard mixture into a mixing bowl and let cool to room temperature. Fold 1 cup of the toasted macadamia nuts into the custard, stirring vigorously with a wooden spoon to soften the mixture and make it easier to spread. Spoon the mixture into the prepared pie shell and spread with a spatula to fill the shell evenly.

Place the cream and granulated sugar into the work bowl of an electric mixer fitted with the whisk attachment and whip until the cream is fluffy and soft peaks form, about 2 minutes. Using a spatula, top the pie with the whipped cream and sprinkle with the remaining ½ cup macadamia nuts. Transfer to the refrigerator for at least 1 hour to set before serving.

CHEF'S NOTE

You will need to prepare the pie shell several hours ahead of time.

NUTRITION FACTS —*1 serving*

| 660 calories | 21G saturated fat | 53G total carbohydrate | 500MG sodium |
| 47G total fat | 215MG cholesterol | 33G sugars | 10G protein |

Cheesecake Lollipops

Yields 5 dozen

These little treats get rave reviews whenever we serve them at events here at Neiman Marcus. They're so simple to make, yet such a nice surprise when served to your guests.

SUGGESTED WINE PAIRING

Two Hands Brilliant Disguise Moscato

Preheat the oven to 375 degrees F. To prepare the crust, place the graham cracker crumbs in a mixing bowl and add the melted butter and cinnamon. Mix well with a fork. Spread out the mixture evenly on a 9-inch by 12-inch baking pan. Transfer to the oven and bake for 5 minutes. Remove the pan from the oven and let cool.

To prepare the cheesecake, place the cream cheese and sugar in the bowl of an electric mixer fitted with the paddle attachment and cream together on medium speed for 8 minutes. In a bowl, mix the sour cream and cornstarch together and then add to the cream cheese mixture on low speed. Fold in the vanilla bean seeds and lemon zest and mix until incorporated. Stop the mixer and use a spatula to scrape down the sides of the bowl. On low speed, add one egg at a time and incorporate; do not overmix.

Turn down the oven to 325 degrees F. Pour the cheesecake mixture into the prepared graham cracker crust and bake for 25 to 30 minutes. Remove from the oven and let the cheesecake cool to room temperature. When cool, transfer to the freezer for at least 4 hours or overnight.

Line a large cookie sheet with parchment paper. With a ¾-inch round cookie cutter, punch out circles of the cheesecake and place on the parchment paper, about ½ inch apart. When you are finished, transfer the cheesecake circles, uncovered, to the freezer for at least 1 or 2 hours.

CHEF'S NOTES

When cutting out the cheesecake circles, have a small bowl of hot water handy to dip your cutter in so you can easily cut out the rounds.

You can find lollipop sticks in the bakery supply aisle of the grocery store or at hobby and craft stores.

After the cheesecake is frozen, gently push the lollipop sticks into the cheesecake circles, halfway into the cheesecake. Return the lollipops to the freezer while you melt the coating chocolate. Place the chocolate wafers in a microwavable bowl deep enough to be able to immerse the lollipops to completely coat. Microwave the chocolate for 2 to 3 minutes or until the wafers are melted. Keep warm until ready to use. Dip the lollipops to coat and then return to the parchment sheet. Keep frozen and remove to serve as needed.

NUTRITION FACTS —*1 cheesecake lollipop*

80 calories	3G saturated fat	6G total carbohydrate	45MG sodium
5G total fat	20MG cholesterol	4G sugars	1G protein

Gristmill Grahams

Yields about 40 bars

This is a spin on my favorite cookie, the venerable Fig Newton. I found the recipe in an old Helen Corbitt cookbook (Helen put Neiman Marcus's Zodiac Room on the map — for more, see page 9) and adapted the ingredients to better suit my desire for a fresh Fig Newton.

¾ cup vegetable shortening

½ cup granulated sugar

1 cup dark brown sugar

2 large eggs

2 cups all-purpose flour

1 teaspoon baking soda

1 teaspoon salt

1 cup whole-wheat graham flour

1 teaspoon ground nutmeg

1 cup minced dried figs *(about 8 ounces)*

2 teaspoons vanilla extract

½ cup confectioners' sugar

SUGGESTED WINE PAIRING

Kracher Beerenauslese Cuvée

Preheat the oven to 375 degrees F. and lightly butter an 11-inch by 17-inch cookie sheet. In the bowl of an electric mixer fitted with the paddle attachment, beat the shortening with the granulated and brown sugars on low speed for 3 to 4 minutes, until light and fluffy. Add the eggs, one at a time, while beating; when they are incorporated, add the all-purpose flour, baking soda, and salt. Add the graham flour, nutmeg, figs, and vanilla. Continue mixing together for about 5 minutes until all the ingredients are thoroughly blended.

Transfer the dough to the prepared cookie sheet and pat out the dough with your knuckles so it fits in an even layer and into the corners of the pan. Score the top of the dough with a sharp knife into serving squares (2-inch squares). Use a fork to punch 2 or 3 small fork holes into the top of each square. Sprinkle the top of the dough with confectioners' sugar and transfer to the oven. Bake for 12 to 15 minutes or until the dough is puffed up and lightly browned.

Remove the pan from the oven and let cool for 15 minutes. When cool enough, cut out the squares and serve.

NUTRITION FACTS —*1 bar*

| 110 calories | 1G saturated fat | 18G total carbohydrate | 85MG sodium |
| 4G total fat | 10MG cholesterol | 11G sugars | 1G protein |

Love, love Fig Newtons, the full-fat kind, not the skinny version! Try this knockoff…

Pecan Sugar Balls

Yields 3 dozen

I love these morsels because of the light, crunchy texture and the sweetness of the sugar on top. My wife, Jody, enjoys them without the confectioners' sugar coating so you may be inclined to leave some without the coating. This would also help keep the confectioners' sugar from getting all over you once you dive in, although I could think of many worse things than getting a little sugar on your clothes!

1	pound unsalted butter, softened
1¼	cups confectioners' sugar, plus ¼ cup for dusting
4½	cups cake flour
2	cups chopped pecans
2	teaspoons vanilla extract

SUGGESTED WINE PAIRING

Kracher Trockenbeeren Auslese NV

Preheat the oven to 300 degrees F. Lightly spray an 11-inch by 17-inch cookie sheet with nonstick cooking spray and set aside. Place the butter, sugar, flour, pecans, and vanilla in the bowl of an electric mixer fitted with the paddle attachment and cream together for 2 to 3 minutes, or until all the ingredients are well mixed. Transfer to a floured work surface and form the mixture into a large ball. Using your fingers or a small scoop, divide the dough and shape into 36 little half-balls (with one side flattened) and place on the prepared cookie sheet.

Transfer to the oven and bake for 30 minutes or until the cookies are dry in the middle. Remove the pecan sugar balls from the baking sheet and let cool on a wire rack. Dust with the remaining confectioners' sugar before serving.

NUTRITION FACTS —*1 cookie*

150 calories	**13G** total carbohydrate
10G total fat	**3G** sugars
5G saturated fat	**65MG** sodium
20MG cholesterol	**1G** protein

Peanut Butter Cookies

Yields about 4 dozen

Who doesn't like peanut butter? And of course everyone has a favorite peanut butter when it comes to the brand or the texture — smooth or crunchy, or extra-crunchy for the hard-cores. My favorite is smooth and creamy peanut butter, which explains why the recipe calls for that. I would suggest having a little of your favorite jelly in a small dish to spread over the cookies — it's a splurge thing.

1¼ cups granulated sugar	2½ cups all-purpose flour
1 cup light brown sugar	¼ teaspoon baking soda
1¼ cups vegetable shortening	¼ teaspoon salt
1½ cups creamy peanut butter	
2 large eggs	
½ teaspoon vanilla extract	

SUGGESTED WINE PAIRING

Fizz 56 Sparkling Moscato d'Asti

Preheat the oven to 300 degrees F. Spray a cookie sheet with nonstick spray. Place the granulated sugar, brown sugar, shortening, and peanut butter in the bowl of an electric mixer fitted with the paddle attachment. Beat on medium speed for 30 seconds, until the mixture is fluffy. Add the eggs and vanilla and beat for about 30 seconds longer, until thoroughly combined. In a mixing bowl, sift together the flour, baking soda, and salt. Add to the mixer while beating on low speed and beat for about 15 seconds, stopping the mixer once to scrape down the sides of the bowl with a spatula.

Using a 1-ounce scoop or a 2-tablespoon measure, drop the cookie dough onto the prepared cookie sheet in dollops about 3 inches apart. Gently press down on the dough with the back of a fork to create small indentations. Transfer to the oven and bake for about 20 minutes or until the edges are nicely browned. Turn out onto a wire rack to cool. Repeat until all the dough is used — cooling and spraying the cookie sheet with more nonstick spray after each batch. Store in an airtight container.

Oatmeal Raisin Cookies

Yields about 3 dozen

I bet there are some people who think that oatmeal raisin cookies are a health food. But don't be fooled — there's nothing healthy about this recipe at all. But you owe it to yourself and those nearest and dearest to you to have a cookie like this available. If nothing else, make the cookie balls and freeze them unbaked. This way when you have that urge you can bake them to order and eat them warm.

½	cup unsalted butter, softened
½	cup granulated sugar
½	cup light brown sugar
1	large egg
¼	teaspoon almond extract
1	cup all-purpose flour
½	teaspoon baking soda
½	teaspoon salt
1½	cups oatmeal
1½	cups raisins

SUGGESTED WINE PAIRING

Il Poggione Vin Santo

Preheat the oven to 300 degrees F. Spray a cookie sheet with nonstick spray. Place the butter, granulated sugar, and brown sugar in the bowl of an electric mixer fitted with the paddle attachment. Beat on medium speed for about 30 seconds, until the mixture is fluffy. Turn down the speed to low and add the egg and almond extract. Beat for 30 seconds longer, until thoroughly combined. In a mixing bowl, sift together the flour, baking soda, and salt and add to the mixer while beating on low speed. Beat for 15 seconds, stopping the mixer to scrape down the sides of the bowl with a spatula. Add the oatmeal and raisins and mix for about 15 seconds longer.

Using a 1-ounce scoop or a 2-tablespoon measure, drop the cookie dough onto the prepared cookie sheet in dollops about 3 inches apart. Gently press down on the dough with the back of a spoon to create small indentations. Transfer to the oven and bake for about 20 minutes or until the edges are nicely browned. Turn out onto a wire rack to cool. Repeat until all the dough is used — cooling and spraying the cookie sheet with more nonstick spray after each batch. Store in an airtight container.

> The fun part of my job is that I get to eat for a living!

NUTRITION FACTS —*1 cookie*

150 calories	1.5G saturated fat	41G total carbohydrate	75MG sodium
3G total fat	10MG cholesterol	37G sugars	2G protein

White Chocolate–Macadamia Nut Cookies with Cranberries

Yields about 4 dozen

I love the chewiness of sun-dried cranberries, and they make such a good match for the chocolate and nuts, but this recipe is great even without the cranberries. Feel free to use white chocolate chunks instead of the morsels for an even more decadent cookie.

½	cup unsalted butter, softened
1	cup granulated sugar
1	cup light brown sugar
2	large eggs
1	teaspoon vanilla extract
2	cups all purpose flour
1	teaspoon salt
¼	teaspoon baking powder
1	cup macadamia nuts, toasted and chopped
¾	cup toasted grated sweetened coconut
1	cup white chocolate chips or morsels
1	cup dried cranberries

SUGGESTED WINE PAIRING

Torresella Prosecco

Preheat the oven to 300 degrees F. Spray a cookie sheet with nonstick spray. Place the butter, granulated sugar, and brown sugar in the bowl of an electric mixer fitted with the paddle attachment. Beat on medium speed for about 30 seconds, until the mixture is fluffy. Turn down the mixer to low and add the eggs and vanilla. In a mixing bowl, sift together the flour, salt, and baking powder. Add to the mixer while beating on low speed and beat for 15 seconds, stopping the mixer once to scrape down the sides with a spatula. Add the macadamia nuts, coconut, white chocolate, and dried cranberries, and mix for 15 seconds longer.

Using a 1-ounce scoop or a 2-tablespoon measure, drop the cookie dough onto the prepared cookie sheet in dollops about 3 inches apart. Gently press down on the dough with the back of a spoon to create small indentations. Transfer to the oven and bake for about 20 minutes or until the edges are nicely browned. Turn out onto a wire rack to cool. Repeat until all the dough is used — cooling and spraying the cookie sheet with more nonstick spray after each batch. Store in an airtight container.

> Like our other cookies, this one is good to have around when you need something sweet.

NUTRITION FACTS —*1 cookie*

| 120 calories | 2.5G saturated fat | 18G total carbohydrate | 75MG sodium |
| 6G total fat | 15MG cholesterol | 13G sugars | 1G protein |

Chocolate, Chocolate Chip Cookies

Yields about 4 dozen

This extra-chocolatey cookie is for the person who loves and craves chocolate. Here we take chocolate cookies to another level and double the pleasure for that afternoon craving.

3½ cups semisweet chocolate chips

½ cup unsalted butter

1 cup light brown sugar

2 large eggs

1½ cups all-purpose flour

⅓ cup cocoa powder

1 teaspoon baking powder

½ teaspoon salt

SUGGESTED WINE PAIRING

M. Chapoutier Banyuls

Preheat the oven to 300 degrees F. Spray a cookie sheet with nonstick spray. Prepare a double boiler by bringing a saucepan with 2 inches of water to a simmer and placing a bowl with 2 cups of the chocolate chips on top, making sure the bottom of the bowl does not touch the water. Once the chocolate has melted, set aside. Place the butter and sugar in the bowl of an electric mixer fitted with the paddle attachment. Beat on medium speed for about 30 seconds, until the mixture is fluffy. Turn down the speed to low and add the melted chocolate and eggs. Mix for about 30 seconds, until incorporated. In a mixing bowl, sift together the flour, cocoa powder, baking powder, and salt. Add to the mixer while beating on low speed. Beat for about 15 seconds on low speed, stopping the mixer once to scrape down the sides with a spatula. Slowly mix in the remaining 1½ cups chocolate chips.

Using a 1-ounce scoop or a 2-tablespoon measure, drop the cookie dough onto the prepared cookie sheet in dollops about 3 inches apart. Gently press down on the dough with the back of a spoon to create small indentations. Transfer to the oven and bake for about 20 minutes or until the edges are nicely browned. Turn out onto a wire rack to cool. Repeat until all the dough is used — cooling and spraying the cookie sheet with more nonstick spray after each batch. Store in an airtight container.

NUTRITION FACTS —*1 cookie*

| 130 calories | 4G saturated fat | 17G total carbohydrate | 40MG sodium |
| 7G total fat | 15MG cholesterol | 11G sugars | 1G protein |

Everyone has their vice, and
mine happens to be cookies.

The Everything Cookies

Yields about 4 dozen

This recipe was probably created by a rogue baker who must have been a troublemaker since early childhood and decided to put all the classic cookie ingredients together to see what happens! When one of something isn't good enough you can have it all with this unique cookie.

¼ cup unsalted butter

3 tablespoons granulated sugar

1 cup light brown sugar

1 large egg

2 teaspoons vanilla extract

¼ cup creamy peanut butter

¾ cup oatmeal

1¾ cups all-purpose flour

½ teaspoon baking powder

½ teaspoon baking soda

½ teaspoon salt

1½ teaspoons Sanka coffee powder

½ cup semisweet chocolate chips

½ cup white chocolate chips

¾ cup raisins

¼ cup chopped walnuts

Preheat the oven to 300 degrees F. Spray a cookie sheet with nonstick spray. Place the butter, granulated sugar, and brown sugar in the bowl of an electric mixer fitted with the paddle attachment. Cream the mixture on medium speed for about 5 minutes, until light and fluffy. Turn down the mixer to low speed, add the egg and vanilla extract, and mix until thoroughly incorporated. Add the peanut butter and oatmeal and mix for 15 seconds. In a mixing bowl, sift together the flour, baking powder, baking soda, and salt. Add the sifted dry ingredients to the mixer in three increments and mix only until incorporated; do not overmix. Turn off the mixer and scrape down the sides of the bowl with a spatula. Stir in the Sanka, chocolate chips, white chocolate chips, raisins, and walnuts just until incorporated.

Using a 1-ounce scoop or a 2-tablespoon measure, drop the cookie dough onto the prepared cookie sheet in dollops about 3 inches apart. Gently press down on the dough with the back of a spoon to create small indentations. Transfer to the oven and bake for about 20 minutes or until the edges are nicely browned. For a crisper cookie, bake a little longer. Turn out onto a wire rack to cool. Repeat until all the dough is used — cooling and spraying the cookie sheet with more nonstick spray after each batch. Store in an airtight container.

SUGGESTED WINE PAIRING

Peller Estates Cabernet Franc Icewine

NUTRITION FACTS —*1 cookie*

120 calories	2G saturated fat	19G total carbohydrate	55MG sodium
4.5G total fat	5MG cholesterol	12G sugars	2G protein

9 DRINKS AND COCKTAILS

DRINKS AND COCKTAILS

This chapter was the most fun to taste-test! We've given beverages their own chapter because at Neiman Marcus, we regard them as an integral part of the dining experience. And our customers also expect interesting, pretty-to-look-at, and, of course, delicious-tasting cocktails when dining at our restaurants. As you would expect, in addition to our cocktail offerings we also have a large selection of local beers and premium wine, rounding out our commitment to providing an upscale, full-service, fine-dining destination that our customers can rely upon and appreciate. During the late 1980s and 1990s, we witnessed a decline in the popularity of alcoholic beverages with lunch, but the last decade has seen a resurgence in interest and an increase in our lunchtime cocktail and wine business. So much so that liquor, beer, and wine vendors are constantly knocking at our doors trying to get their products on the shelves at the Neiman Marcus restaurant bars. Who would have thought, years ago, that the bar shelves at Neiman Marcus are just as important to beverage vendors as the cosmetic shelves are to cosmetics vendors?

We are often asked about which cocktails are the most popular at our restaurants. Overall, our best-sellers are the Bloody Mary and the Mimosa, but as you might imagine, some of our restaurants have their signature drinks, and customer preferences differ from region to region. We find that any sparkling drink or cocktail sells, and red drinks too; they tend to catch the eye, so that when people see a tray of them go by, especially if it's our beautifully presented Bloody Mary, they want one too!

With each of the cocktails that follow, we have suggested a particular spirit or liqueur, usually for good reason involving quality and flavor, but by all means be flexible and use another, similar brand — but for best results, I recommend following the recipes as written. We've organized this chapter so that we start with the alcohol-free drinks and then progress to those that contain Champagne and sparkling wine, then vodka, rum, tequila, bourbon, and gin. We offer specialty cocktails with these and other liquors at many of our restaurants, but these are a sampling of our favorites, chosen with the assistance of Frank Zack, our corporate beverage manager.

My motto, as always, is "Everything in moderation!"

FRANK ZACK, NEIMAN MARCUS BEVERAGE EXPERT

In our last book, *Neiman Marcus Taste*, I felt it was important to ride the current wave of the cocktail that was taking off in the restaurant business here in the United States. It seems that in the last five years, cocktails have become just as important as the food itself in our restaurants. Could we be moving back to the two-martini lunch? Wouldn't that be fun for some? I will tell you this: Frank has made it his mission to get a cocktail or glass of wine in every Neiman Marcus customer's hand when they dine in one of our restaurants. One of the keys to our recent uptick in alcohol sales has been our close relationship with our wine and spirits suppliers like Terlato Wine Group, out of Chicago. One of the reasons I chose to showcase Terlato is the large breadth of their portfolio, with wines and spirits from around the world. From their Santa Margherita Pinot Grigio to their Terlato Chardonnay, Chimney Rock Cabernet Sauvignon, and Bollinger Champagne, Terlato is proving to be a true top-tier importer here in the United States. This is the type of partnership we need to ensure the success of our beverage programs. Frank has been at the helm of this business for ten years and I look forward to his continued success in the promotion of wine and spirits here at Neiman Marcus.

Neiman Marcus Spiced Tea

Yields 7 servings

Spiced Tea has a huge following around the country and people who drink it crave it when they've been away from the Neiman Marcus restaurants for a while. It's an acquired taste that I find you either love or don't care for at all. I was fascinated by the recipe when I first started at Neiman Marcus, especially because the main ingredient is Tang. I remember when Tang was first introduced here in the United States, it was marketed as the choice for astronauts in the early days of space exploration. I'm a big fan of unique food history. Try this recipe and see if you too become a Neiman Marcus Spiced Tea lover.

3   cinnamon sticks

3   whole cloves

⅛   teaspoon ground nutmeg

4   English breakfast tea bags, or Irish Breakfast or Orange Pekoe *(preferably Dammann Frères)*

¼   cup Tang orange drink mix

⅛   teaspoon almond extract

1   orange or lemon, sliced

Place 6½ cups water in a saucepan and add the cinnamon, cloves, and nutmeg. Bring to a boil, turn down the heat to low, cover the pan, and simmer for 5 minutes. Remove the pan from the heat and add the tea bags. Let the tea bags steep for 3 or 4 minutes or up to 5 minutes for a stronger brew. Strain the tea into a clean saucepan, stir in the Tang and almond extract, and let cool to room temperature before refrigerating. Serve over ice in tall 12-ounce glasses and garnish each serving with an orange or lemon slice.

NUTRITION FACTS —*1 cup*

| 50 calories | 0G saturated fat | 15G total carbohydrate | 5MG sodium |
| 0G total fat | 0MG cholesterol | 8G sugars | 1G protein |

Neiman Marcus Lemonade

Yields 20 servings

The important thing with this recipe is to only use fresh lemon juice. Any other type of frozen, bottled, or powdered lemon just won't taste the same as fresh. We make a variety of modifications to this recipe and one of my favorites is to add pomegranate juice to give the drink a bright red color. You could also use your favorite flavor of Monin syrup, available at better liquor stores, to create your own colorful lemonade.

4   cups sugar

4   cups fresh lemon juice

6   lemons, washed and cut in half

2   additional lemons, washed and
    sliced, for garnish

Make a simple syrup by pouring 4 cups water into a small saucepan. Add the sugar and heat on low, stirring until the sugar has dissolved. Remove the pan from the heat and let cool to room temperature. The simple syrup can be stored in an airtight container at room temperature for up to 30 days.

To make the lemonade, mix the simple syrup with the lemon juice and 8 cups water. Feel free to add more or less water and/or lemon juice to taste. Place crushed ice in a glass pitcher and add the lemonade. Place the lemon halves in the pitcher and garnish with some lemon slices. Use the remaining sliced lemons to garnish the serving glasses.

NUTRITION FACTS —*1 cup*

150 calories	**41G** total carbohydrate
0G total fat	**37G** sugars
0G saturated fat	**5MG** sodium
0MG cholesterol	**0G** protein

Summer's Night Tea and Sorbet

Yields 1 serving

This very colorful drink gets its name from a mid-summer night's invitation to experience fresh fruit picked from the garden. Flavors include hibiscus flowers, apple, raspberry, strawberry, and a hint of cream. Here at Neiman Marcus we pair this herbaceous brewed tea with frozen lemon sorbet.

4   scoops *(about 6 ounces)* lemon sorbet
1   cup brewed Dammann Frères Nuit d'été tea, cooled to room temperature
1   strawberry
1   fresh mint sprig

Place the sorbet in a pilsner glass. Add the brewed tea. Garnish the glass with a strawberry and mint sprig. Serve with a straw.

CHEF'S NOTE

You can substitute any brightly colored tea with fresh berry flavors.

NUTRITION FACTS —*1 serving*

200 calories	51G total carbohydrate
0G total fat	50G sugars
0G saturated fat	30MG sodium
0MG cholesterol	0G protein

Grand Champagne Cocktail

Yields 5 servings

Calling anything "Grand" gives the idea that it is truly something special. In fact, we have developed a reputation here at Neiman Marcus for this very special Champagne cocktail. The addition of orange bitters and pomegranate juice gives the drink a wonderful color, helping to persuade other customers to try it as it's paraded through the dining room.

5   raw *(turbinado)* sugar cubes or white sugar cubes

5   dashes orange bitters

5   ounces *(10 tablespoons)* pomegranate juice

1   *(750-ml)* bottle Veuve Clicquot "Yellow Label" Brut Champagne

Place a sugar cube in each of five Champagne coupe glasses. Add a dash of orange bitters over the sugar cubes. Pour 1 ounce of pomegranate juice into each glass and top with the Veuve Clicquot.

CHEF'S NOTE

Coupe glasses are bowl-shaped Champagne glasses that bartending legend suggests (most likely inaccurately) were modeled after Marie Antoinette's breasts. What is more certain is that the glasses were popularized in post-Prohibition days at New York's Stork Club.

NUTRITION FACTS —*1 serving*

150 calories	**11G** total carbohydrate
0G total fat	**7G** sugars
0G saturated fat	**10MG** sodium
0MG cholesterol	**0G** protein

I had an experience where I was able to taste some Champagnes from the 1960s, '70s, and early '80s that unfortunately weren't kept under proper refrigeration over the years. What I learned was that while some of the Champagnes had lost all of their effervescence, and others still retained most of their bubbles, they still had unique flavor characteristics, typically a creaminess and almost syrupy flavor with a long taste finish like a very silky, smooth, white port wine. Lesson learned: Enjoy that lost bottle of Champagne you recently found after 30 years. Give it a chill and by all means a taste.

L et's get some facts straight about Champagnes and sparkling wines. Only wines produced in the Champagne region in France can be called Champagne. A sparkling wine produced anywhere else in the world cannot be called Champagne. In Italy, their sparklers are called prosecco, named after the prosecco grape first cultivated in the north of Italy in a small village called Prosecco, near Trieste. Here in the United States, we produce some of the best sparklers in the Sonoma region of northern California, made from the Chardonnay grape that grows so perfectly in the cool climate influenced by the Pacific Ocean. A few years back, when I turned over the Neiman Marcus beverage program to Frank Zack, a fellow graduate of the Culinary Institute of America and a great mixologist in his own right, he was quick to inform me that any drink with Champagne added would sell well to the lady customers who lunch at our restaurants. And boy, was he right! In this section of drink recipes, you'll find certain brands recommended that we particularly like and which, in turn, our guests have also come to admire. Feel free to use your own favorite bottle of Champagne or other type of sparkling wine.

The following recipes are based on full bottles of Champagne or sparkling wine, which makes measuring easier when entertaining guests. At my home, I've invested in a Champagne bottle stopper; after a bottle gets opened I can extract the air in the bottle by creating a vacuum that seals it up tight. This way, I can enjoy another taste from that bottle up to a week after opening. Maybe the outcome isn't quite as perfect as a newly opened bottle, but I'm never complaining when I'm drinking a great Champagne or sparkling wine.

Arancia Spritz

Yields 6 servings

Arancia, the Italian word meaning "orange," was the name we chose for this popular cocktail because of the Aperol and the blood orange juice. I guess you could say this is a very special Mimosa. It is the type of drink that conjures up memories of your last trip to Italy. I don't know about you, but after a glass, I'm ready to go back immediately!

12 ounces *(1½ cups)* Aperol

6 ounces *(¾ cup)* freshly squeezed blood orange juice

1 *(750-ml)* bottle Santa Margherita prosecco

6 slices blood orange

Add the Aperol, orange juice, and enough prosecco to almost fill a cocktail shaker filled with ice. Stir together for about 10 seconds and strain into six tall wine glasses. Top with the remaining prosecco. Stir once, garnish each glass with an orange slice, and serve.

CHEF'S NOTES

Aperol is an Italian aperitif with a similar flavor profile to Campari, but with half the alcohol content and a less bitter flavor. Bitter orange and rhubarb are among the ingredients.

Prosecco has become increasingly popular as people branch out and try alternatives to Champagne. It is great for mixing and, of course, Italian-themed cocktails.

NUTRITION FACTS —*1 serving*

310 calories	**28G** total carbohydrate
0G total fat	**28G** sugars
0G saturated fat	**5MG** sodium
0MG cholesterol	**0G** protein

Frutti di Bosco

Yields 6 servings

This cocktail translates from the Italian as "fruits of the forest," referring to the mixed wild berries that give it an attractive rich color. Best advise your guests not to wear white when you serve this at a party — just the littlest splash might mean a complete wardrobe change, and that's never fun!

2½   ounces *(5 tablespoons)* wild berry puree *(preferably Monin)*
2½   ounces *(5 tablespoons)* pineapple juice
3   ounces *(6 tablespoons)* fresh lemon juice
1   *(750-ml)* bottle Santa Margherita prosecco

Pour the wild berry puree, pineapple juice, and lemon juice into a large cocktail shaker filled with ice. Shake for about 10 seconds and strain into six Champagne flutes. Top with the prosecco. Stir once to release the thicker part of the puree at the bottom of the flute and serve.

CHEF'S NOTE

Instead of berry puree, you can buy frozen mixed berries and puree them in a blender. If you can't find frozen mixed berries then by all means use frozen strawberries or raspberries or some other type of berry. Monin products are available at upscale liquor stores throughout the United States or you can order from Monin directly: www.moninstore.com.

NUTRITION FACTS —*1 serving*

140 calories	8G total carbohydrate
0G total fat	3G sugars
0G saturated fat	10MG sodium
0MG cholesterol	0G protein

Neiman Marcus Mimosa

Yields 6 servings

We never do anything simple here at Neiman Marcus restaurants — even the simple mimosa gets a makeover. Sure, you can continue to mix orange juice with Champagne or some other type of sparkling wine and call it a mimosa, but why not take it up a few notches? The Solerno liqueur will also make a great addition to your favorite margarita recipe.

3   ounces *(6 tablespoons)* Solerno blood orange liqueur
4   ounces *(½ cup)* fresh orange juice
1   *(750-ml)* bottle Domaine Chandon Brut sparkling wine
3   orange slices, halved
6   ribbons orange peel, 6 to 8 inches long *(see Chef's Note)*

Pour the blood orange liqueur and orange juice into a large cocktail shaker filled with ice. Shake for about 10 seconds and strain into six Champagne flutes. Top with the Domaine Chandon, stir once, and drop an orange half-slice into the flute. Garnish each glass with a ribbon of orange peel hanging from the rim.

CHEF'S NOTE

For the orange peel, use a vegetable peeler to peel away a long strip of the orange zest. Be sure you only peel the outer orange skin and not the white pith, which leaves a bitter taste. The peel adds an attractive touch as well as a fragrant aroma.

NUTRITION FACTS —*1 serving*

170 calories	18G total carbohydrate
0G total fat	15G sugars
0G saturated fat	5MG sodium
0MG cholesterol	1G protein

Rudolph's Red Nose

Yields 6 servings

This cocktail is served each holiday season at the Neiman Marcus restaurants throughout the United States. I think it's a cute name for a very fashionable martini-style drink. Domaine Chandon has done an excellent job with their (dry) Brut Rosé, which is blended from Pinot Noir and Chardonnay grapes to create a sparkler with hints of strawberries and peach. If you haven't stocked your home bar with a bottle of Grand Marnier Raspberry Peach liqueur, it's time to go out and get some. I love it simple — neat in a snifter glass — after a great meal.

1   pint *(about 2 cups)* fresh raspberries

8   ounces *(1 cup)* Grand Marnier Raspberry Peach *(Signature Collection No. 2)*

3   ounces *(6 tablespoons)* Monin sugar-free sweetener

   Juice of 1 lime

1½ ounces *(3 tablespoons)* fresh orange juice

1   *(375-ml)* bottle Domaine Chandon Brut Rosé

Place half of the raspberries (about 1 cup) in a cocktail shaker and muddle. Add 1 cup ice, the Grand Marnier Raspberry Peach, sweetener, lime juice, and orange juice. Shake for about 5 seconds and strain into six martini glasses. Top each glass with the Domaine Chandon and garnish with the remaining raspberries.

CHEF'S NOTE

The term "muddling" refers to crushing an ingredient to release its full flavor; good wine stores or kitchen and bar equipment retailers sell muddlers, blunt wooden or metal tools that will do the job for you.

NUTRITION FACTS —*1 serving*

230 calories	0G saturated fat	19G total carbohydrate	10MG sodium
0G total fat	0MG cholesterol	14G sugars	1G protein

THE TREE
OF GLASS

...ed, minimal, artisan masterpiece
...ludes more than 500 pieces
...ndblown glass faceted
...inless steel and lit by
...and laser lights-cool!

—VODKA—

Hands down, vodka is the most-consumed alcohol in all of our Neiman Marcus restaurants. The number of vodka makers has exploded here in the United States and at times it seems that every state has five or ten vodkas being distilled somewhere. While we try to support local distillers as much as we can, we also have a big commitment to national labels that you will see featured in our vodka recipes. Our focus in creating vodka-based drinks has been to use some of the more interesting flavored vodkas now available, such as vanilla, Chambord, and citrus, to name a few. One of our challenges is coming up with interesting drinks that appeal across generations, so we've created drinks not only based on different flavors but also on color and combinations of liqueurs that complement one another. I hope you take the time to get adventurous and experiment with mixology in your home. Hey, so what if you mess up? The worst thing that can happen is that you might wake up with a small headache!

Parisian Punch

Yields 1 serving

I was really excited when we started using St. Germain liqueur in our bar recipes — I love the aromatic tones of tropical fruit, pear, and grapefruit of this all-natural elderflower liqueur that originates in the French Alps. When we mixed it with Chambord vodka, which has its own unique black raspberry flavor, we created quite the cocktail that soon became a hit with many of our guests. The name might suggest the drink is strong in alcohol content, but I will tell you it's as soft and delicious as any cocktail I've ever enjoyed.

1½ ounces *(3 tablespoons)* Chambord vodka

½ ounce *(1 tablespoon)* St. Germain liqueur

½ ounce *(1 tablespoon)* fresh lemon juice

3 raspberries

2 lemon slices

1 can ginger ale

1 fresh mint sprig

Place the Chambord vodka, St. Germain, lemon juice, raspberries, and lemon slices in a cocktail shaker filled with ice. Shake for about 10 seconds and strain into a pilsner glass filled with ice. Fill with ginger ale and garnish with a mint sprig.

NUTRITION FACTS —*1 serving*

210 calories	21G total carbohydrate
0G total fat	19G sugars
0G saturated fat	10MG sodium
0MG cholesterol	0G protein

Lemon Drop De-Lite

Yields 1 serving

This is one of our skinny drinks, meaning lower in calories — hence the name De-Lite. But I will tell you that De-Lite also stands for "delightful tasting," and you'll enjoy this cocktail on hot summer evenings when only light and refreshing are on your mind. We use Grey Goose Le Citron, but feel free to use your favorite flavored vodka.

1½ ounces *(3 tablespoons)* Grey Goose Le Citron vodka

1 ounce *(2 tablespoons)* fresh lemon juice

¼ ounce *(½ tablespoon)* fresh orange juice

1 ounce *(2 tablespoons)* Monin sugar-free sweetener

1 lemon slice

Place the vodka, lemon juice, orange juice, and sweetener in a cocktail shaker filled with ice. Shake for about 10 seconds and strain into a chilled martini glass. Float the lemon slice on top as a garnish.

NUTRITION FACTS —*1 serving*

110 calories	3G total carbohydrate
0G total fat	1G sugars
0G saturated fat	5MG sodium
0MG cholesterol	0G protein

Neiman Marcus Bloody Mary

Yields 8 servings

The Bloody Mary is our best-selling cocktail, and this version is based on the recipe perfected at our San Francisco store. I like it because it's an appetizer in a glass, and it's always a good way to begin a weekend morning. You'll notice that we serve our "Bloody" in an oversize glass — that really plays up to the idea of a Bloody Mary being a meal in itself!

FOR THE BLOODY MARY MIX

- 5 ounces *(10 tablespoons)* Worcestershire sauce
- 1 teaspoon prepared horseradish
- 1 ounce *(2 tablespoons)* Frank's RedHot hot sauce
- Dash of Tabasco sauce
- ½ teaspoon freshly ground black pepper
- 46 ounces *(5¾ cups)* canned tomato juice

FOR THE BLOODY MARY COCKTAIL

- 8 paper-thin slices of cucumber
- 8 small cherry tomatoes
- 8 olives stuffed with blue cheese *(store-bought)*
- 1 large lime wedge
- 1 teaspoon Old Bay seasoning
- 8 stalks celery, with leaves still attached, cleaned
- 12 ounces *(1½ cups)* Absolut Peppar vodka or Belvedere Bloody Mary vodka

To prepare the Bloody Mary mix, place the Worcestershire sauce, horseradish, hot sauce, Tabasco, pepper, and tomato juice in a large pitcher and stir well to thoroughly combine. Set aside.

To prepare the cocktails, thread a toothpick through a cucumber slice, followed by a cherry tomato and an olive. Repeat to make eight garnishes. Rub the rims of eight large wine glasses with the lime wedge. Place the Old Bay seasoning on a plate and dip the rim of each glass in the seasoning to coat. Add a celery stalk to each glass and fill with ice. Divide the vodka among the glasses. Stir the Bloody Mary mix and pour evenly into the glasses. Place a toothpick with the vegetable garnish across the rim of each drink.

NUTRITION FACTS —*1 serving*

| 160 calories | 0G saturated fat | 11G total carbohydrate | 750MG sodium |
| 0G total fat | 0MG cholesterol | 7G sugars | 1G protein |

Ready to Wear

Yields 8 servings

Okay, so in case you're wondering about the name, I am here to tell you that the primary — no, the only — purpose of our restaurants is to make you, our customers, happy and content while you spend time shopping and relaxing throughout the Neiman Marcus store. So being the restaurant operator in the number one fashion retailer in the world, I've also become somewhat of a fashionista in my own right and like to play off my surroundings when it comes to creating new recipes. In this case, we wanted to create an orange-colored drink because that was the color of the season. Each season, the fashion-trend colors change, so we are often called upon to create a cocktail that matches your clothes. Now that's fun!

12 ounces *(1½ cups)* Voli Orange Vanilla Fusion vodka

4 ounces *(½ cup)* Cointreau liqueur

12 ounces *(1½ cups)* cranberry juice

1 *(750-ml)* bottle Santa Margherita prosecco

8 ribbons orange peel, 6 to 8 inches long
   (see Chef's Note, page 269)

Pour the vodka, Cointreau, and cranberry juice into a large cocktail shaker filled with ice. Shake for about 10 seconds and strain into eight chilled martini glasses. Top with the prosecco and garnish each glass with a ribbon of orange peel hanging from the rim.

NUTRITION FACTS —*1 serving*

250 calories	12G total carbohydrate
0G total fat	10G sugars
0G saturated fat	20MG sodium
0MG cholesterol	0G protein

Frosted Fig

Yields 2 servings

For sure, this cocktail will impress the most hard-to-impress friends you have. You'll need to shop around for the fig jam but once you locate it, save it in your pantry and you'll be ready to shake away. Be sure to buy a good-quality aged balsamic vinegar; my favorites are from Modena, Italy, because they're more syrupy and sweeter, helping to create a superior cocktail.

1½   ounces *(3 tablespoons)* Belvedere vodka

3   ounces *(6 tablespoons)* Bailey's Vanilla Cinnamon Irish Cream liqueur

2   teaspoons balsamic vinegar

2   tablespoons fig jam

½   ounce *(1 tablespoon)* Monin sugar-free sweetener

1   tablespoon turbinado sugar *(golden raw cane sugar)*

1   fresh fig, halved lengthwise

Pour the vodka, Bailey's, and balsamic vinegar into a cocktail shaker filled one-quarter with ice. Add the fig jam and shake for about 10 seconds. Strain into two chilled martini glasses. Place the sweetener in a small bowl and the sugar on a plate. Dip the fig halves first in the syrup and then roll in the sugar. Cut the fig halves almost in half and push onto the rim of each glass.

NUTRITION FACTS —*1 serving*

510 calories	50G total carbohydrate
14G total fat	38G sugars
8G saturated fat	90MG sodium
50MG cholesterol	3G protein

White Raspberry Cosmopolitan

Yields 1 serving

I'm not sure where the first Cosmopolitan cocktail was made; there are several theories, dating its origins back to the 1970s. In any event, I will say it's probably one of the most popular and most-requested cocktails in all our restaurants. Of course, we needed to give it a twist, so out came the flavored vodka of the season and here it is. White cranberries have a mild, sweet flavor and make a clear juice that's become very popular in cocktails.

1½   ounces *(3 tablespoons)* Chambord flavored vodka

1   ounce *(2 tablespoons)* Cointreau liqueur

5   ounces *(10 tablespoons)* fresh lime juice

1   ounce *(2 tablespoons)* white cranberry juice

1   raspberry

Pour the vodka, Cointreau, lime juice, and white cranberry juice into a cocktail shaker filled with ice. Shake for about 10 seconds and strain into a chilled martini glass. Add the raspberry to the cocktail for garnish.

NUTRITION FACTS —*1 serving*

300 calories	40G total carbohydrate
0G total fat	30G sugars
0G saturated fat	5MG sodium
0MG cholesterol	1G protein

Weightless Mojito

Yields 1 serving

Low-cal cocktails made their way into vogue in the past few years, but only seemed to sell in certain pockets of the United States; however, this version using white rum and sugar-free syrup has grown in popularity in many of our bars.

1½ ounces *(3 tablespoons)* Bacardi Superior white rum
1 ounce *(2 tablespoons)* fresh lime juice
1 ounce *(2 tablespoons)* Monin sugar-free sweetener
5 fresh mint leaves
1 ounce *(2 tablespoons)* club soda
1 lime, quartered

Pour the rum, lime juice, and sweetener into a cocktail shaker filled with ice. Add the mint leaves and shake for about 10 seconds. Strain into a pilsner glass filled with ice and top with the club soda. Drop the lime quarters into the glass for garnish.

NUTRITION FACTS —*1 serving*

110 calories	4G total carbohydrate
0G total fat	1G sugars
0G saturated fat	30MG sodium
0MG cholesterol	0G protein

—RUM—

Rum hasn't come back in vogue yet with the Neiman Marcus customer base. But I will say that when you're next in South Florida, treat yourself to a good handmade mojito. If you've never had one, you'll become a fan. Here we've included a couple of our customers' favorite rum concoctions that I'm sure you'll enjoy.

Mermaid Bar Mai-Tai

Yields 1 serving

Our Mariposa restaurant at Ala Moana in Honolulu has really perfected this cocktail. The key — as with any successful recipe — is to use only the freshest ingredients. So while you will be hard pressed to find fresh pineapple juice, if you have a juicer, you should try making your own from a fresh pineapple and see what a difference it makes. However, I've written the recipe using easily available canned pineapple, so you shouldn't be deterred from trying it.

1 ounce *(2 tablespoons)* Bacardi Superior white rum
1 ounce *(2 tablespoons)* Myers's dark rum
½ ounce *(1 tablespoon)* Blue Curaçao liqueur
2 ounces *(¼ cup)* pineapple juice
2 ounces *(¼ cup)* fresh orange juice
1 maraschino cherry
1 pineapple wedge

Pour the Bacardi and Myers's rum into a cocktail shaker and add the Curaçao, pineapple juice, and orange juice. Shake for about 10 seconds and strain into a pilsner glass or tall glass filled with ice. Garnish with a cherry and a pineapple wedge.

NUTRITION FACTS —*1 serving*

260 calories	25G total carbohydrate
0G total fat	22G sugars
0G saturated fat	10MG sodium
0MG cholesterol	0G protein

Blood Orange Agave Margarita

Yields 1 serving

I'm a huge fan of blood oranges and, in turn, their juice. I find the juice has a slight hint of raspberries, making this a great alternative to the classic Mexican Margarita. Squeezing fresh juice will help this cocktail stand out. Enjoy!

1½ ounces *(3 tablespoons)* Herradura Silver or Reposado tequila

½ ounce *(1 tablespoon)* Solerno blood orange liqueur

1 ounce *(2 tablespoons)* agave nectar

1 ounce *(2 tablespoons)* fresh lime juice

1 ounce *(2 tablespoons)* fresh blood orange juice

1 lime slice

Pour the tequila, Solerno, agave nectar, lime juice, and orange juice into a cocktail shaker filled with ice. Shake for 10 seconds and strain into a Champagne coupe glass. Garnish with a lime slice.

NUTRITION FACTS —*1 serving*

240 calories	32G total carbohydrate
0G total fat	29G sugars
0G saturated fat	0MG sodium
0MG cholesterol	0G protein

Margarita Royale

Yields 1 serving

What makes a margarita royal, you ask? We think it's the marriage of one of the best tequilas from Mexico and Chambord from central France.

1½ ounces *(3 tablespoons)* Herradura Silver or Reposado tequila

¼ ounce *(½ tablespoon)* Chambord liqueur

½ ounce *(1 tablespoon)* Monin sugar-free sweetener

½ ounce *(1 tablespoon)* Monin sugar-free blackberry syrup

1 ounce *(2 tablespoons)* fresh lime juice

1 lime slice

Pour the tequila, Chambord, sweetener, syrup, and lime juice into a cocktail shaker filled with ice. Shake for 10 seconds and strain into a Champagne coupe glass. Garnish with a lime slice.

NUTRITION FACTS —*1 serving*

130 calories	6G total carbohydrate
0G total fat	3G sugars
0G saturated fat	20MG sodium
0MG cholesterol	0G protein

—TEQUILA—

Over the last 20 years, we've seen a huge growth in the tequila market, driven primarily by the popularity of margaritas (the best-selling cocktail in the country) and Mexican cuisine. We've had the pleasure to work with some of the best tequilas on the market and have included our versions of a couple of different types of margarita so you can make them at home.

—BOURBON—

Bourbon seems to be the new "everyman's drink" all over the country. Many of the long-time distillers in Kentucky and Tennessee have received lots of press over the past few years, and the bourbon trend sweeping the United States has fueled the resurgence in the popularity of brands such as Jim Beam, Maker's Mark, Jack Daniel's, Wild Turkey, and my favorite, Woodford Reserve. We've also become fond of some more recent bourbons such as Blanton's and Eagle Rare.

Autumn in Manhattan

Yields 1 serving

This cocktail can be served warm or cold. I like the warm version as a winter warmer. Hudson Baby Bourbon is a single-grain bourbon, and the first to be distilled in New York State. The maker tells us it's made from 100 percent New York corn and aged in special American oak barrels. The bourbon has a mildly sweet, smooth taste with hints of vanilla and caramel.

2	ounces *(¼ cup)*	Hudson Baby Bourbon
½	ounce *(1 tablespoon)*	Grand Marnier
½	teaspoon	Monin sugar-free sweetener
2	ounces *(¼ cup)*	apple juice, preferably fresh
1		Amarena cherry, soaked in Grand Marnier overnight

For a chilled cocktail, pour the bourbon, Grand Marnier, sweetener, and apple juice into a cocktail shaker filled with ice. Shake for about 10 seconds and strain into a chilled martini glass. Garnish with the marinated cherry.

For a warm beverage, pour the bourbon, Grand Marnier, sweetener, and apple juice into a microwave-safe glass mug. Warm for 30 seconds in the microwave or until warm, but no longer than 1 minute. Garnish with the marinated cherry.

CHEF'S NOTE

Amarena cherries are small, dark, sour Italian cherries that are available in bottles at specialty grocery stores or from online sources.

NUTRITION FACTS —*1 serving*

180 calories	17G total carbohydrate
0G total fat	16G sugars
0G saturated fat	10MG sodium
0MG cholesterol	0G protein

Fall Gem

Yields 1 serving

Again, we've used our retail savvy to come up with a cute name for a cocktail that evokes fashion, yet also sounds like something you'll enjoy. Eagle Rare is a ten-year-old Kentucky bourbon, and the makers describe its tones as "bold, dry, oaky flavors with notes of candied almonds and very rich cocoa."

1	ounce *(2 tablespoons)*	Eagle Rare Single Barrel Bourbon
1	ounce *(2 tablespoons)*	St. Germain liqueur
½	ounce *(1 tablespoon)*	pomegranate juice
		Juice of ½ lemon
2	dashes	orange bitters
1		ribbon orange peel *(see Chef's Note, page 269)*

Fill a double old-fashioned glass with ice, then transfer the ice to a cocktail shaker. Add the bourbon, St. Germain, pomegranate juice, and lemon juice to the shaker. Shake for about 10 seconds and pour the mixture back into the glass. Holding the pith side of the orange peel over the glass, squeeze the peel to release the oils. Rub the rind around the rim and upper third of the glass exterior and then drop the peel into the cocktail.

NUTRITION FACTS —*1 serving*

180 calories	11G total carbohydrate
0G total fat	10G sugars
0G saturated fat	0MG sodium
0MG cholesterol	0G protein

Spiced 46

Yields 1 serving

What better way to spice up the classic Neiman Marcus Spiced Tea than with Maker's 46? We gave this classic bourbon a real twist by mixing it with peach puree, making it a perfect summer cocktail to be enjoyed by the pool.

1½ ounces *(3 tablespoons)* Maker's 46 bourbon

1½ ounces *(3 tablespoons)* Neiman Marcus Spiced Tea *(page 263)*

1 ounce *(2 tablespoons)* peach puree

½ ounce *(1 tablespoon)* fresh lemon juice

4 fresh mint leaves

Pour the bourbon, spiced tea, peach puree, and lemon juice into a cocktail shaker filled with ice. Shake for about 10 seconds and strain into a chilled martini glass. Garnish with the mint.

NUTRITION FACTS —*1 serving*

170 calories	**7G** total carbohydrate
0G total fat	**6G** sugars
0G saturated fat	**0MG** sodium
0MG cholesterol	**0G** protein

English Cucumber Martini

Yields about 12 servings

As a foodie, I need to tell you that the name of this cocktail comes from the elongated cucumber that's sometimes called a "hothouse cucumber," but more commonly, an "English cucumber." It has no seeds and is the cucumber of choice for those dainty finger sandwiches. What better partner with the great Oxley gin . . . I'll take one right away, as my equally English co-author, John Harrisson, would say!

FOR THE BASIL SYRUP

1 cup sugar

50 fresh basil leaves

FOR THE MARTINIS

1 *(750-ml)* bottle Oxley gin

3 cups peeled, seeded, and diced English cucumber

12 ounces *(1½ cups)* Fever-Tree bitter lemon tonic

12 cucumber slices

To prepare the basil syrup, pour 1 cup water into a saucepan, add the sugar, and bring to a boil. Stir to dissolve the sugar, then add the basil. Remove from the heat immediately and let cool. Transfer to an airtight container and refrigerate overnight. Remove from the refrigerator, transfer to a blender, and puree.

To prepare the martinis, combine half of the gin, the cucumber, 1 tablespoon of the basil syrup, and some crushed ice in a large cocktail shaker and muddle for 5 seconds. (This can also be done in batches if using a small shaker.) Add the remaining gin. Shake for about 10 seconds and strain into chilled martini glasses. Top each glass with 1 ounce (2 tablespoons) bitter lemon soda and garnish with a cucumber slice.

NUTRITION FACTS —*1 serving*

130 calories	**0MG** cholesterol	**20MG** sodium
0G total fat	**6G** total carb	**0G** protein
0G saturated fat	**3G** sugars	

ACKNOWLEDGMENTS

Thank you to my crew here at Neiman Marcus: Anita Hirsch, Frank Zack, Lynda Klempel, and Kevin Combs for helping to continue the great legacy of Neiman Marcus Restaurants.

I'm fortunate to have really great bosses in Karen Katz, our President and CEO of Neiman Marcus Group; Jim Gold, President, Chief Merchandise Officer, Neiman Marcus Stores and Online; John Koryl, President, Neiman Marcus Stores and Online; and my direct boss, Neva Hall, Executive Vice-President of Neiman Marcus Stores. These individuals understand firsthand the importance of the restaurants at Neiman Marcus through their many years of service both in the stores and in our corporate offices. Thank you all for keeping the Neiman Marcus restaurants an integral part of the exemplary customer service we strive toward every day.

Before turning to the special group that made this book possible, I'd like to acknowledge my fellow cooks who inspired me over the years: John Gould (Topnotch Inn, Stowe, VT), whom I met right after the Culinary Institute of America (the other CIA) and our times reading *Larousse Gastronomique*; Uwe Henze (Waiohai Resort, Kauai, HI), who taught me the importance of managing a kitchen staff; Heinz Guggisberg (Sheraton Resort, Steamboat Springs, CO), who made me count my *mise en place* twice when it came to banquet production; and Daniel Boesiger (Amfac Hotel, Minneapolis, MN), who reminded me every day that the reason I got into this business was because I loved to cook. And finally, to Jean Banchet, the man who took me under his wing, brought me into his home, and shared with me his love of the stove — RIP my friend.

What a great team of people who came together to help create *Neiman Marcus Cooks!*

I always wanted to do a book with Rizzoli Publications, and my hard-working agent, David Hale Smith, helped to arrange a meeting with Christopher Steighner of Rizzoli, who became my editor. Thanks, Chris and David, for understanding Neiman Marcus restaurants and the mystique of retail dining in today's world.

For me, one of the most fun things about writing a cookbook is getting to know the people who help guide your vision through to the final published product. Each of these individuals played a vital role in the book you are holding today:

Jody ("Where's the light?") Horton, our photographer. Thanks for making the drive from Austin and taking thousands of photographs. They make the book what it is — beautiful! Kate LeSueur, our cover girl and Jody's able-bodied prop stylist, food stylist, and photo assistant, you're the best. Zeena Khalaf, a gal who withstood the heat of Dallas in August to find the light: Thank you.

I also made new friends with Jim and Roxanne Wisniewski, owners of Culinary Focus in Irving, Texas, where we shot and tested all the recipes. You couldn't ask for two better hosts to photograph a book. I never imagined a fellow Archbishop Ryan Raider would be part of any cookbook of mine! And to Terry Wright, the man behind the nutritionals ever so important in today's dining scene.

A special thank-you to Liz Barrett, VP of corporate communications and PR of Terlato Wine Group and their corporate chef, Colin Crowley, for their matching of all the recipes with their outstanding portfolio of wines and Champagnes.

One of the most important jobs in creating a cookbook is the recipe tester, and I had the best in the business in Katherine Shaw. Her attention to detail was impressive, not to mention her quick wit and keen sense of what's needed next.

A new experience for me while working on *Neiman Marcus Cooks* was working hand-in-hand with the book designer, and in this case it was Blair Richardson. Ideas would pop into my head and then, with the exchange of simple two- or three-word e-mails between us, I always felt that we were both on the same page. I consider myself lucky to have met and worked with Blair, with her boundless creativity.

Three times are a charm in the case of my good friend and British coauthor John Harrisson. Seems the more time he spends here on this side of the pond, the less and less I need to edit his Britishisms when he wordsmiths my work! John's been a key player in each Neiman Marcus cookbook, and it's his talented writing that's made all three books the collector's item they've become. Thank you, John.

BERNARDAUD

bernardaud.fr

chilewich.

chilewich.com

COOKIES CRUMBS AND CRUST

cookiescrumbsandcrust.com

CULINARY FOCUS

culinary-focus.com

DAMMANN FRÈRES

dammann.fr

24karrot.com

Elegant Cakery
Special Occasion Cakes

elegantcakery.com

empire
BAKING COMPANY

empirebaking.com

FALKSALT

falksalt.com

Fernando Pensato

pensato.com

illy

shop.illy.com

JAN BARBOGLIO.

janbarboglio.com

Juliska

juliska.com

LYNX

lynxgrills.com

MATCH

match1995.com

Nachtmann
FINE BAVARIAN CRYSTAL

nachtmann.com

nambe
MUSEUM-QUALITY DESIGNS SINCE 1951

nambe.com

Neily on Nutrition

neilyonnutrition.com

Rosenthal
&
sambonet

rosenthalusa.com

staub
en France

staub.fr

steveconnollyseafood.com

TERLATO WINES
ALWAYS EXCEPTIONAL

terlatowines.com

The Tested Recipe

thetestedrecipe.com _ Katherine Shaw

CONVERSION CHART

Liquid Conversions

U.S.	METRIC
1 tsp	5 ml
1 tbs	15 ml
2 tbs	30 ml
3 tbs	45 ml
¼ cup	60 ml
⅓ cup	75 ml
⅓ cup + 1 tbs	90 ml
⅓ cup + 2 tbs	100 ml
½ cup	120 ml
⅔ cup	150 ml
¾ cup	180 ml
¾ cup + 2 tbs	200 ml
1 cup	240 ml
1 cup + 2tbs	275 ml
1 ¼ cups	300 ml
1 ⅓ cups	325 ml
1 ½ cups	350 ml
1 ⅔ cups	375 ml
1 ¾ cups	400 ml
1 ¾ cups + 2 tbs	450 ml
2 cups (1 pint)	475 ml
2 ½ cups	600 ml
3 cups	720 ml
4 cups (1 quart)	945 ml

(1,000 ml is 1 liter)

Weight Conversions

U.S./U.K.	METRIC
½ oz	14 g
1 oz	28 g
1 ½ oz	43 g
2 oz	57 g
2 ½ oz	71 g
3 oz	85 g
3 ½ oz	100 g
4 oz	113 g
5 oz	142 g
6 oz	170 g
7 oz	200 g
8 oz	227 g
9 oz	255 g
10 oz	284 g
11 oz	312 g
12 oz	340 g
13 oz	368 g
14 oz	400 g
15 oz	425 g
1 lb	454 g

Oven Temperatures

°F	GAS MARK	°C
250	½	120
275	1	140
300	2	150
325	3	165
350	4	180
375	5	190
400	6	200
425	7	220
450	8	230
475	9	240
500	10	260
550	Broil	290